The New Population Problem: Why Families in Developed Countries Are Shrinking and What It Means

D1713588

THE PENN STATE UNIVERSITY
FAMILY ISSUES SYMPOSIA SERIES

Series Editors
Alan Booth and Ann C. Crouter
Pennsylvania State University

Booth/Dunn • *Stepfamilies: Who Benefits? Who Does Not?*

Booth/Dunn • *Family-School Links: How Do They Affect Educational Outcomes?*

Booth/Crouter/Landale • *Immigration and the Family: Research and Policy on U.S. Immigrants*

Booth/Crouter • *Men in Families: When Do They Get Involved? What Difference Does It Make?*

Booth/Crouter • *Does It Take a Village? Community Effects on Children, Adolescents, and Families*

Booth/Crouter/Clements • *Couples in Conflict*

Booth/Crouter • *Just Living Together: Implications of Cohabitation on Families, Children, and Social Policy*

Crouter/Booth • *Children's Influence on Family Dynamics: The Neglected Side of Family Relationships*

Crouter/Booth • *Work-Family Challenges for Low-Income Parents and Their Children*

Booth/Crouter • *The New Population Problem: Why Families in Developed Countries Are Shrinking and What It Means*

The New Population Problem: Why Families in Developed Countries Are Shrinking and What It Means

Edited by

Alan Booth
Ann C. Crouter
The Pennsylvania State University

LAWRENCE ERLBAUM ASSOCIATES, PUBLISHERS
2005   Mahwah, New Jersey   London

Lawrence Erlbaum Associates, Inc., Publishers
10 Industrial Avenue
Mahwah, New Jersey 07430
www.erlbaum.com

Cover design by Kathryn Houghtaling Lacey

Library of Congress Cataloging-in-Publication Data

The new population problem : why families in developed countries are shrinking and what it means / edited by Alan Booth, Ann C. Crouter.
    p. cm.
Includes bibliographical references and index.
ISBN 0-8058-4978-5 (cloth : alk. paper)
ISBN 0-8058-4979-3 (pbk. : alk. paper)
1. Family size—Developed countries—Congresses. 2.Fertility, Human—Developed countries—Congresses. I. Booth, Alan, 1935– II. Crouter, Ann C. III. Series.
HQ766.5.D44D43 2005
304.6'3—dc22

2004062484
CIP

Books published by Lawrence Erlbaum Associates are printed on acid-free paper, and their bindings are chosen for strength and durability.

Printed in the United States of America
10 9 8 7 6 5 4 3 2 1

Contents

Preface

One of the most dramatic demographic trends today is that increasing numbers of women throughout the developed world are electing to have fewer children or no children at all. Sometimes fertility decisions of this kind take the form of delayed childbearing. Thanks to new opportunities, women are able to pursue educational goals and to establish themselves in jobs and careers. Many wait for the right time to have children, often putting off childbearing until the chances of becoming pregnant are greatly reduced. Delaying may also mean that women who might have wanted to have two, three, or more children in fact have one or two children. A parallel but related trend is that increasing numbers of women are bearing children outside of marriage. Moreover, there is a sense, at least for some, that adults appear to be less interested in investing in children—who are an increasingly expensive investment—than they have been in the past. The papers in this volume address some of the antecedents and consequences of the recent steep declines in fertility in developed countries from different theoretical and disciplinary angles.

Ironically, only a few years ago, the major fertility-related social issue was the population explosion and the accompanying fear that the earth's population was increasing at rates that would soon become unsustainable. While fertility rates are still high in some less-developed parts of the world, as the title of this volume suggests, the new population problem in many countries in Europe, Asia, and North America is declining fertility. With fertility decline comes a reshaping of the population age pyramid. In countries experiencing a population decline, the percentage of the population in mid-life or old age is growing, while the base of young people whose production activities typically support the older generation is becoming smaller and smaller. The effects of population decline in the United States have been mitigated an influx of immigrants who often bring children with them or produce relatively large families after settling down. Different countries react differently to the prospect of immigration, however, because it stirs up anxieties about national identity. Thus, the topic of fertility declines is interesting not only at the level of the individuals and the couples who are making these decisions but at the level of the societies that must come to grips with their long-term implications.

This volume is based on the presentations and discussions from a national symposium on "Creating the Next Generation: Social, Economic, and Psychological Processes Underlying Fertility in Developed Countries", held at the Pennsylvania State University, October 9–10, 2003, as the eleventh in a series of annual interdisciplinary symposia focused on family issues. The book is divided into four sections, each dealing with a different aspect of the topic. Each section includes a chapter by the lead author(s), followed by shorter chapters by discussants.

In the first section of the volume, S. Philip Morgan, a demographer, and Kelly Hagewen set the stage for the entire volume by looking at contemporary trends in U.S. fertility. His chapter builds on theoretical work by demographer Bongaarts. Other chapters in this section by demographer Kelly Raley, social psychologist

Belinda Tucker, and demographer Suzanne Bianchi build on Morgan's overarching vision of the broad mechanisms through which people make decisions about family size.

Social and cultural values and attitudes are at the heart of the second section of the volume. Here demographers Jennifer Barber and William Axinn explore how changing values and attitudes in such areas as gender roles and materialism may underlie (and reflect) changing patterns in fertility. Their remarks weave together insights from demography, sociology, and social psychology. In their chapters, economist Shelly Lundberg, demographer Hans-Peter Kohler, and sociologist Duane Alwin build on Barber and Axinn's ideas in interesting and novel ways to consider the role of changing social and cultural values and attitudes and their implications for individuals' decisions about fertility and family size.

In the third section of the volume, demographer Elizabeth Thomson moves away from the individual as the unit of analysis to the country level. In her skillful hands, a more detailed portrait of fertility patterns arises. Fertility decisions vary widely from country to country, and Thomson's analysis attempts to identify some of the reasons why, including the possible role of the rise in cohabiting unions and the concomitant decline in the centrality of marriage in many parts of the world. Psychologist Sara Jaffee and demographers Harriet Presser and Nancy Landale each use insights from data from different parts of the world to shed light on Thomson's key ideas.

The final section of the volume focuses on the possible long-term consequences of current fertility trends for individuals, families, and societies. Here, writers draw from years of experience to look into the future and imagine how it may unfold. Three noted social scientists play the role of "seer": demographer Christine Bachrach, sociologist Lynn White, and demographers Daniel Lichter and Jillian Wooten. Their chapters are followed by a synthesis of a panel discussion in which Drs. Bachrach, White, and Lichter were joined by Drs. Morgan, Barber, Axinn, and Thomson. The group proposed ways in which today's fertility patterns will matter for the next generation and what societies and nations can do about them.

The final chapter is an integrative commentary by Tanya St. Pierre and Jacinda Dariotis, graduate students at Penn State in the Departments of Sociology and Human Development and Family Studies, respectively. This interdisciplinary team summarizes the themes woven throughout the volume and suggests next steps for research.

Acknowledgments

The editors are grateful to the many organizations at Penn State that sponsor the annual symposium and book series, including the Population Research Institute, the Social Science Research Institute, the Children, Youth, and Families Consortium, the Prevention Research Center, the Center for Human Development and Family Research in Diverse Contexts, the Center for Work and Family Research, and the Departments of Human Development and Family Studies, Labor and Industrial Relations, Psychology, Sociology, Crime Law and Justice Program, and the Women's Studies Program. The editors also gratefully acknowledge core financial support in the form of a five-year grant funded by the National Institute of Child Health and Human Development (NICHD), as well as ongoing, substantive guidance and advice from Christine Bachrach and Lynne Casper of NICHD. We also acknowledge the ongoing support and commitment of Lawrence Erlbaum Associates, especially Bill Webber, to publish the volumes in this growing series. The support of all of these partners, year after year, has enabled us to attract the excellent scholars from a range of backgrounds and disciplines, on whom the quality and integrity of the series depends.

A lively, interdisciplinary group of scholars from across the Penn State community meets with us annually to generate symposia topics and plans and is available throughout the year for brainstorming and problem solving. We appreciate their enthusiasm, intellectual support, and creative ideas. We are especially grateful to Gordon De Jong, Rukmalie Jayakody, David Shapiro, and Leif Jensen for presiding over symposium sessions and for steering discussion in productive directions. The many details that go into planning a symposium and producing a volume are always under-estimated by the organizers. In this regard, we are especially grateful for the strong efforts of our administrative staff, including Tara Murray, William Harnish, Diane Mattern, and Sherry Yocum. Finally, we could not have accomplished this work without the incredible organizational skills, hard work, and commitment of Ann Morris and Barbara King. Their attention to the many details that go into organizing a good conference make it possible for us to focus on the ideas, a luxury many book editors do not enjoy. We simply could not create this series of books without them.

—Alan Booth
—Ann C. Crouter

I

Contemporary Patterns and Trends in U.S. Fertility: Where Have We Come From, and Where Are We Headed?

1

IS VERY LOW FERTILITY INEVITABLE IN AMERICA? INSIGHTS AND FORECASTS FROM AN INTEGRATIVE MODEL OF FERTILITY

S. Philip Morgan[1]
Kellie Hagewen
Duke University

Introduction

The United States has an exceptional level of overall fertility—among the highest for economically developed countries. In addition, its fertility is approximately the level required for population replacement (2.1 children per woman). In contrast, fertility is well below replacement in many other developed countries, raising serious concerns for national governments. These low rates of fertility are also well below the number of children that many women intend (Bongaarts, 2002; Kohler, Billari, & Ortega, 2002), creating personal crises for some women (e.g., Hewlett, 2002). Why is the U.S. fertility level high relative to that in other developed countries? Is the very low fertility observed in some other countries transitory? Or are the forces of economic development and concomitant changes inevitably anti-natalist and do they portend low fertility in the American future?

A common response to the "American exception" is that the high fertility rates in the United States can be attributed to the Hispanic and African American sub-populations. True, Hispanic fertility, at 2.75 children per women (TFR= 2.75), is substantially above, and African-American fertility, at 2.05 children per woman, is moderately above (TFR 2.05), that for non-Hispanic Whites, at 1.84 children per woman (TFR= 1.84).[2] But the White non-Hispanic estimate is higher than the overall fertility of most developed countries. (Note that many of those countries contain minorities who also have higher fertility than do natives.) Higher U.S. fertility cannot be "written off" to the behavior of its large minority groups.

In this chapter we describe and build on a model suggested by Bongaarts (2001, 2002). The model posits fertility intentions as the key factor augmented by a set of other factors altering the extent to which these intentions are realized. This framework allows us to integrate much of what we know about low fertility and to

---

[1] Contact S. Philip Morgan: pmorgan@soc.duke.edu. This research was supported by a grant from the National Center for Child health and Human Development at the National Institutes of Health, R01 HD41042.
[2] These are revised estimates based on vital registration birth data and 2000 Census data. See Hamilton et al. (2003).

explain much of what we see in contemporary cross-national fertility. The model also makes clear the assumptions inherent in forecasting fertility into the future.

An Integrative Model of Fertility

While concerns about low fertility have arisen, much of the world is still characterized by high fertility—high in terms of women's stated intentions and relative to levels required for population replacement. At its heart, both the fertility decline and any eventual stabilization will reflect the fertility intentions of women and their partners. The heart of the fertility transition everywhere has been the decline in family size, driven by a desire for small families. Figure 1.1 shows a stylized version of a fertility transition from high to low levels of fertility. Note that before fertility began its decline, the intended parity (*IP*) or intended family size was high but the level of observed fertility (*TFR*) was higher still. The difference in IP and TFR expands for countries undergoing transition. Finally, for post-transition (low fertility) societies the reverse occurs: women have fewer children than they intend. This stylized transition obscures the exact experience of particular countries because there is variation in IP and TFR within each of these stages. Finally, these stages reflect past experience and do not guarantee that countries that now have high and medium levels of fertility will follow this pattern.

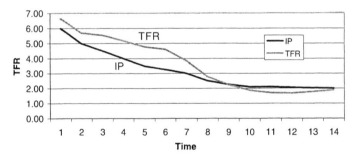

Figure 1.1. Stylized Trends: TFR and IP

Our goal is to explain this general, historic pattern in fertility and variation for countries at particular stages. This explanation allows us to contemplate likely future scenarios, specifically, to forecast future fertility levels and to illustrate the uncertainty inherent in such forecasts.

An Aggregate and Integrative Model

Bongaarts (2001, 2002) offers a useful accounting framework that captures many of the factors that need to be considered. This framework can account for the decline in fertility over time as well as contemporary cross-sectional differences.

Specifically,

$$TFR = IP \acute{} F_u \acute{} F_r \acute{} F_g \acute{} F_t \acute{} F_i \acute{} F_c \acute{} E$$

In Bongaarts' conceptualization, the level of current fertility (i.e., the total fertility rate, *TFR*) equals the intended parity (*IP*) of young women (e.g., those aged 21–25) increased or de-creased by a set of model parameters that reflect forces not incorporated into their reports of childbearing intentions. F_u: *Unwanted fertility.* Demographers define unwanted births as those resulting from conceptions that occurred when women reported that they intended to have no more children (at the time they became pregnant). Thus, these pregnancies (and births) would not have occurred in a "perfect contraceptive" society. Unwanted fertility increases TFR relative to IP (and $F_u > 1.0$).

- F_g: *Gender preferences.* Some couples who intend, say, two children, will decide after having two that the gender composition is not acceptable and that they will revise upwards their *IP*. Given that one cannot control sex of offspring, couples are not expected to incorporate gender preferences in their *IP*. In the United States, evidence shows that couples prefer having at least one son and one daughter and that couples with two sons or two daughters are more likely to have additional children. Such preferences and behavior would increase *TFR* relative to *IP* (and $F_g > 1.0$).

- F_r: *Replacement effect.* Some couples will have additional children because one of their children dies. Replacement is a *response* to a child death. Some couples have additional children as insurance against a future child loss. This factor increases *IP* and, thus, we do not include its impact here. (See Preston, 1978.) Replacement will increase fertility (i.e., $F_r > 1.0$) most in settings where infant and child mortality is highest.

- F_t: *Tempo effect.* The TFR is a period measure of fertility; it measures births in a given calendar year. Thus, if women are having births at later ages (and in subsequent years), the TFR is depressed. Bongaarts and Feeney (1998) have described and documented this effect, which can be both powerful and enduring. ($F_t < 1.0$ when age at childbearing is increasing and > 1.0 when age at childbearing is declining.)

- F_i: *Sub/infecundity.* Fecundity is the biological ability to have children. In general, women (and men) will not know if they are, or when they will become, sub or infecund and thus they cannot incorporate the likelihood of infecundity into their reports of *IP*. A small proportion of women are infecund at young ages (1 or 2%; see Bongaarts, 1978) but the proportion increases with age (especially after age 35; see Bongaarts, 1978; Menken, 1985). Thus, infecundity increases *IP* relative to *TFR* (and $F_i < 1.0$).

- F_c: *Competition.* Women can also revise their fertility intentions upwards or downwards depending upon their experiences, opportunities, and constraints (that encourage or compete with childbearing). Some of this competition may be anticipated and incorporated into IP. Some may not be, e.g., the contemporary difficulty of combining a job and a family or of finding a suitable partner may be underestimated. In contemporary settings F_c is expected to be < 1.0.

To show the value of this framework, we continue with the stylized example in Figure 1.1. First, at the broadest level we see a strong association between intended parity and the TFR. The plotted values are shown in Table 1.1. Both show that fertility falls because people want fewer children. Of course, this begs a further question: why do people want fewer children? This question and its answer are fundamental in discussions of current and future fertility levels; we will return to them in detail below. In Table 1.1 we show a stylized, plausible version of the "rest of the story"—trends in other factors that explain the varying relative levels of the TFR and IP.

Table 1.1.
Hypothetical Model Values Consistent With Trends in Figure 1.1

Time Period	IP	Fu	Fg	Fr	Ft	Fi	Fc	TFR	
1	6.00	1.05	1.01	1.10	1.00	0.95	1.00	6.65	Pre-transition
2	5.00	1.10	1.01	1.09	0.99	0.95	1.00	5.69	
3	4.50	1.20	1.02	1.08	0.98	0.95	1.00	5.54	
4	4.00	1.30	1.03	1.07	0.97	0.95	0.98	5.18	
5	3.50	1.40	1.04	1.06	0.96	0.95	0.97	4.78	
6	3.25	1.50	1.05	1.05	0.95	0.95	0.95	4.61	In-transition
7	3.00	1.40	1.05	1.04	0.95	0.95	0.93	3.85	
8	2.50	1.25	1.05	1.03	0.95	0.94	0.92	2.78	
9	2.25	1.20	1.04	1.02	0.92	0.93	0.91	2.23	
10	2.10	1.15	1.02	1.01	0.91	0.92	0.90	1.87	
11	2.10	1.09	1.02	1.00	0.90	0.90	0.90	1.70	Post-transition
12	2.05	1.09	1.02	1.00	0.90	0.91	0.90	1.68	
13	2.02	1.09	1.01	1.00	0.95	0.93	0.90	1.77	
14	2.00	1.09	1.01	1.00	1.00	0.95	0.90	1.88	Future 2020

In this framework, a value of 1.0 means that the model parameter has "no effect", net of intended parity (IP) in increasing the TFR. The most striking pattern in Table 1.1 is the dramatic increase in unwanted fertility (F_u) for societies in transition from high TFR to low TFR, and then its subsequent decline in the post-transition period. Note that unwanted fertility does not disappear in the post-transition period and that we do not forecast its disappearance. Replacement (F_r) is substantial in pre-transition (when infant and child mortality is high) but our stylized view shows a secular decline to "no effect". Interestingly, the gender composition effect has little influence when fertility is high, but its impact increases as fertility falls. In late periods, a counterbalancing effect (an emergence of gender indifference; see Pollard & Morgan, 2002) attenuates the effect of gender preference (F_g). We project a very modest effect of gender preference that raises TFR relative to IP.

In the post-transition stage, IP is greater than TFR, implying that the remaining factors are <1.0 and of a magnitude to overcome the factors discussed above. Bongaarts (2002) shows that delayed fertility is a major factor lowering the TFR. At the heart of the "second demographic transition" is the increase in age at childbearing. This factor operates as long as age at childbearing continues to increase. We anticipate that the increase will stop in the future as ages of childbearing increase to ages where sub- and infecundity become major concerns (when women delay childbearing to a point where biological constraints on childbearing become a significant factor). Also lowering fertility relative to intentions is infecundity and competition. Future trends in these components are highly speculative and are core issues taken up below.

Before moving to a discussion of the individual factors, let us consider country variation within the post-transition category. Italy and the United States produce a striking contrast. We assume (Table 1.2) that intended parity varies modestly across countries, consistent with data presented by Bongaarts (2001, 2003).[3] Further, unwanted fertility (F_u) increases the *TFR* by 10% in the United States and by 4% in Italy. The next two components are additional births resulting from attempts to achieve a given sex preference (F_g) or to "replace" a child who has died (F_r). These model parameters are very small and do not vary in this example. The remaining three model parameters are important in low fertility settings and reduce observed fertility relative to intent. The tempo effect (F_t) represents the effects of fertility postponement that is greater in Italy than in the United States. The sub/infecundity parameter (F_i) increases as the pattern of childbearing moves later (or if relevant diseases are prevalent). Here we assume a greater reduction in Italian fertility due to its later mean age at childbearing. Finally, there is *competition* (F_c) with other activities (e.g., women's career) or obstacles (e.g., the absence of a suitable partner)

---

[3] Simple means of desired or intended parity vary little across low-fertility countries. But more nuanced analyses (e.g., Micheli & Bernardi, 2003) or more recent data (e.g., Goldstein, Lutz & Testa, 2003) make this an active area of inquiry.

that lead one to adjust intended parity. This adjustment could be upwards or downwards for individuals, but in the low fertility context there is evidence that the predominant shift is downwards (Quesnel-Vallee & Morgan, 2002). Note that a set of modest but complementary differences in each of the model parameters can cumulate to produce substantial differences, like those we posit below for Italy and the United States. Note these differences emerge in the absence of major differences in intended parity (*IP*).

Table 1.2.
Bongaarts' Conceptual Model of Factors Affecting Period: Illustrative Values for Italy and the United States

		Country	
		Post-transition (Italy)	Post-transition (United States)
Component	Description		
IFS	Intended family size	2	2.2
Fu	Unwanted fertility	1.04	1.10
Fg	Gender preferences	1.02	1.02
Fr	Replacement effect	1.005	1.005
Ft	Tempo effect	0.85	0.92
Fi	Sub/infecundity	0.90	0.92
Fc	Competition	0.75	0.90
TFR=		1.22	1.89

TFR= IFS* Fu * Fg * Fr * Ft * Fi * Fc

Thus, this formulation is a compact way to account for differences across time or across countries in various components affecting fertility. The formulation helps us think through which aspects of fertility are responsible for differences in fertility levels across groups. What, more precisely, needs to be explained? Answers allow us to contemplate behavioral models on the most important aspects separating U.S. fertility levels from those in other countries.

To determine whether or not U.S. fertility will fall below replacement level and whether or not low fertility countries will remain below replacement level, we must answer a set of questions structured by the above framework:

- How many children do young adults intend and what level of certainty is attached to these plans? Is there any evidence of secular decreases in recent decades?
- What proportion of individuals will have mistimed and unwanted births? How is this related to the availability of reproductive health services and contraceptives?
- How strongly will the desire for a child of each sex influence fertility?
- To what extent will individuals' intended or desired fertility be frustrated by subfecundity or infecundity? Will new technologies reduce the number of women unable to have the children they intend?
- Will competition from non-childbearing desires/interests lead to shifts in intended parity over the life cycle? What is the impact of increasing female labor force participation and how will it be offset by institutional adjustments? How important is the establishment of a stable long-term relationship for achieving intended parity?

Below we address these questions. Together, these answers provide the reasons for low fertility, and why it is lower in some places than in others.

The Total Fertility Rate and Period Approach

The total fertility rate (TFR) is the most widely used measure of fertility. It has several desirable features: it is a single summary measure over all childbearing years, is age-standardized, and has an intuitive description. Specifically, the TFR is the mean number of children a woman would have if she were to experience (over the course of her life) the age-specific fertility rates of a particular period. Below (Table 1.3), we present TFRs for selected countries that illustrate the level and range observed in the contemporary period.

The TFR is a "period measure" (as opposed to a cohort measure). While strong arguments for a cohort approach have been made (see Ryder, 1965), most agree that fertility rates are better described from a "period" perspective. Rates tend to increase or decrease in concert across a broad age range, and there is little inherent in observed behavior that can be traced to earlier, unique, "formative" experiences (i.e., cohort—see Ni Bhrochain, 1990). From a decision maker's standpoint, the relevant question is: do I/we attempt to have a child now (at this age and in this time period) or not.

Table 1.3.
Selected Low TFRs

Country	TFR
Spain	1.16
Italy	1.20
Greece	1.30
Germany	1.33
...	...
France	1.89
U.S.	2.03
U.S. White Non-Hispanic	1.84

Source: United Nations Population Division (2002).
U.S. Data for 2001 from Ventura et al. (2003).

Fertility Intentions

The cornerstone of our approach is the concept of a target family size or intended parity. If all women realized their fertility intention, then (given a fixed age-pattern of fertility) the TFR = IP. This is the same as saying that all other factors in the model above equal unity, 1.0. But is intended parity sufficiently stable and predictive to make this formulation useful? A large theoretical and empirical literature addresses the *predictive validity* of reproductive intentions. Morgan (2001) has recently reviewed this literature and notes that intended parity is not an accurate predictor of completed fertility for individuals or aggregate fertility for cohorts. However, Morgan argues that the pattern of *errors* is predictable/interpretable so that an *adjusted IP* could be useful for projection purposes. The current model is a version of this approach focused on a period (as opposed to a cohort).

As a period measure of IP, we take the mean target number of children for a group of women at early stages of family formation (e.g., women aged 21–25). In effect, we assume that older women would have exactly this IP were they to "start over" (i.e., were they now at this earlier life cycle stage) and that older women represent exactly the response pattern to existing period constraints of younger ones were they to experience these period conditions at each subsequent age. In this way, we "construct" a synthetic cohort of intentions/behavior that parallel the

TFR synthetic measure. Are these counterfactuals plausible? We respond: yes. Over the past 30 years in low-fertility countries, intended parity has been quite stable. So older age groups actually had an IP equal to that currently reported by younger women. Also, age-period-cohort analyses show that women of all ages respond similarly to period conditions. As evidence of the stability of IP over the past few decades, we show intended parity for women ages 20–26 from the General Social Survey (see Hagewen & Morgan, 2003). (See Figure 1.2.)

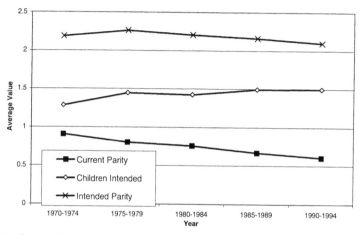

Figure 1.2. Current Parity, Intended Number of Children and Intended Parity, Women 20-26

The top line in the figure shows little change in IP, the sum of additional children intended and current parity. In 1970–1974 and 1990–1994, IP was 2.18 and 2.10, respectively. Beneath this stability one can see clear declines in current parity, an indicator of fertility delay/postponement. We interpret this decline as postponement because of the observed mirror-image increase of additional children intended. At the aggregate level, this postponement did not lead to substantial declines in intended parity for young women.

Why have the intentions of young women remained roughly the same over highly variable periods? Our answer (also see Morgan, 2003) focuses on the importance of and rationale for low parity births in contemporary, low-fertility societies. Regarding importance, first- and second-order births account for 75–90% of all births in many contemporary, low-fertility societies. Fertility rates and trends, now and in the future, will be driven primarily by the births of first and second children. Regarding their rationale, long-standing norms have discouraged childlessness and one-child families (Blake, 1972). The sanctions for violating these norms are weaker because there is an expanded set of circumstances that legitimate them. However, these circumstances legitimate *not having children—* not *the desire to have none.* Very few young women state an intended parity of 0 or 1 child. Also, we argue that norms have emerged against having a large number of children. Large families are seen as incompatible with good parenting and with providing children the resources and attention they need and deserve. These norms discourage reports of large intended parity. Taken together, these norms prescribe a narrow range for intended parity. Two children is invariably the modal response, usually accounting for over 50% of all respondents.

These intentions for a small family size fit with other structural constraints and with biological predispositions. For instance, norms about space, safety, and child development mean that more than two children require larger houses, larger cars, and extended periods of childcare and education. Our final point may be more controversial: biological predispositions reinforce a number of these tendencies, especially the affective reasons for having kids (that parents fall in love with their children) (Miller, 2002; Morgan & King, 2001), and that parents are willing to have fewer children to increase their children's life chances (see Lam, 2003). Biological predispositions do not "cause" anything. As Pinker notes, the gene associated with risk taking does not make you take risks. It does, however, increase the pleasure sensation resulting from things like jumping out of a plane or driving fast. Likewise, neural circuitry producing a warm glow when you hold your helpless, big-eyed infant did not make you have that baby but it does help you to fall in love with him or her. In fact, this warm glow, love, may be the root of altruism toward our children. Hrdy (2000) asserts that maternal attachment is conditional—the strongest evidence, she argues, is the co-evolution of babies to extract maternal commitment. In short, having few and heavily investing in them "fits" well with our evolutionary inheritance and, thus, with neural wiring in our **and** our children's brains (i.e., from our genes).[4]

Thus, despite their *central role* in our argument and model, we do not see intentions as playing a *dynamic role* in contemporary change/differences. Rather, we believe that there is a remarkably pervasive desire (and supporting norms, structure, and biological predispositions) for *two children when and if one can afford them and care for them.* The dynamic parts of the model reflect the constraints present across countries and over time. We now characterize the influence of such constraints.

---

[4] On a longer time scale (century versus a decadal one), such predispositions might be expected to strengthen due to natural selection.

Unwanted Births

Recent surveys suggest that 7–12% of births in the United States can be classified as "unwanted." There is widespread misunderstanding beyond demography, and some within, about this important concept of *unwanted fertility.*[5] A birth is considered unwanted if the respondent reports that, prior to becoming pregnant with this child, she did not want more children. The question relates to intentions prior to pregnancy and has no necessary link to how parents feel about a child (at birth or afterwards). If unwanted fertility has negative consequences for children it is likely spread over the full set of siblings, who may suffer from the diminution of resources available per child. Powerful and long-standing norms of equal treatment of one's children would seem to guarantee this result (see Parsons, 1974).

The current U.S. rate of 7–12% is high by international standards[6] and has declined over the past half century, but little of this decline is evident in the past fifteen years. Will unwanted fertility decline further in the future? We forecast contemporary levels of unwanted fertility into the indefinite U.S. future. To explain, unwanted fertility depends on two phenomena: unintended conceptions and the acceptability of abortion. The United States has high rates of unintended pregnancy, and abortions are stigmatized, with access sometimes difficult. Of course, this answer is unsatisfactory because it replaces one question with two difficult-to-answer questions: why are unintended pregnancies so frequent and why is abortion stigmatized (compared to other developed countries)?

Only brief answers can be sketched here, but neither portends secular change. High rates of unintended pregnancies occur because contraceptives are not used effectively. A range of contraceptives is available that have high theoretical effectiveness. In practice, these contraceptives are not used because they have perceived risks, are not convenient, or sex was not planned or expected (Glei, 1999; Sable, Libbus, & Chiu, 2000). Our prediction of stability does not suggest that these factors are immutable, but rather that they are anchored in contemporary culture, little influenced by secular factors and unlikely to be influenced by coherent public policy. Likewise, the future of abortion acceptability and access is anybody's guess. A few decades ago, powerful ideologies of equality spawned seemingly secular shifts toward women's right to control their own reproduction (Rossi & Sitaraman, 1988). But the right-to-life movement has succeeded in making many

---

[5] The concept "unintended births" (or pregnancies) includes those who did not want a birth now (a timing failure) and those who wanted no more children ever (a number failure). Unwanted births refer to the latter. Mosher and Bachrach (1996) report that 57% of pregnancies are unintended and that 40% of U.S. births result from unintended pregnancies. Kost and Forrest (1995) report 7% unwanted using the 1988 National Maternal and Infant Health Survey; Forrest and Singh (1990) report 12% using the 1988 National Survey of Family Growth. Chandra et al. (1997) report 10% of births as unwanted using the 1995 NSFG.

[6] Estimated unwanted fertility rates in the United States are more than twice as high as in Sweden, France and Japan, for instance (see AGI [1999], chart 2.6, p. 17).

reconsider women's rights vis-à-vis those of unborn children. Coupled with the increasing acceptability of having children outside marriage, many now construct/ interpret an unwanted birth to an unmarried woman as the best (even noble) choice given the alternatives.

Other Unpredictable Demographic Events That Increase Fertility

An unwanted birth is, by definition, a demographic event that increases fertility relative to intentions. Other demographic events, likewise unintended, can lead to decisions to increase fertility relative to earlier stated intentions. Two events that have received substantial attention in the literature are child deaths and the sex composition of children. Infant and child mortality are rare and most couples do not factor the possibility of a child death into their statement of intentions. Nevertheless, were one of their children to die, parents might replace this child by an additional birth. The evidence for volitional replacement of this sort is modest in places with high to moderate infant mortality,[7] and its potential impact on fertility in low-mortality contexts is very small.[8] Forecasting a secular decline in this component seems straightforward.

The sex composition of children is another example. In situations where the sex of children cannot be manipulated, couples will not know their sex composition at parity two (when they have two children). Thus, their stated intention (as asked in most surveys) cannot take account of the as yet undetermined sex of their future children. Thus, if parity two is reached and the current sex composition is unsatisfactory, fertility intentions may be revised upwards. The potential of such an effect is substantial but it depends on the type and intensity of the sex preference.

For instance, assume that couples have a strong sex preference, say of one boy and one girl, and thus report wanting two children. If they keep having children until they have one boy and one girl their mean family size would be 3.0—one child more than intended (Bongaarts & Potter, 1983, Table 9.1). Of course, some couples would only have two children (50%) while some would have 3 (25%), some 4 (12.5%), and the rest more than 4. Similar estimates can be made for any sex composition. These calculations represent the maximum effect of sex preferences. Few couples would consider sex composition so important that they disregard family size. Behavioral estimates in the United States clearly indicate that couples with two same-sex children are more likely to have a third, more likely by a factor of

---

[7] Preston (1978) points out that there are multiple pathways by which infant mortality can influence fertility. The "biological replacement mechanism" operating through cessation of breastfeeding when an infant dies can be substantial, as can the behavioral mechanism of "hoarding" (i.e., having additional children as protection against possible child loss). Replacement of children who die certainly occurs but has only modest effects on fertility, even in high-mortality contexts.

[8] U.S. infant mortality rates slipped below 7 per 1,000 (to 6.8) in 2001 (Matthews, Menacker, & MacDorman, 2003). Child mortality rates are very low in the United States so that fewer than 8 per 1,000 die by age 5 (Arias & Smith, 2003). These rates are substantially higher than those for many other developed countries, although lower than those of developing countries.

1.23 for cohorts of women born 1915–1954 (see Pollard & Morgan, 2002). If we were to assume that couples were willing to "try once, but only once" to have the daughter or son they have not had, then the fertility of these women would increase moderately, perhaps from 2.0 children to 2.07.[9] Pollard and Morgan (2002) argue that this effect is becoming smaller as the result of fundamental gender change (emerging gender indifference).[10] Such a trend suggests this factor's influence, quite modest already, will fade further.

In short, the influence of gender preference is currently very modest, and this weak effect will likely only diminish in the future. This small and weakening effect is forecast in the absence of sex selection technology that will likely become widely available in the coming decade. Such technology would weaken further or eliminate this pronatalist effect.

Fertility Timing

Demographers have long known that when the age at childbearing shifts upward, period rates (such as the TFR) are depressed relative to cohort rates (e.g., Ryder's 1980 important and classic work). Bongaarts and Feeney (1998; Bongaarts, 2001, 2002) have made important contributions to this understanding in the past decade. First, they propose a simple calculation to estimate the magnitude of this "tempo distortion." This work suggests that current TFRs for many countries are 5–20% below levels that would be observed in the absence of fertility postponement. Second, they show that the tempo distortion remains as long as increases in age at childbearing persist. For many countries, this implies that the tempo distortion can last for three or more decades. Third, while these tempo effects can persist for decades, they argue that the trend toward older ages at childbearing must eventually end (and may be nearing an end in countries with mean age at childbearing over 30 years of age). Taken together, the import of their argument is that the underlying level of number of births per woman is greater than that implied in contemporary TFRs. In fact, for many contemporary countries, nearly one half of the difference in current TFRs and replacement-level fertility can be attributed to this "tempo distortion."

---

[9] Using estimates from Pollard and Morgan (2002), the odds of an additional birth to a parity 2 woman are increased by a factor of 1.23 if her children are of the same sex. Using a parity progression ratio (the proportion of women who had at least *n* live births who go on to have at least one more) to parity 3 of .6 for those with one boy and one girl, the higher odds of a birth for those with children of the same sex implies 69 extra births per 1,000 women (assuming 50% of women have same sex children). If the parity progression drops to .4, then this differential by sex of children produces 46 extra births. In Appendix Table A2, we show the possible effects of sex preference of this magnitude at parity 2 on overall fertility. This exercise suggests that 1.02 (or a 2% increase in fertility) is an appropriate estimate for U.S. fertility in the period 1960–1990.

[10] The calculations implied in endnote 5 make clear that the impact of sex preference on overall fertility also declines as the progression ratio to parity 3 declines. So, while the differential risk of having a child may remain, its impact on overall fertility declines as fewer women overall have a third child or as fewer women reach parity 2.

    The case for the United States is illustrative but moderate in impact. In Figure 1.3, the observed TFR shows the well-known 20th-century swings in U.S. fertility. The adjusted TFR (TFR') shows the underlying period quantum of fertility (the predicted level of period fertility in the absence of fertility postponement). The baby boom was amplified by a *decline* in ages at childbearing that pushed TFR>TFR'; in contrast, the baby bust was amplified by an *increase* in ages at childbearing (TFR<TFR'). Note the TFR'>TFR for the period 1960–1995. For the 1975–1994 period, TFR/TFR' equals .92, our estimate of the contemporary effect of fertility postponement (F_p) in Table 1.2.

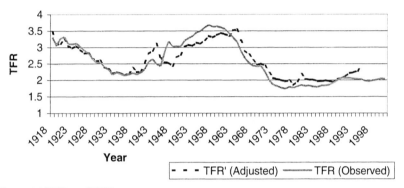

Figure 1.3. TFR and TFR'

    Thus, this component may have cyclical effects (that can now be well measured and monitored) but the secular effect of this factor in many low-fertility countries has nearly run its course (because further delays in childbearing are becoming difficult). Modest fertility increases will accompany the leveling off of increases in mean ages at childbearing.

Infecundity/Subfecundity

Without changing their intention, couples can have fewer children than intended because of unanticipated sub/infecundity. The prevalence of sub/infecundity increases with fertility postponement. Thus, this factor becomes a stronger anti-natalist factor as ages at childbearing rise.[11] As a counterforce, effective treatments for sub/infecundity allow many women to have children. In 2000, nearly 1% of U.S. births were the result of assisted reproductive technology (ART) (i.e., in vitro fertilization embryo transfer [IVF] Wright et al., 2003).[12]

---

[11] We ignore here differences across social contexts in the disease environments that may increase sub/infecundity.

[12] Reports from ART clinics in the United States reported 35,025 live births from 25,228 live birth deliveries in 2000. The number of ART procedures was 99,629 in 2000. The number of births and the success rate has increased dramatically over the past decade. See Wright et al. (2003). There were approximately 4 million births in 2001 (4,026,000). Thus, the percent resulting from ART equals 0.87%.

How rapidly does fecundity decline with age? Table 1.4 shows estimates accepted by most demographers. A few women are unable to have children even at the youngest ages (our estimate is 2% at age 17.5) The increase by age (shown in this table) is plotted on a log scale in Figure 1.4. Note that, on a log scale, the increase is linear with a slope of approximately 1.0. This indicates that infecundity increases by doubling approximately every 5 years. At age 42.5, 60% of women are infecund; five years later nearly all are infecund.

Table 1.4.
Percent Infecund by Age

Age	% Infecund
17.5	2
22.5	5
27.5	10
32.5	15
37.5	25
42.5	60
47.5	100

Source: Menken (1985).

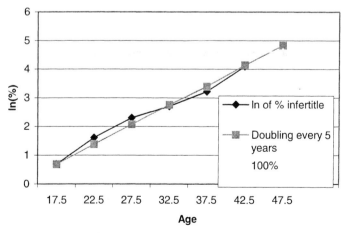

Figure 1.4. Increase in Infecundity With Age

Since infecundity increases with increasing age and ages at first birth are rising, this antinatalist factor should be strengthening. An indication of the effects of the "biological clock" is illustrated by simulations carried out by Bongaarts and Potter (1983) and reproduced in Table 1.4. The table shows the percent of women who would not realize their family size goals given marriage ages of 20, 25 and 30 and three "spacing regimes". No spacing implies no use of contraception until desired family size is attained. Medium spacing means two years of effective contraceptive use following each birth. Wide spacing assumes two years of effective contraception following marriage and three years following the birth of each child. Two levels of contraceptive effectiveness are shown (90% and 100% effective). No spacing and early marriage implies that very few will not realize their goals for 1, 2 or 3 children. Postponement of marriage (and first birth) and wide spacing contribute significantly to the percent falling short of intentions. Twenty-seven (26.9) percent of women marrying at age 30 and adopting wide spacing will fail to have three children prior to the end of their fecund years.

Mean age at first birth increased from 21.4 in 1970 to 25.0 in 2000 (Mathews & Hamilton, 2002). Using the data in Table 1.5 and assuming "marriage" at age 25, a desire for two children, wide spacing, and perfect contraceptive use, nearly 8% (7.8%) would have fewer than two children. A precise estimate of this factor is very difficult but a current estimate of .9 (a 10% overall reduction in TFR) seems reasonable.

As mentioned above, a counterforce is improved technologies that can alter fecundability (i.e., the monthly probability of conception). As noted previously, 1% of births now result from in vitro fertilization embryo transfer. These procedures and new ones will likely offset in part the increased infecundity one would expect from further advances in mean maternal age. Leridon (2003) offers these estimates of the current impact of in vitro fertilization embryo transfer: at ages 30, 35 and 40, the 2-year success rate for couples is 32, 21 and 15% above that expected in the absence of in vitro fertilization embryo transfer treatments. Thus, in vitro fertilization embryo transfer partly offsets the effects of this factor and there is room for substantial progress in the future. At the current time these levels of effectiveness and their expense of treatment (which limits the numbers receiving these treatments) reduce the impact of this counterforce.

Table 1.5.
Proportion Failing to Attain Desired Family Size

Marriage Age and Number of Children Desired	No Spacing	Medium Spacing		Wide Spacing	
		$e = .90$	$e = 1.00$	$e = .90$	$e = 1.00$
Marriage at Age 20					
1 child desired	3.0%	3.0%	3.0%	3.1%	3.1%
2 children	3.4%	3.7%	3.7%	4.5%	4.7%
3 children	4.3%	4.7%	4.8%	6.0%	6.2%
Marriage at Age 25					
1 child desired	5.1%	5.1%	5.1%	5.5%	5.7%
2 children	6.1%	6.3%	6.3%	7.5%	7.8%
3 children	7.3%	8.1%	8.2%	10.8%	11.3%
Marriage at Age 30					
1 child desired	8.8%	8.8%	8.8%	9.7%	9.9%
2 children	11.0%	11.5%	11.6%	14.6%	15.4%
3 children	14.7%	16.4%	16.7%	25.3%	26.9%

Source: Bongaarts (1983), Table 7.1.

Life Course Competition Between Fertility Intentions and Other Goals

The above model parameters have fairly predictable effects. They can cumulate to produce modest differences. But an additional set of factors, ones we group together and label *competition* (F_c), can lead to much lower fertility than originally intended (or conceivably to higher fertility). In this category, we discuss factors that lead persons to alter their intention for children, say after age 25. Fertility intentions at ages 21–25 are driven primarily by normative expectations and general preferences and attitudes. Later in the reproductive life-course they are altered by practical considerations and constraints.

In many contexts, forming a stable union is a pre-requisite to childbearing, and in most such unions provides the most appropriate contexts for childbearing (see Thomson, this volume). When intentions are stated in young adulthood, most respondents are assuming they will be married (or will be in "marital-like" stable unions). Thus, in some cases the failure to have children can be traced directly to the absence of a suitable partner. If women decide to have a child without a partner, they may choose to have fewer children than intended because of the difficulty of raising children as a single parent. Thus, changing proportions of married and the stability of unions can account for family sizes falling below those intended. For instance, using Current Population Survey data, O'Connell and Rogers (1983, p. 369) find that the fertility expectations of women aged 18–24 and married in 1971 were realized by the end of the decade (1981). However, unmarried women's expectations were not met, explaining the "failure" of birth expectations data "to predict the period fertility downswing of the 1970s" and for the underestimation of completed fertility for the age group as a whole. Quesnel-Vallee and Morgan have used longitudinal data from the National Longitudinal Survey of Youth to address this same question over the period 1982–2000 (for birth cohorts 1957–1961). They find substantial aggregate stability in the fertility intentions of women aged 18–24 and a strong correspondence between aggregate intentions and behavior. However, there is substantial individual level inconsistency with "being unmarried at age 24", a strong correlate of not realizing intentions by age 40.

Thus, a key area for study is the link between union formation and fertility. Rindfuss, Guzzo and Morgan (2003) show that countries with high levels of nonmarital childbearing have higher levels of overall fertility. It would seem that marriage postponement and strong injunctions against nonmarital births set the stage for very low fertility. Women's and society's willingness to accept nonmarital childbearing, possibly in cohabiting unions, stands out as a key question in determining "how low fertility will go."

Other important factors are linked to roles that compete with childbearing and rearing. Broadly conceived, some contexts are more conducive to combining work or other activities and being a parent. Rindfuss, Guzzo and Morgan (2003) identify the following as important factors:

- Availability, acceptability, accessibility, quality, and cost of childcare
- Market substitutes for goods/services formerly produced in the home
- Labor market accommodations (e.g., flex time)
- Public policy interventions (e.g., family leave)
- Gender role flexibility and men's contributions to housework and childcare

While not measuring these components specifically, Rindfuss et al. estimate the degree of "incompatibility" of childbearing and female labor force participation across 22 low-fertility countries. These results are reproduced in Table 1.6.

Table 1.6.

Sensitivity/Elasticity[1] of Female Labor Force Participation (FLFP) and the Total Fertility Rate (TFR)

Country	Years Since the TFR First Fell Below 2.0	Average FLFP Increase	Sensitivity[1]	1997 TFR
Italy	21	0.40	-3.15	1.19
Portugal	15	0.78	-2.26	1.43
West Germany[2]	20	0.34	-1.64	1.45
Austria	25	0.44	-1.48	1.37
Greece	15	0.54	-1.44	1.32
Spain	16	0.48	-1.38	1.16
Japan	23	0.51	-1.38	1.44
Switzerland	26	0.46	-1.02	1.40
France	23	0.49	-0.84	1.69
Belgium	25	0.41	-0.82	1.50
Sweden	29	0.53	-0.80	1.58
UK	24	0.52	-0.54	1.71
Denmark	29	0.52	-0.48	1.75
Canada	26	0.52	-0.44	1.66
Finland	29	0.93	-0.39	1.76
Australia	20	0.58	-0.38	1.80
Netherlands	25	0.38	-0.30	1.53
Ireland	5	1.61	-0.29	1.87
Luxembourg	28	0.33	-0.24	1.71
Norway	23	0.60	-0.20	1.85
New Zealand	16	0.71	0.02	1.96
U.S.	25	0.53	0.27	2.06

[1] Sensitivity or elasticity = $\ln(TFR_t/TFR_1) / \ln(FLFP_t/FLFP_1)$, where subscript 1 = first year in series TFR<2.0 and year t=1997 or last year with observed data.

Compatibility is measured by the "sensitivity or elasticity" of period fertility (the TFR) with respect to changes in female labor force participation. The countries are listed in order of sensitivity. The estimate for Italy, -3.15, indicates that a 1% increase in female labor force participation was associated with a 3.15% reduction in fertility. Such sensitivity suggests very high incompatibility in childbearing and women's work. The U.S. estimate, on the other hand, is .27, suggesting no decline in fertility (and actually a trivial positive effect, a .27 increase in fertility associated with an increase of 1% in female labor force participation) with increasing female labor force participation. This Italy/U.S. difference is reflected in the parameters for this component shown in Table 1.6.

How large are the effects of competition (F_c)? Given our model $(TFR = IP´F_u´F_g´F_r´F_t´F_i´F_c´E)$ and assuming no measurement error, we can solve for F_c. Specifically, $F_c = TFR / (IP´F_u´F_g´F_r´F_t´F_i)$. Using values in Table 2, we derive a value of .9 for the contemporary United States (competition, F_c, lowers fertility by .9, or 10%) due to revised intentions after age 25 resulting from this class of factors. Conversations with Bongaarts reveal his view that the importance and difficulty of measurement of this factor are the major weakness of this model. Clearly, this is an area requiring more work, but longitudinal data offer the opportunity to estimate this component or to measure it in combination with other components. For instance, Quesnel-Vallee and Morgan (2003) show that recent U.S. cohorts have substantial inconsistency between fertility intent and outcomes between ages 22 and 40. But the *NET* shift is -.33 births. Since Quesnel-Vallee and Morgan focus on cohort fertility, their model reduces to: $(TFR = IP´F_u$ $´F_g´F_r´F_i´F_c)$ and $(TFR / IP = F_u´F_g´F_r´F_i´F_c)$. U.S. estimates shown earlier in Table 1.2 suggest that the first four components are roughly offsetting. Thus, competition (F_c) equals, using the Quesnel-Vallee and Morgan estimates, 2.05/2.29 TFR/IP =.89 (very close to the .9 we have suggested).[13] These calculations give us some confidence in parameters suggested for Table 1.2. However, much additional work will be needed to refine these estimates.

---

[13] See Appendix Table A.1.

Conclusion

At a 2003 Population Association of America session on low fertility, a speaker expressed concern that "fear of population decline" and very low fertility might lead to coercive pronatalist policies. Such a concern is justified; limiting access to contraceptives and abortion has been justified elsewhere as a necessary response to low fertility (Berelson, 1979; Kligman, 1998) and could conceivably increase fertility by increasing unwanted fertility (F_u). In contrast, consider Judith Blake's (1972) reaction to suggested antinatalist coercion as a remedy for the "high fertility" of the 1950s and early 1960s. Specifically, Blake suggested that before imposing *new layers of coercion* we should examine and perhaps relax the existing *pronatalism inherent in contemporary American society*. These pressures included homophobia, norms against premarital sex (encouraging individuals to form marital unions), norms to marry and have children as early as possible, structural barriers to women's equal participation in the labor market, etc. In parallel, contemporary concerns about low fertility should lead us to think about existing antinatalist coercion that could be weakened or removed, allowing persons to achieve their personal preferences that, luckily, seem to mirror the needs of the collective. Specifically, women report family size intentions that are very close to levels needed for population replacement. The interest of the collective lies in assisting women in realizing their intentions.

The framework used here indicates where some of this effort could be directed. First, the state could invest in infertility research and subsidize infertility treatments. Over 1% of U.S. births are now conceived through in vitro fertilization embryo transfer procedures—in short, reduce the impact of the sub/infecundity (F_i) parameter. An equally large impact could result from making childbearing/ childrearing more compatible with women's labor force work (reducing competition (F_c)). Public policy could play a role here by making daycare, flex time, maternity leave, and healthcare for mothers and children available. Public policy can also encourage more egalitarian gender roles that make men better helpmates and parents. Demographic research plays a key role because it is unclear yet what policies and what features of the social context are most crucial to women and couples.

But the comments above construct the problem too narrowly. First, low fertility is not a contemporary problem in the United States. Current levels of fertility and immigration will keep the U.S. population growing slowly throughout the next century. Second and more importantly, the welfare of children and families are linked to the same factors discussed above. Thus, helping women and couples realize their family intentions and reducing contemporary competition between work and family spheres will benefit children, women, and families. Societal changes aims at promoting family welfare should have widespread appeal and also lay the groundwork for continuing levels of replacement level fertility.

Table A1.
Actual Parity at Age 40 and Intended at Age 25: Selected Cohorts of U.S. Women from NLSY 1979

Birth Cohort (1)	Intended Parity at Age 25 (2)	Achieved Parity at Age 40 (3)	Col (3) / Col (2) (4)	Number of Women NLSY '79 (5)
1961	2.35	2.2	0.94	178
1960	2.25	1.94	0.86	391
1959	2.34	2	0.85	349
1958	2.29	1.94	0.85	370
1957	2.24	2.17	0.97	59
All	2.29	2.05	0.89	1347

Source: Quesnel-Vallee & Morgan (2003).

Table A.2.

The Effects of Sex Preference: Effects on TFR of Desire for a Child of Each Sex Operating Only at Parity 2

(1) Cohort size	(2) P0->P1 Parity Prog.	(3) P1->P2 Parity Prog.	(4) # of Births P0 & P1	(5) % women reaching parity 2	(6) P2-->P3 Prog. No SP	(7) Effect of Same Sex	(8) % at P2 w/ Same Sex	(9) Parity 2 births	(10) Births added by SP	(11) Births P4+ (PPR=.15)	(12) Implied TFR P0-p3	(13) Impact on TFR
With Sex Preference									0.15			
1000	0.82	0.85	1517	0.7	0.7	1.23	0.5	300.1	56.1	45.0	1862.1	1.036
1000	0.82	0.85	1517	0.7	0.6	1.23	0.5	257.2	48.1	38.6	1812.8	1.031
1000	0.82	0.85	1517	0.7	0.5	1.23	0.5	214.3	40.1	32.1	1763.5	1.027
1000	0.82	0.85	1517	0.7	0.4	1.23	0.5	171.5	32.1	25.7	1714.2	1.022
1000	0.82	0.85	1517	0.7	0.3	1.23	0.5	128.6	24.0	19.3	1664.9	1.017
Without Sex Preference												
1000	0.82	0.85	1517	0.7	0.7	1	0.5	244.0	0.0	36.6	1797.5	
1000	0.82	0.85	1517	0.7	0.6	1	0.5	209.1	0.0	31.4	1757.5	
1000	0.82	0.85	1517	0.7	0.5	1	0.5	174.3	0.0	26.1	1717.4	
1000	0.82	0.85	1517	0.7	0.4	1	0.5	139.4	0.0	20.9	1677.3	
1000	0.82	0.85	1517	0.7	0.3	1	0.5	104.6	0.0	15.7	1637.2	

Note on Table A.2. The above provides justification for our estimates of 1.02 for the parameter Fg. Beginning with a cohort of 100 women (Col. 1), the P0->P1 and P1->P2 progression ratios produce 1517 births (Col. 4) with 70% of women reaching parity 2 (Col. 5). We allow the P2->P3 progression ratio to vary from .7 to .3. In the upper panel we allow these P2->P3 ratios to be increased by a factor of 1.23 (Col 7) for the 50% of women with same-sex children (Col. 8). With this structure of sex preference we obtain the number of P2 births (Col. 9).

In the lower panel we make the same calculation but assume no sex preference. Col. 10 shows the number of births added by sex preference. We assume a .15 parity progression for P3+ that adds the high parity births in Col 11. Adding Columns 4, 9 and 11 we obtain the TFR. Col. 13 shows the ratio of the TFR with and without sex preference. This range of estimates includes our suggested parameter of 1.02. This value remains in the range when we choose other parameters observed in the U.S. over the last several decades.

References

Alan Guttmacher Institute. (AGI). (1999). *Sharing responsibility: Women, society and abortion worldwide.* New York: Author.

Arias, E., & Smith, B. L. (2003). Deaths: Preliminary data for 2001. *National Vital Statistics Reports, 51*(5), 1-48.

Berelson, B. (1979). Romania's 1966 anti-abortion decree: The demographic experience of the first decade. *Population Studies, 33,* 209–222.

Blake, J. (1972). Coercive pronatalism and American population policy, in R. Parke, Jr. & C. F. Westoff (Eds.), *U. S. Commission on Population Growth and the American Future, Aspects of Population Growth Policy* (pp. 85–109). Washington, DC: Government Printing Office.

Bongaarts, J. (1978). A framework for analyzing the proximate determinants of fertility. *Population and Development Review, 4,* 105–132.

Bongaarts, J. (2001). Fertility and reproductive preferences in post-transitional societies. In R. A. Bulatao & J. B. Casterline (Eds.), *Global fertility transition* (pp. 260–281). New York: Population Council.

Bongaarts, J. (2002). The end of fertility transition in the developed world. *Population and Development Review, 28,* 419–444.

Bongaarts, J., & Feeney, G. (1998). On the quantum and tempo of fertility. *Population and Development Review, 24,* 271–291.

Bongaarts, J., & Potter, R. G. (1983). *Fertility, biology and behavior.* New York: Academic Press.

Chandra, A. J., Mosher, W. D., Peterson, L., & Piccinino, L. J. (1997). Fertility, family planning, and women's health: New data from the 1995 National Survey of Family Growth. *Vital and Health Statistics, 23*(19), 1–114.

Forrest, J. D., & Singh, S. (1990). The sexual and reproductive behavior of American women, 1982–1988. *Family Planning Perspectives, 22,* 206–214.

Glei, D. A. (1999). Measuring contraceptive use patterns among teenage and adult women. *Family Planning Perspectives, 31,* 73–80.

Goldstein, J., Lutz, W., & Testa, M. R. (2003, May). *The emergence of sub replacement family size ideals in Europe.* Paper presented at the annual meetings of the Population Association of America, Minneapolis, MN.

Hagewen, K. J., & Morgan, S. P. (2003). *A trend analysis of intended parity and ideal family size in the United States, 1970–2002.* Unpublished manuscript, Duke University.

Hamilton, B. E., Sutton, P. D., & Ventura, S. J. (2003). Revised birth and fertility rates for the 1990s and new rates for Hispanic populations, 2000 and 2001: United States. *National Vital Statistics Reports, 51,* 1–96.

Hewlett, S. A. (2002). *Creating a life: Professional women and the quest for children.* New York: Miramax.

Hrdy, S. B. (2000). The optimal number of fathers: Evolution, demography, and history in the shaping of female mate preferences. *Annals of the New York Academy of Sciences, 907,* 75–96.

Kligman, G. (1998). *The politics of duplicity: Controlling reproduction in Ceausescu's Romania.* Berkeley: University of California Press.

Kohler, H.-P., Billari, F. C., & Ortega, J. A. (2002). The emergence of lowest-low fertility in Europe during the 1990s. *Population and Development Review, 28*, 641–680.

Kost, K., & Forrest, J. D. (1995). Intention status of U.S. births in 1988: Differences by mother's socioeconomic and demographic characteristics. *Family Planning Perspectives, 27*, 11–17.

Leridon, H. (2003, May). *Age and fertility: What are your chances of bearing a child at each age?* Paper presented at the annual meetings of the Population Association of America, Minneapolis, MN.

Matthews, T. J., & Hamilton, B. E. 2002. *Mean age of mother, 1970–2000.* Hyattsville, MD: National Center for Health Statistics

Matthews, T. J., Menacker, F., & MacDorman, M. F. (2003). Infant mortality statistics from the 2001 period linked birth/infant death data set. *National Vital Statistics Reports, 52*(2), 1–28.

Menken, J. (1985). Age and fertility: How late can you wait. *Demography, 22*, 469–484.

Micheli, G. A., & Bernardi, L. (2003, May). *Two theoretical interpretations of the dissonance between fertility intentions and behaviour.* Paper presented at the annual meetings of the Population Association of America, Minneapolis, MN.

Miller, W. B. (2002). The role of nurturant schemas in human reproduction. In J. Lee & H.-P. Kohler (Eds.), *The biodemography of human reproduction and fertility* (pp. 43–56). Boston: Kluwer.

Morgan, S. P. (2001). Should fertility intentions inform fertility forecasts? In G. K. Spencer (Ed.), *Proceedings of U.S. Census Bureau Conference: The direction of fertility in the United States* (pp. 153–184). Washington, DC: U.S. Census Bureau.

Morgan, S. P. (2003, May). *Is low fertility a 21st Century crisis?* Presidential address at the annual meeting of the Population Association of America, Minneapolis, MN.

Morgan, S. P., & King, R. B. (2001). Why have children in the 21st century? *European Journal of Population, 17*, 3–20.

Mosher, W. D., & Bachrach, C. A. (1996). Understanding U.S. fertility: Continuity and change in the National Survey of Family Growth, 1988–1995. *Family Planning Perspectives, 28*, 4–12.

Ni Bhrochain, M. (1992). Period paramount? A critique of the cohort approach to fertility. *Population and Development Review, 18*, 599–629.

O'Connell, M., & Rogers, C. C. (1983). Assessing cohort birth expectations data from the Current Population Survey, 1971–1981. *Demography, 20*, 369–384.

Parsons, T. (1974). Age and sex in the social structure. In R. L. Coser (Ed.), *The family: Its structure and functions* (pp. 243–255). New York: St. Martins. (Reprinted from *American Sociological Review, 7*, 604–616, 1942).

Pollard, M. S., & Morgan, S. P. (2002). Emerging gender indifference: Sex composition of children and the third birth. *American Sociological Review, 67*, 600–613.

Preston, S. H. (1978). Introduction. In S. H. Preston (Ed.), *The effects of infant and child mortality on fertility* (pp. 1-18). New York: Academic Press.

Quesnel-Vallée, A., & Morgan, S. P. (2002, August). *Do women and men realize their fertility intentions?* Paper presented at the annual meeting of the American Sociological Association, Chicago.

Rindfuss, R. R., Guzzo, K. B., & Morgan, S. P. (in press). The changing institutional context of low fertility. *Population Research and Policy Review.*

Rossi, A. S., & Sitaraman, B. (1988). Abortion in context: Historical trends and future changes, *Family Planning Perspectives, 20*, 273–281, 301.

Ryder, N. B. (1965). The cohort as a concept in the study of social change. *American Sociological Review, 30*, 843–861.

Ryder, N. B. (1980). Components of temporal variations in American fertility. In R. W. Hiorns (Ed.), *Demographic patterns in developed societies* (pp. 15–54). London: Taylor and Francis LTD.

Sable, M. R., Libbus, M. K., & Chiu, J.-E. (2000). Factors affecting contraceptive use in women seeking pregnancy tests: Missouri, 1997. *Family Planning Perspectives, 32*, 124–131.

Wright, V. C., Schieve, L. A., Reynolds, M. A., & Jeng, G. (2003). Assisted reproductive technology surveillance—United States, 2000. *MMWR Surveillance Summaries, 52*, 1–16.

2

THE ROLE OF NONMARITAL BIRTHS IN SUSTAINING REPLACEMENT FERTILITY IN THE UNITED STATES

R. Kelly Raley

The University of Texas

In 2002, the total fertility rate was 2.01, down slightly from 2.13 in 2000, but certainly not as low as one would expect from looking at trends prior to 1975 or what one would expect by looking at fertility rates in the United Kingdom (1.71) or West Germany (1.45) (Hamilton, Martin, & Sutton, 2003; Rindfuss, Guzzo, & Morgan, in press). Why has fertility not declined substantially below replacement in the United States, and can we expect it to drop to very low levels in the foreseeable future?

Applying Bongaarts' (2001) model for fertility in post-transitional societies, Morgan and Hagewen's analysis demonstrates the best aspects of the way in which demographers attack important social questions. A demographic approach sections out the contributing factors and determines how responsive fertility patterns are to possible changes in each factor. In so doing, Morgan and Hagewen produce a convincing argument that unwanted fertility, replacement fertility for children who die, and preferences for a certain gender composition for offspring will not have much impact on fertility trends in the United States, even in the near future. By definition, tempo effects also should not be important in the long term. The impact of infecundity is somewhat offset by advances in technology to enable infertile parents to have children. Consequently, the key factor determining whether fertility in the United States will drop to "very low" levels (say, a TFR of 1.3) involves competition between other aspects of the life course and fertility. This factor is the focus of my comments.

Aside from fertility intentions, competition is clearly the most important factor in determining the future course of fertility in the United States. It is also the most ambiguously defined in the Bongaarts model. It includes a wide range of potential influences, ranging from the ability to find a suitable partner, to opportunities for leisure. Much of the literature on the factors contributing to fertility decline focuses on the role of female labor force participation. Increasing labor force opportunities encourage women to invest in the accumulation of human capital early in the life course. This delays both union formation and the start of childbearing. After leaving school, the majority of college-educated women eventually marry, but in the absence of maternity leave and adequate alternative childcare, labor force participation may encourage couples to revise their fertility intentions downwardly because having a child may jeopardize the woman's income and career opportunities.

If women's employment is incompatible with replacement levels of fertility, then growth in women's labor force participation since 1975 should have led to much lower levels of fertility. Morgan's research with others suggests that important institutional changes in the workplace/family lessened the strain women experience when combining childbearing with labor force participation. Today, the employee role may conflict less with the mother role, as childcare, flextime, and family leave, as well as services to replace home production, are more acceptable and available. Furthermore, in the United States men do an increasing share of the work involved with rearing children (Bianchi, this volume). These "institutional accommodations" could reduce the strain of childrearing, enabling women to participate in the labor force without sacrificing their own or their children's well-being. Moreover, because women probably take into account the strain involved with working and raising children when forming their fertility intentions in adolescence and early adulthood, a reduction in this incompatibility might induce women to revise their fertility intentions upward. In the Bongaarts model this translates into an increase in F_c, possibly to a value of over 1.

A second factor captured under the heading "life course competition" is the ability to find a suitable partner for reproduction. Some of the delay in marriage is due to the rise in women's educational attainment and labor force participation. For some women this has resulted in delayed fertility and this factor is reflected in the growing mean age at childbearing (Mathews & Hamilton, 2002). This part of the influence of delayed marriage is incorporated in the influence of women's labor force participation described above. Women's labor force participation is an incomplete explanation for marriage trends, however. Labor force opportunities for men, particularly men without college education, have declined (Levy, 1998). Consequently, some young women who would start a family if they were married delay childbearing because they have no husband and nonmarital childbearing is personally and socially unacceptable. Some women will never marry and some will marry too late to completely recover their fertility intentions, resulting in declines in the total fertility rate.

As long as nonmarital fertility is unacceptable, delays in marriage are likely to result in declines in fertility. However, a second institutional accommodation reducing the negative impact of delayed marriage is the relaxation of the imperative that women be married before bearing children. We can observe this institutional change in studies both on attitudes and behavior. A declining proportion of high school seniors view bearing children outside of marriage as immoral (Thornton & Young-DeMarco, 2001) and an increasing proportion of births is nonmarital (Ventura & Bachrach, 2000). The increasing acceptability of nonmarital childbearing discounts the negative impact of delayed marriage on F_c, keeping fertility levels higher than they otherwise would be.

Life course competition impacts levels of fertility in at least three ways. First, competing activities can influence the other factors in the Bongaarts framework. For example, nonmarital fertility can keep the mean age at childbearing from increasing despite delays in marriage, minimizing tempo effects (F_t). However, the accumulation of human capital often pushes childbearing to older ages, which influences the importance of another factor—infecundity. Even if technological advances make childbearing at older ages possible, those who delay childbearing until these ages may decide that they are attached to their life as it is and do not want to be putting a child through college post-retirement. This leads to the second way competition influences fertility. As Morgan and Hagewen suggest, women (and men) adjust their childbearing intentions downward when they are faced with competing draws on their time and energy. Third, competition may have feedback effects on the fertility intentions of future generations, to the extent that intended parity is driven by social (instead of biological) factors. Cultural norms are maintained and/or changed depending on the behavior of successive generations. If a large enough proportion of women face sufficient competition that they forgo childbearing altogether, norms that legitimate not having children could shift to support not wanting children as well. This feedback effect could be reinforced as the workplace and other institutions face less pressure from the family to accommodate women who bear children.

Not All Institutional Accommodations Are Equal

If delays in marriage and increases in female labor force participation are the primary sources of life course competition, then four types of changes will account for the majority of the variability in F_c: levels of labor force participation, the degree of incompatibility between women's employment and childrearing, the marital status of women in childbearing ages, and the acceptability of nonmarital childbearing. Certainly other factors may contribute to F_c, but it seems likely that these are the biggest components. A problem with combining all these factors into one is that these influences may offset one another. For example, the depressing effect of labor force participation is discounted when workplaces and husbands accommodate women's employment. Additionally, factors associated with delayed union formation may offset the influence of factors associated with female labor force participation. It may be that increasing compatibility between female labor force participation buoys fertility despite a strong downward force exerted by delayed marriage.

Teasing out the different forces involved would be less important if it were not for the fact that they imply different levels of investment in the next generation. Women's labor force participation increases family income, enabling families to invest more in their children. If mothers' employment is facilitated by fathers' increased role in childrearing, children may benefit from the greater involvement of another adult. In fact, mothers may have incentives to invest more in their children when another adult monitors her behavior and indirectly benefits from her effort. Moreover, female labor force participation may allow companies to invest in the next generation, for example, by providing childcare at reduced cost or offering extended paid maternity leave. In contrast to the first type of institutional accommodation, easing mothers' ability to combine work and childrearing, an increase in nonmarital fertility implies reduced investments in children. Men who are not married to the mothers of their children invest less time and money in those children, and more of the onus of childrearing falls on women's shoulders. Numerous studies document that, while most children in single parent families do fine, on average growing up in a single parent family is associated with lower levels of educational attainment and more idleness (Cherlin, 1999; McLanahan & Sandefur, 1994). This is likely the case even when mothers cohabit with the fathers of their children, as a large proportion of these unions will dissolve while the child is young (Graefe & Lichter, 1999; Manning, Smock, & Majumdar, in press). Consequently, not all institutional adjustments contribute equally to our ability to create the next generation. If F_c is near 1.0 because of workforce and gender role accommodations to women's employment, this implies at worst steady, and probably net increased, investments in children. However, if nonmarital fertility is the dominant force, then it implies reduced investments in children.

An additional dimension to this problem is that the factors impacting fertility likely vary by class status. The mean age at childbearing has increased substantially over the past 30 years for marital births, but has changed little for nonmarital births (Wu, Bumpass, & Musick, 2001). Young adults with greater economic potential typically delay marriage and childbearing until they have established their careers but, once they have completed schooling, have higher marriage rates than those with less education (Lichter, McLaughlin, Kephart, & Landry, 1992; Oppenheimer, Kalmijn, & Lim, 1997). In contrast, women with fewer resources are ready to begin childbearing at younger ages, in part because they have less incentive (or opportunity) to invest in human capital. However, they also have more difficulty finding a suitable mate and consequently are more likely to have nonmarital birth. Of the two institutional accommodations discussed, the labor force accommodation is more likely than the increasing acceptability of nonmarital childbearing to enable middle- and upper middle-class women realize their fertility intentions. Conversely, the rise in nonmarital fertility has likely been more important for working- and lower-class women, because the many of the labor force accommodations are probably not available to them. Maternity leave is usually unpaid and positions available to women without at least some college education usually do not provide flexible work schedules. Moreover, while some of the newly available market goods and services that replace domestic production are available to almost everyone (e.g., fast food), a good many are not (e.g., laundry and housekeeping service).

How Important Is the Increase in Nonmarital Fertility?

It is beyond the scope of this paper to present a comprehensive model for
evaluating how the four factors identified above influence the fertility rate. Instead,
I wish to examine the role of only one factor—the rise in nonmarital fertility—in
sustaining fertility in the United States. One way to discern the influence of a
factor is to examine what would have happened to fertility rates if there had been
no institutional accommodation. In other words, what would have happened if
nonmarital fertility remained unacceptable and fertility rates outside marriage
remained low? If I assume that levels of marital fertility are unaffected by nonmarital
fertility, I can answer this question by examining trends in marital fertility.
Figure 2.1 presents trends in the total marital fertility rate[1] and total fertility rate in
the United States along with estimates for two very low fertility countries, Japan
and Spain. The thick line shows trends in the United States total fertility rate (TFR)
from 1972 to 2002. In the early 1970s fertility continued a downward course but by
1977 the TFR leveled off. In the late 1980s and then again for the year 2000, the
total fertility rate jumped upward. Since 2000, fertility rates have declined. Examining
only births to married women, we see that the total fertility rate would have generally
declined to very low levels over the past 30 years if not for nonmarital births. The
marital fertility rate was 1.79 births per woman in 1972, dropped to 1.43 in 1985, and
sits at 1.33 in 2002. Interestingly, the marital fertility rates in the United States in the
1990s fall between those of Japan and Spain, both countries with very low levels of
nonmarital fertility (Thomson, this volume).

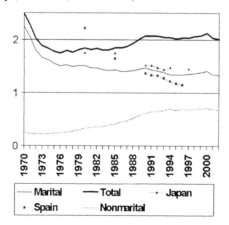

Figure 2.1. The Role of Nonmarital Fertility in Sustaining a Near-Replacement TFR in the
United States

---

[1] I calculate the marital fertility rate using a formula similar to that for the Total Fertility Rate except that only
births to married women are included in the numerator. All women, regardless of marital status, are included in the
denominator.

Of course, the line showing trends in the marital fertility rate probably does not reflect what truly would have happened if nonmarital fertility had not become more acceptable, because the assumption that marital fertility is unaffected by nonmarital fertility is unrealistic. For example, some women who have children prior to marriage have fewer births while married than they would have had had they not started childbearing premaritally. Nonetheless, the analysis suggests that nonmarital fertility plays a big role in maintaining fertility levels in the United States. Future research could use longitudinal data to examine women's fertility intentions in young adulthood and whether nonmarital births are offset by fewer marital births.

An important next step will be to examine more directly whether nonmarital fertility can account for all of the decline in life course competition between other goals and fertility (F_c). A group that has been less affected by this change is women with college degrees. Premarital fertility is still uncommon for women will a college education, despite this group's late age at marriage. Only 7% of premarital first births in 1990–1994 were to women with a college degree (Bachu, 1999). Thus, Murphy Brown notwithstanding, it seems unlikely that nonmarital fertility has been relevant for enabling college educated/career women to realize their intended parity.

If college-educated women with careers are increasingly able to realize their fertility intentions, factors enabling women to combine work with marital childbearing are more important than increasing nonmarital fertility. Recent research on fertility trends and differentials by educational attainment provides some support for this part of the institutional accommodation argument. Consistent with the argument that for women, career building competes with childrearing, women with college degrees have lower levels of fertility in their early 20s than other women (Martin, 2000; Rindfuss, Morgan, & Offutt, 1996). However, increasingly women with college degrees make up for children they did not have in their 20s by bearing children in their 30s. Whereas among women who reached age 30 childless in the 1970s, fertility rates past age 30 were low for women at all levels of educational attainment, in the 1990s fertility rates after 30 have increased for women with a college degree (Martin, 2000). This increase suggests workplace and family accommodations have enabled women to combine career and childrearing, at least for women with college degrees.

Taken together with the earlier discussion on nonmarital fertility, these findings suggest that the institutional accommodations that are available to college-educated women differ substantially from the accommodations available to those without a college degree. Among women with lower levels of education, increases in the acceptability of nonmarital fertility, but not workplace accommodations, have reduced life-course competition (F_c). In contrast, women with college degrees face increased workplace and family accommodations that enable them to achieve desired levels of fertility despite continued low levels of nonmarital fertility.

Conclusion

An examination of fertility trends in the United States, or a comparison of U.S. fertility rates to those of other countries, raises an important question. Why are fertility rates so high? Morgan and colleagues suggest the importance of two institutional accommodations—the increasing acceptance of nonmarital fertility and changes in the family and workplace that enable women to participate in the labor force without compromising childbearing. In this chapter I have provided evidence to support the claim that nonmarital fertility has been key. Marital fertility in the United States is near that of very low fertility countries like Spain, Italy, and Japan. Additional work should investigate more directly whether increases in the availability of maternity leave, childcare, services to replace domestic production, and men's participation in housework enable women to realize their desired number of children. Although the argument is intriguing, the evidence for this second accommodation is, thus far, weak. Morgan and colleagues show that in countries with near replacement fertility, female labor force participation is not negatively correlated with fertility. However, a number of confounding factors, including men's employment opportunities, could impact this correlation analysis. Martin (2000) shows that among women childless at age 30, fertility rates past age 30 increased among college-educated women, but we cannot be sure whether this is due to other period influences (such as income growth) or to the increasing availability and acceptability of childcare. For this part of the story to become established fact, we need more direct evidence that variation in work place accommodations such as flextime, in the availability and affordability of childcare, and in husbands' contributions to domestic production is associated with variation in fertility.

Investigating which of the institutional accommodations was most instrumental in maintaining near replacement fertility in the United States is important because each implies different trends in the amount of resources we are investing in the next generation. I have argued that changes that enable employed women to have children may be associated with increased investments in children. However, nonmarital fertility is associated with reduced investments and consequently poorer outcomes in terms of educational attainment and employment. Future research should also investigate how the factors that help maintain fertility vary by class status. If middle-class women enjoy accommodations that enable them to invest more in their children, while lower- and working-class women are able to have children by bearing and rearing them nonmaritally, these forces are important for the intergenerational transmission of inequality.

References

Bachu, A. (1999). *Trends in premarital childbearing, 1930–1994* (Current Population Reports P23-197). Washington, DC: U.S. Department of Commerce.

Bongaarts, J. (2001). Fertility and reproductive preferences in post-transitional societies. In R. A. Bulatao & J. B. Casterline (Eds.), *Global fertility transition* (pp. 260–281). New York: Population Council.

Cherlin, A. J. (1999). Going to extremes: Family structure, children's well-being, and social science. *Demography, 36*(4), 421–428.

Graefe, D. R., & Lichter, D. T. (1999). Life course transitions of American children: Parental cohabitation, marriage, and single motherhood. *Demography, 36*(2), 205–217.

Hamilton, B. E., Martin, J. A., & Sutton, P. D. (2003). Births: Preliminary data for 2002. *National Vital Statistics Reports, 51*(11).

Levy, F. (1998). *The new dollars and dreams: American incomes and economic change.* New York: Russell Sage Foundation.

Lichter, D. T., McLaughlin, D., Kephart, G., & Landry, D. J. (1992). Race and the retreat from marriage: A shortage of marriageable men? *American Sociological Review, 57*, 781–799.

Manning, W. D., Smock, P. J., & Majundar, D. (In press). The relative stability of cohabiting and marital unions for children. *Population Research and Policy Review.*

Martin, S. P. (2000). Diverging fertility among U.S. women who delay childbearing past age 30. *Demography, 37*, 523–533.

Mathews, T. J., & Hamilton, B. E. (2002). Mean age of mother, 1970–2000. *National Vital Statistics Reports, 51*(1), 1-14.

McLanahan, S. S., & Sandefur, G. D. (1994). *Growing up with a single parent: What hurts, what helps?* Cambridge, MA: Harvard University Press.

Oppenheimer, V. K., Kalmijn, M., & Lim, N. (1997). Men's career development and marriage timing during a period of rising inequality. *Demography, 34*(3), 311–330.

Rindfuss, R. R., Guzzo, K. B., & Morgan, S. P. (In press). The changing institutional context of low fertility. *Population Research and Policy Review.*

Rindfuss, R. R., Morgan, S. P., & Offutt, K. (1996). Education and the changing age pattern of American fertility: 1963–1989. *Demography, 33*, 277–290.

Thornton, A., & Young-DeMarco, L. (2001). Four decades of trends in attitudes toward family issues in the United States: The 1960s through the 1990s. *Journal of Marriage and the Family, 63*(4), 1009–1037.

Ventura, S. J., & Bachrach, C. A. (2000). Nonmarital childbearing in the United States, 1940–99. *National Vital Statistics Reports, 48*(16 Revised). 1-39.

Wu, L. L., Bumpass, L. L., & Musick, K. (2001). Historical and life course trajectories of nonmarital childbearing. In L.Wu & B. Hareven (Eds.), *Out of wedlock: Causes and consequences of nonmarital fertility* (pp. 3–48). New York: Russell Sage Foundation.

3

WHEN THE RULE APPLIES: COMMENTARY ON "IS VERY LOW FERTILITY INEVITABLE IN AMERICA?" BY S. PHILIP MORGAN AND KELLIE HAGEWEN

M. Belinda Tucker

University of California, Los Angeles

S. Philip Morgan and Kellie Hagewen have presented valuable insights regarding the somewhat peculiar fertility patterns displayed in the United States, as compared to other more economically endowed nations and societies. Their model effectively integrates diverse theories and schools of thought and highlights many of the issues related to fertility that require innovative and directed social policy. In particular, a reduction in competition between the spheres of work and family is one of the most desperately needed tasks for contemporary society—especially given the ever more central economic role played by women.

This commentary has several aims. The first is to discuss one group in the United States that *is* conforming to the patterns displayed by other economically advanced nations and to offer explanations for this exception that may inform the more general model. That portion will be developed through reference to preliminary findings from my own program of research. Second, the paper will highlight one aspect of the Morgan and Hagewen model that, in my view, could be deconstructed and more fully developed. The last aim is to comment briefly on the inherent conflicts in what I perceive to be national goals regarding fertility.

Given my orientation as a social psychologist, the perspective on fertility that frames this discussion differs somewhat from that represented in the lead paper. My interest in childbearing behavior revolves around a desire to understand how individual family formation behaviors and attitudes are shaped by larger sociocultural and societal forces, including group norms, public policy, demographic trends, cultural beliefs and practices, and technological innovations (medical and otherwise), among others. However, my work with anthropologists over the last twenty years has given me another angle of vision on such concerns. I now conduct large-scale national surveys as well as community ethnographies and have been enriched by the challenge of mapping and integrating the two "ways of knowing." Through this process I've gained an appreciation for the understanding that can be derived from examining the particular—that is, an in-depth analysis of a single case (a single subpopulation in this instance) that seems to defy the more general trends. By so doing, we may gain greater insight into the more global processes.

The "Non-Exception"

Morgan and Hagewen note that some have erroneously attributed the relatively high fertility rates of the United States to higher birthrates among Latinos primarily, but also African Americans. This is somewhat ironic since the U.S.-based Black[1] population, in particular, has displayed rapidly declining birthrates. As has been pointed out in U.S. Department of Health and Human Services press releases and numerous media reports, the fertility rate of Black teenagers (15–19) has reached historic lows, declining by 37% between 1991 and 2001 and by 8% during 2000 alone (Martin, Hamilton, Ventura, Menacker, & Park, 2002; U.S. Department of Health and Human Services, 2002). Still, birthrates of Black adolescents remain considerably higher than the current U.S. average.

A less known and less told tale is that of married African American women, whose birthrates have been declining steeply for several decades. The fertility rate of married Black couples is now below replacement level. Table 3.1 displays birthrates (number of births per 1,000 women) of married women ages 15–44 overall by race and Hispanic origin between 1970 and 1999. The birthrate for married Black women declined by 52% between 1970 and 1999—from 130 in 1970, to 89 in 1980 and 67 in 1999 (Centers for Disease Control and Prevention, 2000). By comparison, the decline in birthrates for married women overall in the United States over the same time period was 28%. The fertility of married Black women is three quarters the level of that for U.S. married women overall and four fifths the level of White married women. In fact, as recently as 1971, the pattern was exactly reversed, with birthrates of 121 for married Black women and 117 for their White counterparts.

Table 3.1.
Birthrates for Married Women by Race: 1970–1999

Year	All Races	Blacks	Whites	Non-Hispanic Whites
1999	86.5	67.3	87.8	81.7
1990	93.2	79.7	94.1	—
1980	97.0	89.2	97.5	—
1970	121.1	130.3	119.6	—

Source: Centers for Disease Control and Prevention. 2000
Note: Birthrates defined as number of live births to married women per 1,000 married women in the specified group.

---

[1]The term African Americans is used here to refer to the subpopulation of U.S.-born persons of African descent. The more general term Black is used to refer to persons of African descent more generally. Census data do not make a distinction between native-born African Americans and foreign-born or culturally distinctive persons of African descent who also reside in the United States.

What might account for such a dramatic reversal of trends? First, we must acknowledge that the population of married Black women is becoming more select and more homogeneous. As marriage becomes less prevalent in the African American population more generally, those who chose to or are able to marry may be more conventional in obvious ways—more educated (up to a point) and more middle-class in jobs, income, resources, and even outlook. This alone is unlikely to account, however, for the marked decline in childbearing. Most likely, the factors contributing to this phenomenon lie almost entirely under F_c—the "competition" component of the Morgan and Hagewen model.

Though married Black women are seldom considered in social science literature, existing discussions tend to include acknowledgment that African American women play a more central role in the economic well-being of their families than do women of other racial or ethnic groups. Data from the March 2002 Current Population Survey show that Black married women have incomes that are 37% higher than those of single women ($15,137 to $20,790) (Bureau of Labor Statistics, 2002). The proportionate difference is considerably less for White women, with White married women making only 9% more than those who are single—$15,993 to $17,371 (Bureau of Labor Statistics, 2002), and, in fact, making less money than married Black women. This would speak to the distinctive nature of married Black women, but also the greater reliance of couples and families on their incomes: Overall, in 2001, Black wives' earnings were 77% those of Black husbands, while White wives earned only 55% of White husbands' salaries (Bureau of Labor Statistics, 2002).[2] Of course, this is due largely to the fact that White male incomes are so much higher than anyone else's.

Still, is income dependency sufficient to account for the steep decline in married Black female fertility? Some scholars have examined the increasing cost of children as a deterrent to greater fertility. Despite the cost, however, the desire for children remains high as data from our own surveys reveal. The following discussion will refer specifically to data from the first wave of the Survey of Families and Relationships that was conducted in 1995–1996 and consists of interviews with 3,407 African Americans, Mexican Americans, and native-born Whites in 21 cities across the United States. A second wave has just been collected, but is not yet ready for analysis.

---

[2] Clearly a significant number of Black husbands and wives are not married to other Black persons, so these ratios are distorted by the level of interracial marriage. In 1990 (the most recent published Census data), just over 7% of all couples with one Black partner were interracial (U.S. Bureau of the Census, 1998).

Survey Findings

In an effort to determine whether married African American women hold attitudes or engage in other behaviors that might help explain their distinctive fertility patterns, their responses on a range of related topics were compared to those of Mexican American and White married women. Table 3.2 presents results from one-way analyses of variance—a preliminary step for analysis of this issue.

Table 3.2.
Attitudes of Married Women by Race/Ethnicity: Survey of Families and Relationships

	Black (*n*=242)	Mexican American (*n*=67)	White (*n*=392)	F
No. other children	.50	.19	.15	10.76***
Religiosity	7.74	6.84	6.33	26.29***
Marriage will last five years	8.99	9.13	9.58	10.56***
Chance of remarriage	3.14	3.40	4.16	9.70***
Man should be main earner	5.94	6.50	3.80	45.26***
Working mom just as good	7.89	7.46	6.99	7.41***
Woman's most important task is kids	4.82	6.87	4.21	22.23***
Living standard w/o marriage worse/better	5.24	4.90	4.16	18.47***

***p<.0001.
Source: Author's analysis of data from the Survey of Families and Relationships.

Having children. The respondents were asked about live births, as well as other categories of children that the women might have raised. Although there was little difference among the groups of women in childbearing and no difference in adoption, African American married women were significantly more likely than either Whites or Mexican Americans to be raising children who were neither biological offspring nor adopted (an average of .5 children per woman). The value placed on having children was equally high among all three groups. African American and Mexican American women were significantly younger than whites when they had their first child (22, 21, and 24.9, respectively), but all were equal in their determination that having more children was highly unlikely: on a scale of 1 (highly likely) to 10 (extremely likely). Blacks reported a mean of 2.3 and Mexican Americans and Whites scored 2.5. This was not unexpected since the mean age for each group was late 30s.

Surprisingly, given the greater economic pressures among African Americans, among those married women who were childless, White women were significantly more likely than Blacks to cite both financial constraints and even not having met the right partner as reasons for not having children (there were too few Mexican Americans in this category to include in the analysis). In some sense, this may reflect the high value married African American women place on childbearing. Neither financial constraints nor limitations of one's partner were sufficient to forego having children altogether. Notably, the groups as a whole felt little pressure from family and virtually none from friends to have children.

Religion. Black married women were significantly more religious than either White or Mexican American women. This is further evidence that married Black women may be more conventional in a range of ways than the African American population more generally. For such women, marriage may be more than a "love match", but for them also a measure of respectability—especially given the rhetoric of the national political debate on family values.

Relationships. There was no difference among the groups in the mean number of marriages they had experienced (1.3 for all groups). At the same time, married African American women expressed significantly greater uncertainty about the future of their relationships than did the other women, when asked what the chances were that their relationship would last another five years. Furthermore, White women had significantly greater confidence than Black women that they would find another partner if their current relationship did end. (Both of these concerns are realistic, given the much higher divorce rates and lower likelihood of remarriage for married Black women—Tucker & Mitchell-Kernan, 1999.)

Summary

So not only are married African American women carrying more of the family economic load, but they also have other children besides their own to raise and are uncertain about the chances that their current family arrangement (and the attendant economic benefits) will last. Moreover, data from the Bureau of Labor Statistics demonstrate that African Americans in general have been at greater risk for layoff than others—and had greater difficulty finding new work (Bureau of Labor Statistics, 2002). Under such circumstances, why would you bring another child into this world, regardless of your deep desires? It would be perfectly rationale to limit the number of children you have under such conditions. Evidence that this may be the mindset of many African American women is available in Centers for Disease Control health data. In 1995, ever-married Black women were twice as likely as Whites to have had tubal ligations or hysterectomies (comparable sterilization rates result from greater reliance among Whites on male vasectomy) (Chandra, 1998). Black women are also more likely to obtain abortions—57.2 per 1,000 compared to 11.9 for White women and 31.4 for Hispanic women (Ventura, Abna, Mosher, & Henshaw, 2003). Both tendencies are indicative of a strong determination to not give birth.

Burt Landry's award-winning book, *Black Working Wives* (2000), offers some insight into these findings. Subtitled, "Pioneers of the American Family Revolution," his book presents a compelling analysis of labor force entry by Black women and its meaning for women, families, and the larger community. Landry argues that Black women had little choice but to embrace employment outside the home (for the economic survival of families), yet in doing so they also discovered that life outside the hearth was a route to greater equality within the home. He maintains that in a revolutionary sense, African American women have constructed a new vision of womanhood—one that is based on a strong commitment to work and community as well as their responsibilities at home. To have additional children would mean taking leave of powerful commitments on several fronts. In the end, it would mean letting other people down. Parenthetically, both African American and Mexican American women were more strongly supportive of a dominant economic role by men (Taylor, Tucker, & Mitchell-Kernan, 1999). Although they endorsed men doing more at home and women sharing the economic responsibilities, married women of color still appear to be less inclined to openly challenge the traditional male role. (For a more complete discussion of this apparent contradiction, see Taylor, Tucker, & Mitchell-Kernan, 1999.)

Another Angle

Despite the insight derived from analysis of these survey responses, other factors, less realized by quantitative approaches, are possibly at play. It was noted earlier that African American married women in our survey begin having children at younger ages than the other groups of women (though clearly at an adult age). Does this represent cultural preference? I happened upon significant data on this topic one day while in a hair salon. (From an ethnographic perspective, Black barber shops and hair solons are particularly rich sources of insight on community behavior.) On this particular day, the topic of conversation was news correspondent Connie Chung's decision to take a leave from her career in order to attempt to conceive a child with her husband. Chung's actions were roundly criticized by the customers and stylists, with most expressing the sentiment that if she wanted to have children she should have had the sense to begin earlier. She was, in effect, reaping what she had sowed. Given that this hair salon was located in upscale Westwood Village, adjacent to UCLA, and not in an African American community, these were the opinions of women who were solidly middle class.

I want to suggest that this strong sentiment is more than simply culturally rooted. My own life experience is instructive in this regard (as a single case study). Before I gave birth to my second son, I signed papers to obtain a tubal ligation for two key reasons: First, my pregnancies were made enormously difficult by the presence of fibroid tumors. Second, the financial costs of additional children would have been too great, in terms of both the loss of my essential income and the long-term financial obligations attendant to successfully raising a child. The latter reason has been long cited and studied in fertility studies. However, the first has been virtually ignored in behavioral research. African American women are at least three times more likely than White women to develop fibroid tumors and their tumors tend to be more numerous and larger (Agency for Healthcare Research and Quality, 2001). Moreover, Black women are typically diagnosed at much younger ages: in their mid to late 30s compared to White women who are more likely to be diagnosed in their 40s (Marshall, Spiegelman, Barbieri, et al., 1997). The racial differences are so substantial and striking that an RFA on the topic has been issued by the National Institutes of Health (NIH, 2002). Until recently, resolution was possible only through hysterectomy or, if you could last that long, menopause. Since fibroids can impair fertility, this circumstance would come under F_i in the Morgan and Hagewen model. Indeed, statistics on infertility by race are suggestive of such a link. The 1995 National Survey of Family Growth found that 10.5% of Black women are infertile compared to 6.4% of White women and 7% of Hispanic women (U.S. Department of Health and Human Services, 1997). Short of preventing conception, however, fibroids can also make the experience of pregnancy so unappealing that a woman would be reluctant to go through it again.

But there may be something else afoot here that does not fit so neatly into the model. There are numerous websites concerning fibroids among Black women. The testimonials are extensive, with some women reporting that virtually everyone they know has some form of fibroids. I am suggesting that the impact on fertility is not simply subfecundity, per se. Rather, the admonishment to have children early may be based on observations of older generations and their experiences with fibroids. This translates into a developing group perception, turned into cultural expression, based on observations of physiological realities.

The key to a future of understanding and affecting (if that is the desire) fertility patterns in the United States may lie in deeper observations of women as they and their partners make these decisions. It also lies, I believe in unpacking/deconstructing the competition element (F_c) of the proposed model—which, in my view, is where the most interesting and illuminating processes occur.

Social Policy

The final point in this discussion has to do with national policy regarding fertility. Public policy relevant to family welfare has, in my view, been a contorted effort to encourage fertility and more "traditional" lifestyles among what some would view as the more "desirable" members of society, while at the same time discouraging fertility among impoverished groups and populations of color. Higher-income women are being encouraged to stay at home, while welfare reform legislation continues to raise the number of hours worked by women receiving public assistance. I am aware of no serious proposal to address the below replacement dilemma facing Black married couples (and I will be amazed if and when such a development occurs). As Morgan and Hagewen have proposed, the need to make the spheres of work and family more compatible is paramount. Where I perhaps differ is that I do not see a societal will to do so. Despite the massive increase in women's and mothers' employment, I do not believe that for the average working mother things are significantly better than they were a decade ago. In fact, with the tightened economy, many women are working harder than ever before, with less support, and likely to be even more reluctant to request anything resembling special treatment. This society has a very long way to go to make maternal employment and childrearing responsibilities compatible.

References

Agency for Healthcare Research and Quality. (2001). *Management of uterine fibroids. Summary, evidence report/technology assessment: No. 34* (AHRQ Publication No. 01-E051). Rockville, MD: Author.

Bureau of Labor Statistics. (2002). *Table 1. Displaced workers by age, sex, race, Hispanic origin, and employment status in January 2002.* Retrieved from the Bureau of Labor Statistics Web site: www.bls.gov/news.release/dispt01.htm

Centers for Disease Control and Prevention. (2000). *Table 1–19. Birth rates for married women by age of mother, according to race and Hispanic origin: United States, 1950 and 1955 and each year 1960–99.* Retrieved from the Centers for Disease Control and Prevention Web site: www.cdc.gov/nchs/data/statab/t991x19.pdf

Chandra, A. (1998). Surgical sterilization in the United States: Prevalence and characteristics, 1965–95. *Vital Health Statistics, 23*(20).

Landry, B. (2000). *Black working wives: Pioneers of the American family revolution.* Berkeley: University of California Press.

Marshall, L. M., Spiegelman, D., Barbieri, R.L., et al. (1997). Variation in the incidence of uterine leiomyoma among premenopausal women by age and race. *Obstetrical Gynecology, 90*, 967–973.

Martin, J. A., Hamilton, B. E., Ventura, S. J., Menacker, F., & Park, M. M. (2002). Births: Final data for 2000. *National Vital Statistics Reports, 50*(5).

National Institutes of Health (2002). RFA:Uteri—Basic Science And Translational Research. http://grants1.nih.gov/grants/guide/rfa-files/RFA-HD-03-005.html, Release date: November 18, 2002

Taylor, P. L., Tucker, M. B., & Mitchell-Kernan, C. (1999). Ethnic variations in perceptions of men's provider role. *Psychology of Women Quarterly, 23*, 759–779.

Tucker, M. B., & Mitchell-Kernan, C. M. (Eds.). (1995). *The decline of marriage among African Americans: Causes, consequences and policy implications.* New York: Russell Sage Foundation.

U.S. Bureau of the Census. (1998). *Table 2. Race of couples: 1990.* Retrieved from the U. S. Census Bureau Web site: http://www.census.gov/population/socdemo/race/interractab2.txt. Release date: June 10, 1998.

U.S. Department of Health and Human Services. (1997). Fertility, family planning, and women's health: New data from the 1995 National Survey of Family Growth. *Vital and Health Statistics, 23*(19).

U.S. Department of Health and Human Services. (2002). *HHS report shows teen birth rate falls to new record low in 2001* (Press Release). Retrieved from the U.S. Department of Health and Human Services Web site: http://www.hhs.gov/news/press/2002pres/20020606.html

Ventura, S. J., Abna, J. C., Mosher, W. D., & Henshaw, S. (2003). Revised pregnancy rates, 1990–97, and new rates for 1988–99: United States. *National Vital Statistics Reports, 52*(7).

4

TIME AND MONEY: MARKET WORK, NONMARKET WORK, GENDER EQUALITY, AND FERTILITY

Suzanne M. Bianchi
University of Maryland

Morgan and Hagewen (this volume) effectively use Bongaarts' model to help us think about U.S. fertility levels: where they have been, where they are headed, how they compare to those in Western Europe, and what we most need to understand if we want to accurately predict the future of U.S. fertility. Those of us who have been following Morgan's work, most recently highlighted in his 2003 PAA Presidential Address (Morgan, 2003), can see in this paper the coherence in Morgan's fertility research agenda—an agenda that has documented fertility trends, motivations, and timing issues (Morgan, 2001; Morgan & King, 2001), evaluated the usefulness of fertility intentions in predicting fertility behavior (Morgan, 2001; Quesnel-Vallee & Morgan, 2002), returned to the question of son preference in U.S. fertility decisions (Pollard & Morgan, 2002), and become increasingly interested in the institutional context surrounding fertility levels and trends in developed economies (Rindfuss, Guzzo, & Morgan, 2003).

The paper raises interesting questions: do individuals know their work and family preferences early in life and subsequently act to realize those goals (as Catherine Hakim [2003] has recently suggested)? If so, what happens when life throws them a wrench? What "gives" when life unfolds differently than planned and is it having children or having as many children as one might ideally like?

To answer these questions, fertility cannot be studied narrowly but must be studied in conjunction with opportunities in the marriage market, labor market conditions, and state policies that alter markets and affect ideational factors like norms, intentions, and preferences. To predict U.S. fertility, we need to understand what is happening to marriage and its relationship to childbearing because delayed marriage can inhibit the realization of fertility intentions for population subgroups who feel strongly that one should be married to have children. On the other hand, childbearing that is early, often mistimed, and largely outside marriage also alters subsequent intentions and completed family size.

Most importantly, we have to pay attention to women's (and men's) time and resources and factors that compete with having children. A partial list of these resources and factors is provided in the Morgan-Hagewen chapter (availability of childcare and market substitutes for housework, labor market accommodations for parents and public policies that require such accommodations, and men's role in the home). It is this "competition" component, F_c, in Morgan and Hegewen's work that I find most interesting. First, this component is the unmeasured residual and is illustratively estimated to be the factor that most depresses Italian fertility and also has a large effect on U.S. fertility (Morgan & Hagewen, this volume, Table 1.2). The authors solve for its size by placing a value on each of the other components in the Bongaarts model, assuming no measurement error. Like many of our most important and interesting social science explanations for behavior (e.g., discrimination in wage regressions), the most important area for understanding low fertility is measured only indirectly, as a residual, after estimating those components that are easier to quantify. The framework is elegant but unfinished.

This is partly why I like this work. For one thing, it suggests that I have been laboring in the right vineyard in my own research. Although I have not been preoccupied with the issue of low fertility per se, I have been consumed with trying to understand women's changing time allocation between market and nonmarket work, how this change might be related to changes in men's time allocation, and how changes in women's lives have altered family life. It has been a largely descriptive exercise for me, focusing first on changes in women's market work that could be measured with Census and CPS data on cohorts, and more recently collecting and using time diary data on nonmarket activities.

From this research, we know a number of things about factors that may be relevant to low fertility, particularly this F_c "competition" component. We could ask: If a young woman today were to read the social science literature and base her fertility decisions on what she learns, what could she know about her likely future work and family life?

- Although women's time allocation to market work has increased, her likelihood of employment remains responsive to parenting. So, if past predicts future, a young woman planning her career and family today can know that she is likely to curtail market work when she has children (Table 4.1).

- Mothers have drastically reduced the hours they spend doing housework (exclusive of childcare). Fathers have added a little time in this area, and the ratio of mother's to father's housework hours has dropped dramatically (from mothers doing 7 times what fathers did in 1965 to about twice what fathers did in 2000). A young woman who marries today can look ahead and expect to get more household help from her husband than was true for her mother. But she still must recognize that more of this work is likely to fall on her than on the father of her children (Table 4.2).

4. TIME AND MONEY

Table 4.1.
Percent of Mothers and Fathers, Age 25-54, with Any Weeks Worked in the Previous Year by Presence and Age of Children, 2000

	Mothers	Fathers
Ages of Children		
All Over Age 6	72.8	89.4
At Least One < Age 6	58.4	90.8
At Least One < Age 4	56.0	91.1
At Least One < Age 1	46.3	91.0
Number of Children		
One	72.1	89.4
Two	67.8	90.6
Three	60.1	89.9
Four+	47.4	85.9

Source: Author's tabulations from the March 2000 Current Population Survey.

Table 4.2.
Weekly Hours of Housework (Excluding Childcare) of Mothers and Fathers, 1965-2000

	1965	1975	1985	1995	2000
Mothers	32.1	23.7	20.5	18.8	18.6
Fathers	4.4	7.5	10.3	10.8	9.8
Ratio (Mothers/Fathers)	7.3	3.1	2.0	1.7	2.0

Source: Author's tabulations from the 1965, 1975, 1985, 1995, and 2000 time diary collections.

- On the childcare front, women who marry today can also expect more, but not equal, sharing of childcare responsibilities. Again, if current levels were to persist into the future, (married) mothers will be doing about twice the amount of childcare that (married) fathers do (Figure 4.1). If men continue to take on more childrearing tasks, the gender difference may narrow. However, at this point in time, women who want children must consider that they will likely do more of the childrearing than the child's father, especially if they take into account the fact that, should their partnership disrupt, they will likely be the parent with custody of the children.

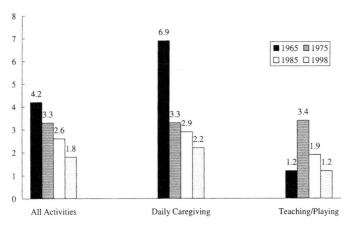

Source: Author's tabulations from the 1965, 1975, 1985, and 1998 time diary collections.

Figure 4.1. Ratio of Mothers' to Fathers' Time in All Childcare Activities, Daily Caregiving Activities, and Teaching and Playing With Children, 1965-1998

- Women also recognize that as mothers they will be busy, perhaps busier than in the past, with total weekly workloads (unpaid plus paid hours) exceeding 60 hours per week (Table 4.3).

- Women might also conclude that if they marry, they will share fairly equal workloads with a spouse, despite doing more of the childrearing and housework. That is, the ratio of married women's to men's total workload is near unity in the U.S. (Table 4.4). However, women must consider that when they curtail market work to rear children, which many of them are going to do even in today's less gender-differentiated world, their greater allocation of time to nonmarket activity may compromise their economic security in the event that the marriage does not last. When couples with children divorce, mother's and children's economic well-being drops by one third and they enjoy only about one half the standard of living, on average, of the fathers of their children after divorce (Bianchi, Subaiya, & Kahn, 1999).

Table 4.3.
Total Work Loads (Paid and Unpaid) of Parents, 1965 and 2000*

	Hours per Week		
	1965	2000	Change
Married Mothers	59	65	+6
Married Fathers	60	63	+3
Single Mothers	59	66	+7

* Paid work includes market work and commuting; unpaid work includes housework, childcare and other caregiving, and shopping for household goods and services.

Source: Author's tabulations from the 1965 and 2000 time diary data.

Table 4.4.
Gender Differences in Hours per Week of Work (Paid + Unpaid) Among All Adults and Married Parents, 1965 and 1998

	All Adults		Married Parents	
	1965	1998	1965	1998
Market Work				
Women	15.1	29.8	6.0	25.0
Men	46.4	37.7	47.8	40.2
Ratio (women/men)	0.3	0.8	0.1	0.6
Nonmarket Work				
Women	40.9	29.3	52.7	39.6
Men	10.9	18.4	12.3	23.5
Ratio (women/men)	3.7	1.6	4.3	1.7
Total Work				
Women	56.0	59.1	58.8	64.6
Men	57.3	56.1	60.1	63.7
Ratio (women/men)	1.0	1.1	1.0	1.0

Source: Author's tabulations from the 1965 and 1998 time diary data.

In fact, one factor I would add to the Morgan/Hagewen discussion of competition is the likelihood of marital dissolution. It is not only marriage (or union) formation that may enter into the calculations about when to have children and how many to have. Union dissolution and its likelihood may also enter into calculations about allocation of time to work and family. Marital disruption becomes one of those life events that "throws a wrench" into the realization of life goals, work plans, and fertility intentions.

A second factor missing from the "competition" list is changing norms and expectations that surround the rearing of children. It is difficult to amass evidence of change over time in this factor but anecdotal evidence suggests that parental estimates of what children "need" in terms of time and money may be increasing. What parents think children need will affect how many children they think they can afford. Despite a trend toward more egalitarianism on gender role attitude questions, there remains considerable ambivalence on attitude questions about maternal employment and time with children. Parents believe children "need" large doses of parental, especially maternal, time. Again, thinking about what a young woman today might learn from social science evidence, attitude trends are revealing.

- When asked on the General Social Survey (GSS), "Do preschool children suffer if a mother works?" relatively high percentages of men and women, but especially men, continue to answer yes (39% of women and 55% of men in 2002) (Figure 4.2).
- When we asked whether parents feel they spend enough time with their children, spouse, and self, a high percentage of mothers and fathers express feelings of "too little" time in all these relationships (Figure 4.3). Parental guilt is rampant.

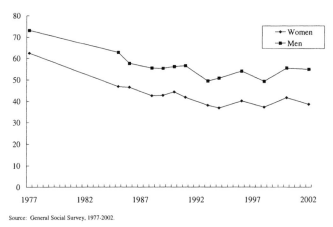

Source: General Social Survey, 1977-2002.

Figure 4.2. Percent Who Say a Preschool Child is Likely to Suffer if Mother Works, 1977-2002

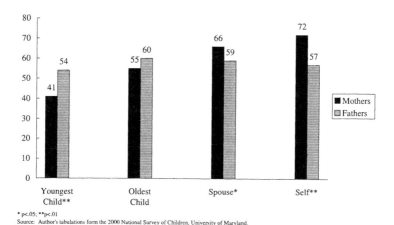

* p<.05; **p<.01
Source: Author's tabulations form the 2000 National Survey of Children, University of Maryland.

Figure 4.3. Percent Reporting "Too Little" Time with Youngest Child, Oldest Child, Spouse, and for Oneself, 2000

Parents' strong feelings of too little time with their children coexist with trends that suggest that parents spend at least as much time with their children as in the past. Despite rapid changes in the work roles of women and increases in single parenting, a number of studies find that mothers currently spend as much time caring for children as in the past and (married) fathers spend a lot more time in childcare (Bianchi, 2000; Bittman, 1995; Sandberg & Hofferth, 2001). Those who become parents increasingly are those who want to invest in parenting. Others who are not interested face less normative pressure to become parents than they once did.

Other factors may also be relevant. For example, in today's urban environments, parents' fear for their children's safety may encourage them to structure and supervise their children's time more closely—enrolling them in more extracurricular activities and accompanying them on these activities. Additionally, norms about parental caregiving and the need to invest in children are high, perhaps higher than in the past. Lareau (2002) argues this is particularly true of the middle class, where parents impart a sense of entitlement in their children through their intensive (verbal) interaction with children, the myriad of activities in which they enroll their children, and the travel and cultural experiences they provide for their children. It would follow from theoretical predictions in the demographic, sociological, and economic literatures that as individuals have fewer children, each child becomes more "precious," more "worthy" of heavy investments of time and money. Yet there are limits to both time and money, and as expectations for what children need rise, more individuals may come to feel they can't afford children or at least not many children.

Morgan and Hagewen conclude that according to clear norms operating in the United States, one is still supposed to want children but not a lot of them. This proscribes a narrow range of family sizes. Postponement does not mean individuals do not want children—they just want them later. Yet infertility looms large if childbearing gets pushed too late—although technology may change this threat to realized fertility intentions. Currently, those who can afford it, go to great lengths to have children through infertility treatments, a testimony to the strong desire for children on the part of many.

If the goal is to encourage replacement fertility, Morgan and Hagewen suggest that we need to make childbearing/rearing and women's labor force participation more compatible. We must make it easier for women to do market work and men to do family caregiving. This is one possible solution: a call for less gender-differentiation in the work and family-balancing act. But there are other solutions. For example, some might see wisdom in a partial return to a more gender-specialized solution. Public policy could facilitate having one full-time wage earner when children are young (and that person will undoubtedly most often be the father in heterosexual couples) and the return of one person to the home during the childrearing years (with that person undoubtedly the mother in most, but not all, heterosexual couples). Some of the family leave proposals in the United States and in existence in the most liberal democratic regimes in Scandinavia solve the problem of time constraints with this type of solution. Some argue that this is the strong preference of a minority of women and we should pay attention to it (Hakim, 2003). Another solution would be to reduce consumption standards and openly question whether affluent and middle-class children "need" all the material resources being lavished upon them or whether instead they, and their less economically fortunate peers, "need" even more parental time than they are currently receiving. If more parental time in childrearing is needed, making market work and childrearing more compatible for women may not achieve the desired end. Far broader changes may be implicated.

In conclusion, what must be clear to young women in the United States today, as they face their future work and family choices is that no perfect solution exists to the inevitable conflict between caregiving and doing other things. Children take time and money and those resources have to come from somewhere. It is increasingly acceptable to choose not to have children but, for those who choose to become parents, it may be increasingly required that one invest heavily in those children. Where does this leave the young women at the beginning of their childbearing years today? My guess is that most women remain certain that they want to "be a mother," but they are also certain that they want to be more than "just a mother," and uncertain about how to pull it all off.

References

Bianchi, S. M. (2000). Maternal employment and time with children: Dramatic change or surprising continuity? *Demography, 37*, 401–414.

Bianchi, S. M., Subaiya, L., & Kahn, J. R. (1999). The gender gap in the economic well-being of nonresident fathers and custodial mothers. *Demography, 36*, 195–203.

Bittman, M. (1995). *Recent changes in unpaid work* (Occasional Paper No. 4154). Canberra: Australia Bureau of Statistics.

Hakim, C. (2003). Preference theory: A new approach to explaining fertility patterns. *Population and Development Review, 29*, 349–374.

Lareau, A. (2002). Invisible inequality: Social class and childrearing in black families and white families. *American Sociological Review, 67*, 747–776.

Morgan, S. P. (2001). Should fertility intentions inform fertility forecasts? In G. K. Spencer (Ed.), *Proceedings of the U.S. Census Bureau Conference: The direction of fertility in the United States* (pp. 153–178). Washington, DC: U.S. Bureau of the Census.

Morgan, S. P. (2003). Is low fertility a 21st century crisis? *Demography 40*, 589-603.

Morgan, S. P., & King, R. B. (2001). Why have children in the 21st century? *European Journal of Population, 17*, 3–20.

Pollard, M. S., & Morgan, S. P. (2002). Emerging gender indifference: Sex composition of children and the third birth. *American Sociological Review, 67*, 600–613..

Quesnel-Vallée, A., & Morgan, S. P. (2002, August). *Do women and men realize their fertility intentions?* Paper presented at the annual meeting of the American Sociological Association, Chicago.

Rindfuss, R. R., Guzzo, K. B., & Morgan, S. P. (In press). The changing institutional context of low fertility. *Population Research and Policy Review*.

Sandberg, J. F., & Hofferth, S. L. (2001). Changes in children's time with parents: United States, 1981–1997. *Demography, 38*, 423–436.

II

How Do Social and Cultural Values and Attitudes Shape Fertility Patterns in the Developed World?

5

HOW DO ATTITUDES SHAPE CHILDBEARING IN THE UNITED STATES?

Jennifer S. Barber
William G. Axinn
University of Michigan

Introduction

In this chapter we examine the role of attitudes, preferences, and expectations in shaping childbearing behavior in the United States. Theoretical models of childbearing behavior consistently include attitudes[1] as central components in understanding this important human behavior (Lesthaeghe & Wilson, 1986; Lesthaeghe, 1998; Preston, 1986). For example, structural or demand theories suggest that higher levels of education and labor force participation for women increase the opportunity costs of childbearing and thereby reduce the *demand* or desire for children (Becker, 1981; Bulatao & Lee, 1983; Easterlin & Crimmins, 1985; Notestein 1953; Rindfuss, Swicegood, & Rosenfeld, 1987). Ideational theories hypothesize that the spread of new *ideas* through institutions like schools and the mass media lead to the incorporation of new *preferences* for delayed parenthood and smaller families (Caldwell, 1982; Lesthaeghe & Willems, 1999; Lesthaeghe & Surkyn, 1988; Rutenberg & Watkins, 1997; Valente et al., 1997; Watkins, 1995). Still other theories posit that increasing consumption aspirations lead to delayed marriage and childbearing as young people put off family formation until they have fulfilled their *preferences* for consumer goods (Easterlin, 1980; Freedman, 1979). Likewise, the family mode of social organization framework argues that macro-level social changes influence couple-level childbearing behavior by altering the social organization of families in ways that change individual *preferences* for family versus non-family behavior (Axinn & Yabiku, 2001; Thornton & Lin, 1994).

---

[1] We follow Alwin and Scott's (1996) definition of attitudes—"attitudes are latent predispositions to respond or behave in particular ways toward attitude objects." However, in this chapter, we use the term "attitude" broadly, to encompass a wide variety of subjective phenomena. We agree with Alwin and Scott (1996) that "distinctions can often by fuzzy" and that "attitudes should be distinguished from other related concepts" (p. 76). Throughout the chapter, we also refer to desires, preferences, etc., when referencing a particular survey question or research finding. When referring broadly to research relating subjective phenomena such as attitudes, beliefs, and value, we use the shorthand "attitudes".

The empirical literature is also consistent with the hypothesis that attitudes are an important determinant of childbearing behavior in the United States. For instance, research from the 1970s demonstrates the strong impact of family size preferences on completed family size in the United States (Coombs, 1974, 1979; Vinokur-Kaplan, 1978). Later research shows a relationship between spousal agreement on family size preference and the transition to another birth (Thomson, 1997; Thomson, McDonald, & Bumpass, 1990). Other studies provide evidence that a relatively wide range of attitudes, such as those concerning gender roles, education, work, and self-esteem, may affect the transition to parenthood (Morgan & Waite, 1987; Plotnick, 1992), in particular first-birth timing and premarital pregnancy (Barber, 2000, 2001). Numerous other studies indicate that attitudes predict key proximate determinants of childbearing, including cohabitation, marriage, contraceptive use, and abortion (e.g., Axinn & Thornton, 1992, 1993; Barber & Axinn, 1998a, 1998b; Beckman et al., 1983; Brazzell & Acock, 1988; Chilman, 1980; Goldscheider & Waite, 1991).

In this paper we begin by considering the relationship between individual attitudes and childbearing behavior in the United States, reviewing the theoretical reasoning and empirical evidence for this relationship and discussing key caveats. We then consider the impact of the attitudes of others, including peers, parents, and partners, on childbearing behavior. Again, our review touches on both theoretical reasoning and empirical evidence. Next, we review changes over the past 50 years in childbearing attitudes and consider their impact on trends in childbearing behavior. Finally, we consider the likely sources of change and variation in attitudes, and their implications for childbearing behavior.

Attitudes as Predictors of Childbearing Behavior

Fishbein and Ajzen's theories of Reasoned Action and Planned Behavior—the mostly widely used frameworks for linking attitudes and behavior in the social sciences—predict that positive attitudes toward a behavior increase the likelihood of that behavior (Fishbein & Ajzen, 1975). They define an attitude as "a disposition to respond favorably or unfavorably to an object, person, institution, or event" (Ajzen, 1988, p. 4). In this framework, attitudes toward a particular behavior, along with subjective norms (social pressure), predict intentions, and intentions predict behavior. In the case of childbearing, positive attitudes toward childbearing, coupled with social pressure or social support, increase its likelihood (Fishbein & Ajzen, 1975; Vinokur-Kaplan, 1978). Thus, individuals with positive attitudes toward children and childbearing are likely to enter parenthood earlier and have more children than their peers who have more negative attitudes toward children and childbearing.

However, the finite nature of our time and resources limit our behavioral choices. As a result, attitudes toward a wide variety of behaviors are likely to affect the timing of family formation. As young people make the transition to adulthood, they must choose among a variety of possible roles. Furthermore, decisions about which roles to fulfill often must be made simultaneously. Choosing one role may make the fulfillment of other roles quite difficult (Rindfuss, 1991; Rindfuss, Swicegood, & Rosenfeld, 1987), or it may subsequently ease the transition to other roles. With respect to childbearing, these roles involve behaviors that fall under two broad categories: behaviors that *facilitate* childbearing and behaviors that *compete* with childbearing. We use the terms "facilitate" and "compete" not to suggest that individuals cannot fulfill multiple roles simultaneously, but rather to suggest that some combinations of roles are *more difficult* to fulfill simultaneously than other combinations. We expect particularly difficult role combinations to lead to the postponement of one of the roles, although not necessarily the avoidance of that role altogether. This is akin to the F_c component in Morgan's model (see Morgan, this volume).

For example, because parenting roles are particularly difficult to fulfill in combination with labor force participation and educational enrollment, selecting roles that involve these behaviors tends to delay first births among women (Barber, 2001; Crimmins, Easterlin, & Saito, 1991; Kasarda, Billy, & West, 1986; Rindfuss & St. John, 1983; Rindfuss, Morgan, & Swicegood, 1988). Thus, preferences for roles involving education and careers compete with preferences for early childbearing, and thus tend to delay childbearing (Barber, 2000, 2001). Although preferences for education and labor force participation are likely to impact first-birth timing simply because they impact actual school and work behavior, they may also have a more independent effect on childbearing behavior. That is, young people may express their preferences for education and careers by delaying family formation even when actual career choices and educational options may be beyond their control (Stolzenberg & Waite, 1977; Waite & Stolzenberg, 1976). For example, positive attitudes and expectations for careers have been linked to reduced family size *expectations* among women (Stolzenberg & Waite, 1977; Waite & Stolzenberg, 1976); positive attitudes and expectations for education have been linked to a lower likelihood of premarital childbearing (Plotnick, 1992); and preferences for education, careers, and consumer spending have been linked to delayed childbearing (Barber, 2001; Crimmins, Easterlin, & Saito, 1991; Easterlin, 1980).

In contrast to roles involving education and career development, other types of roles fulfilled in young adulthood are particularly facilitating for childbearing. For instance, young people whose social lives are organized around marriage are likely to be in situations that are ideal for parenthood. Early marriage leads to early childbearing (Rindfuss, Morgan, & Swicegood, 1988), and early pregnancy leads to early marriage (Manning, 1993). Furthermore, most married couples go on to bear children (Rindfuss, Morgan, & Swicegood, 1988), and most children are born to married couples (Loomis & Landale, 1994; Manning, 1995). Thus, preferences for early marriage and large families are likely to be particularly compatible with early family formation. Preferences for large families speed the entry into marriage, probably because of the desire to begin childbearing within a marital relationship

(Barber & Axinn, 1998b). Preferences for early marriage are likely to lead to early first births partially because they speed the entry into marriage. Preferences for early marriage and large families may also have a strong impact on childbearing behavior independent of marriage. For instance, young people who prefer early marriage or large families may begin childbearing particularly quickly even *after* they marry.

An explanation for the influence of preferences on childbearing behavior can be found in the concept of *role conflict*. For example, the role of parenthood calls for spending time with children, while the roles of student and worker usually involve spending large amounts of time away from home. Similarly, parenthood requires spending substantial amounts of money on children that cannot be used to purchase luxury items. Role conflict theory asserts that individuals will avoid making the transition into roles perceived as conflict- or tension-inducing (Burr et al., 1979; Crimmins, Easterlin, & Saito, 1991; Goode, 1960). We hypothesize that individuals will delay the transition into a role that conflicts with a role that they already occupy.

Attitudes toward competing behaviors, or attitudes toward roles that conflict with childbearing, may impact the attitude-behavior relationship in at least three ways: via attitudes, via intentions, or via behavioral control (Barber, 2001). First, favorable attitudes toward a competing behavior may reduce favorable attitudes toward the focal behavior. For example, positive attitudes toward childbearing and toward careers are negatively correlated (Crimmins, Easterlin, & Saito, 1991; Stolzenberg & Waite, 1977; Waite & Stolzenberg, 1976). This is consistent with the expectancy value framework, which determines attitudes toward a behavior by summing the desirability associated with each possible outcome of that behavior weighted by the likelihood of the outcome (Edwards, 1954). One component of the desirability associated with any behavioral outcome, and thus an influence on attitudes toward the behavior, is its opportunity cost (that is, the sacrifice of not performing competing behaviors). Thus, a young person who holds strong positive attitudes toward education and career development may have negative attitudes toward early childbearing because one of the opportunity costs of early childbearing is sacrificing time for school and work. This effect is also consistent with cognitive consistency theories (e.g., cognitive dissonance theory and balance theory), which posit that holding positive attitudes toward two competing behaviors produces an uncomfortable psychological state that individuals will attempt to reduce (Festinger, 1957; Heider, 1958). For example, holding positive attitudes toward both early childbearing and pursuing a demanding career may produce dissonance, motivating a shift toward a less positive view of career development that is more consistent with wanting early childbearing.

Second, if an individual does form positive attitudes toward two competing behaviors, it may affect the strength of his or her intention to implement one or both of those behaviors. This is also implied by cognitive consistency theories, which suggest that *intending* to perform competing behaviors will produce dissonance that individuals will attempt to reduce. For example, an individual who intends to have a large family as well as a demanding career and a luxury lifestyle may hold weaker intentions to form a large family than another individual whose goals do not include a demanding career and a luxury lifestyle.

Third, forming intentions to carry out two or more competing behaviors may compromise an individual's ability to implement one of the behaviors. This is consistent with the notion that external factors are likely to be important determinants of whether individuals are able to achieve their goals (Ajzen, 1988). In this case, competing intentions are "external" factors (external to the concepts explicitly considered by the theory of planned behavior). This effect is also consistent with cognitive consistency theory, except that attempting to perform multiple competing behaviors is likely to produce more than *psychological* discomfort. When fulfilling one role makes the fulfillment of another role difficult in terms of time, money, effort, psychological well-being, or other resources, an individual experiences role conflict. In general, forming intentions for two competing behaviors is likely to diminish the individual's ability to implement either of those intentions. Thus, for instance, a woman who intends to have a baby while attaining a graduate degree may find herself too busy working toward graduation to focus time or energy on her plan to have a baby.

Overall, individuals who hold positive attitudes toward education, careers, and luxury spending are less likely to hold positive attitudes toward family formation. However, those who hold positive attitudes toward both family formation and these alternatives are likely to work toward cognitive consistency by forming intentions that focus on one side of the family formation equation. Those who decide to form families, achieve high levels of education, have demanding careers, and attain a luxury lifestyle are likely to experience difficulty implementing all of those intentions.

Socially Encouraged and Discouraged Behaviors

Contingent consistency models suggest that attitudes have a stronger impact on behavior when there is also social support for the behavior (Grube & Morgan, 1990). In other words, positive attitudes toward a behavior that is not socially supported may not be enough to motivate that behavior. Individuals who are inclined toward a behavior that they perceive as non-normative are likely to be influenced in their intentions by social pressure to avoid the behavior (Ajzen, 1988; Ajzen & Fishbein, 1980; Fishbein & Ajzen, 1975). In addition, they may encounter obstacles in attempting to fulfill their intentions.

Thus, positive attitudes toward premarital childbearing may not have a strong influence on behavior because social pressure operates to discourage premarital childbearing. A young unmarried person with favorable attitudes toward becoming pregnant is likely to face substantial pressure from parents, teachers, and at least some peers to delay premarital sex and pregnancy. One partner of an unmarried couple might insist on using a contraceptive, or if a young unmarried woman actually becomes pregnant, her parents or other important adults may encourage an abortion. In addition, because 58% of premarital pregnancies are unintended (Abma et al., 1997), they are less likely to be the result of intentional behavior.

On the other hand, marital childbearing, which generally enjoys considerable social support, is intended nearly 80% of the time (Abma et al., 1997). Thus, positive attitudes toward children and childbearing are likely to have a much stronger impact on childbearing behavior within marriage.

Attitudes toward competing behaviors may, on the other hand, be better predictors of socially discouraged behaviors than of socially encouraged behaviors. For instance, although attitudes toward childbearing may be better predictors of marital childbearing than premarital childbearing, attitudes toward competing alternatives such as work, school, and consumer spending may be better predictors of premarital childbearing. This is likely because childbearing may conflict more strongly with alternative behaviors if the birth occurs outside of marriage. Married parents may expect more support from their spouse in fulfilling the time and financial demands of raising a child than an unmarried parent. This expectation of support may be particularly influential for women, who tend to be responsible for the majority of childcare responsibilities (Hochschild, 1989). For instance, a married mother may anticipate less role conflict from attending college than would a single mother, because she may expect her husband to care for the children while she is studying or attending classes.

Young Adulthood Experiences

Although theoretical and empirical research on attitude formation and stability suggest that young adulthood is a time of relatively unstable attitudes (Alwin, 1994), we argue that attitudes held during the transition to adulthood are particularly likely to influence family formation behavior for two reasons. First, the transition to adulthood is a period of relatively abundant opportunities, and thus individuals are likely to form their attitudes and intentions in explicit comparison to the alternatives. For instance, attitudes and intentions toward family formation at age 18 are likely to be heavily influenced by attitudes toward pursuing a college education and establishing a career, because educational and career opportunities are abundant at these ages. Similarly, young adults' attitudes toward work and career are likely to be related to attitudes toward family, because family formation opportunities are also abundant. Second, decisions made during the transition to adulthood have a particularly long-lasting influence on the remainder of the life course because they set individuals on paths that are sometimes difficult to change. For instance, young adults who choose early family formation often find it difficult to complete college and establish careers (Hoffman, 1998), and those who choose educational attainment and careers tend to delay marriage and childbearing (Barber, 2000, 2001; Marini, 1978; Thornton, Axinn, & Teachman, 1995).

Attitudes toward family formation may affect family formation behavior via their impact on early adult experiences. For instance, preferences for large families speed the entry into marriage and decrease the likelihood of cohabitation (Barber & Axinn, 1998), which in turn increase the rate of young parenthood (Loomis & Landale, 1994; Manning, 1995; Manning & Landale, 1996). Positive attitudes toward family life in general may also decrease educational attainment, which leads to earlier childbearing. In addition, positive attitudes toward family formation may have direct effects on the entry into parenthood that cannot be explained by early adulthood experiences such as cohabitation, marriage, childbearing, education, or work.

Attitudes toward alternatives to family formation may also affect family formation behavior via their impact on early adult experiences. For instance, expectations for high levels of education are associated with college attendance, which is associated with delayed marriage and childbearing (Rindfuss, Morgan, & Swicegood, 1988; Thornton, Axinn, & Teachman, 1995). Attitudes toward alternatives to family formation may also have a more direct impact on early adult childbearing beyond participation in those alternatives. For instance, the desire for a college education may influence individuals' family formation behavior even if they do not enroll in school. That is, they may postpone marriage or childbearing *in hopes of* achieving a college education, regardless of whether or not this is a realistic possibility. Similar reasoning may be applied to attitudes toward careers.

Attitudes toward luxury spending may also affect family formation behavior via their influence on education, work, cohabitation, marriage, or childbearing behavior. Preferences for high levels of consumer spending are hypothesized to delay family formation because individuals with these preferences tend to accumulate education, build their careers, and earn the money necessary to purchase consumer goods—all of which delay both marriage and childbearing (Easterlin, 1980). Also, preferences for luxury spending may impact family formation, regardless of whether individuals actually accumulate wealth, when marriage and childbearing are delayed in hopes of achieving greater wealth.

Empirical Evidence

We now briefly turn to a presentation of empirical results to illustrate the key points raised above. This presentation focuses on first-birth rates.[2] Table 5.1, excerpted from Barber (2001), shows estimates of the effects of attitudes toward activities with children, the belief that children cause worry and strain, and total family size preferences on premaritally and maritally conceived first-birth rates. (See Barber, 2001 for an explanation of the measures and methods used.) Consistent with other research results, these analyses indicate that attitudes toward children

---

[2] The models estimate effects on the hazard of first birth. When the number of events is very small, the hazard and the rate are similar. Thus, for ease of interpretation, we refer to the first-birth rate rather than the hazard.

and childbearing are strong predictors of first-birth timing. However, this table also shows an important distinction: the influence of attitudes toward children and childbearing is limited to *maritally conceived* first births. While estimates for Models 5–8 illustrate the strong effects of these attitudes on the timing of first births conceived within marriage, none of the coefficients for Models 1–4, which estimate the effects on *premaritally conceived* first-birth rates, is statistically significantly different from zero.

Table 5.1.

Logistic Regression Estimates of Effects of Attitudes Toward Childbearing on Hazard of First Birth

	Hazard of Premarital First Birth				Hazard of Marital First Birth			
	(1)	(2)	(3)	(4)	(5)	(6)	(7)	(8)
Attitude Toward Activities with Children	-.05 (.07)			-.06 (.07)	.01 (.04)			-.02 (.04)
Attitude Toward Activities with Children * Woman	.09 (.10)			.12 (.10)	.16** (.06)			.16** (.06)
Belief that Children Cause Worry and Strain to Parents		-.16 (.13)		-.19 (.13)		-.19** (.07)		-.16* (.07)
Family Size Preference			-.02 (.03)	-.02 (.03)			.05*** (.02)	.04** (.02)
Chi-Square Value	89.07	91.11	91.30	95.45	210.33	200.38	203.00	217.26
Degrees of Freedom	20	19	19	22	20	19	19	22
Number of Person Months	71,346	71,185	70,678	70,517	94,541	94,380	93,710	93,549

Notes:

[†]p < .10, * p < .05, ** p < .01, *** p < .001, one-tailed tests.

All chi-square values are significant at the .001 level.

Coefficients are additive effects on log-odds of first birth.

Standard errors in parentheses.

Models include the following control variables: mother" total number of children, mother's age at first childbearing, average early family income, average later family income, family income decline, family financial assets, parents' average education, mother Catholic, mother divorced and remarried + mother divorced and not remarried (mother continuously married is reference category), gender, and dichotomous measures of age: < age 20 (reference), 20 ≤ age < 22, 22 ≤ age < 24, 24 ≤ age < 26; 26 ≤ age < 28, and age ≥ 28.

Source: Barber, J. S. (2001). Ideational influences on the transition to parenthood: Attitudes toward childbearing and competing alternatives. *Social Psychological Quarterly, 64,* 101–127.

Model 5 shows that positive attitudes toward activities with children significantly speed entry into parenthood; however, this effect is only statistically significant among women. While women who enjoy activities with children enter motherhood significantly earlier than their peers who do not enjoy such activities, the extent to which men enjoy activities with children does not predict how quickly they enter fatherhood. Model 6 shows the influence of believing that children cause worry and strain on first-birth rates. The more strongly both men and women believe that children cause worry and strain, the later they enter parenthood within marriage. Model 7 shows the influence of family size preferences on young adults' entry into parenthood. Both men and women who prefer large families enter parenthood, on average, much more quickly than their peers.

Finally, Model 8 shows that the effects of these attitudes toward children and childbearing on first-birth timing are largely independent of one another. When included in the same model, the effects remain similar in magnitude, and similarly statistically significant. When compared to a base model of marital childbearing that does not include the attitude measures, the chi-square value for Model 8 indicates that the addition of the attitude measures results in a significant improvement in model fit (not shown in tables).

Attitudes Toward Alternative Behaviors

Table 5.2, also from Barber (2001), shows estimates of the effects of attitudes toward school, careers, and consumer spending on premaritally and maritally conceived first-birth rates. The results in this table indicate that these attitudes have a strong impact on the transition to parenthood, in particular on the timing of premaritally conceived first births.

Model 1 shows the influence of expectations for education on premarital first-birth rates. Although the impact of expectations for education is not statistically significant in Model 1, it is in the predicted direction. Previous research indicates that expectations for high levels of education and success in school may have a strong deterrent effect on premarital first births (Plotnick, 1992). Plotnick suggests that this influence is mainly because premaritally pregnant girls with positive attitudes and expectations toward education are more likely to get an abortion or to legitimize the pregnancy through marriage than are their premaritally pregnant peers with less positive attitudes and expectations for education.

Model 2, which shows the influence of attitudes toward careers on premarital birth rates, indicates that those who believe their career will be a source of life satisfaction have lower first-birth rates. Those who strongly believe that work will be a source of satisfaction in their lives have a yearly log-odds of premarital first birth that is 1.17 lower than those who strongly believe that work will *not* be a source of satisfaction in their lives.

Table 5.2.

Logistic Regression Estimates of Effects of Attitudes Toward Competing Alternatives to Childbearing on Hazard of First Birth

	Hazard of Premarital First Birth				Hazard of Marital First Birth			
	(1)	(2)	(3)	(4)	(5)	(6)	(7)	(8)
Educational Expectation	-.07 (.05)			-.07 (.05)	-.01 (.03)			-.01 (.03)
Attitude Toward Careers		-.39** (.14)		-.36** (.14)		-.13* (.08)		-.11 (.08)
Attitude Toward Luxury Goods			-.38* (.16)	-.33* (.16)			-.21* (.10)	-.19* (.10)
Chi-Square Value	90.57	95.81	93.89	102.13	192.36	196.76	201.18	200.72
Degrees of Freedom	19	19	19	21	19	19	19	21
Number of Person Months	70,921	71,318	71,276	70,879	93,800	94,384	94,326	93,742

Notes:

† p < .10, * p < .05, ** p < .01, *** p < .001, one-tailed tests.

All chi-square values are significant at the .001 level.

Coefficients are additive effects on log-odds of first birth.

Standard errors in parentheses.

Models include the following control variables: mother's total number of children, mother's age at first childbearing, average early family income, average later family income, family income decline, family financial assets, parents' average education, mother Catholic, mother divorced and remarried + mother divorced and not remarried (mother continuously married is reference category), gender, and dichotomous measures of age: < age 20 (reference), 20 ≤ age < 22, 22 ≤ age < 24, 24 ≤ age < 26; 26 ≤ age < 28, and age ≥ 28.

Source: Barber, J. S. (2001). Ideational influences on the transition to parenthood: Attitudes toward childbearing and competing alternatives. *Social Psychological Quarterly, 64*, 101–127.

Model 3 shows the influence of consumer spending preferences on premarital first-birth rates. This model strongly supports existing theories predicting that preferences for luxury goods delay entry into parenthood (Crimmins, Easterlin, & Saito, 1991; Easterlin, 1980). Each one-point increase on the four-point scale reduces the log-odds of a premarital first birth by .37. This translates into 1.11 lower log-odds of premarital childbearing among those individuals who, on average, rated the consumer goods as "very important" compared to those who rated them as "not at all important" overall. Note also that attitudes toward luxury goods similarly delay *marital* childbearing (Model 7). Each one-point increase on the four-point scale reduces the log-odds of a marital first birth by .24.

Model 4 demonstrates that educational expectations, attitudes toward careers, and attitudes toward consumer spending have independent effects on premarital first-birth rates. In fact, the magnitude and statistical significance of these effects changes only slightly when the measures are included in the same model. Furthermore, the addition of these measures to a base model of premarital childbearing that does not contain measures of attitudes results in a significant improvement in model fit (not shown in tables). In addition, Models 5–8 show that these attitudes have some effects on marital first-birth rates. However, these relationships are much weaker than the relationships with premarital first-birth rates. Also, Model 8 indicates that these relationships are not statistically independent—it appears that attitudes toward careers and attitudes toward consumer spending are related, and the attitude toward careers mainly influences marital first-birth rates.

In addition to these relationships, we note that Plotnick (1992) found a significant relationship between egalitarian gender role attitudes and premarital pregnancy rates. His results indicate that egalitarian attitudes lead to higher premarital pregnancy rates, and that premaritally pregnant girls with egalitarian attitudes were less likely to marry than their counterparts with less egalitarian attitudes.

Overall, the results presented in Tables 5.1 and 5.2 are consistent with the theoretical framework described above, emphasizing that positive attitudes toward a particular behavior increase the likelihood of that behavior, and that positive attitudes toward competing behaviors decrease the likelihood of that behavior. In this case, positive attitudes toward behaviors that facilitate childbearing increase childbearing rates, and positive attitudes toward behaviors that compete with childbearing decrease childbearing rates. Furthermore, the pattern of these results suggests that attitudes toward childbearing-related behaviors are more strongly related to marital than premarital childbearing rates, while attitudes toward competing behaviors are more strongly linked to premarital childbearing rates. This pattern supports our hypothesis predicting that attitude-behavior consistency is contingent on whether the birth is conceived premaritally or within marriage. Lastly, these analyses illustrate that men and women respond quite similarly to their attitudes toward childbearing, education, careers, and consumer spending, while women respond more strongly to their attitudes toward activities with children. In results not shown here, Barber (2001) found that men's and women's attitudes toward these alternatives differ significantly, which indicates that although men and women respond similarly to similar attitudes, they may actually behave differently in part because they tend to have different attitudes.

Mediating Role of Early Adulthood Experiences

Tables 5.3 and 5.4 illustrate the role of early adulthood experiences with education, union formation, and work in mediating the effects of attitudes on childbearing behavior (for more details regarding the measures and models displayed in Tables 5.3 and 5.4, see Barber, 2001). Table 5.3 shows how early adulthood experiences mediate the impact of attitudes toward school, careers, and luxury goods on premarital childbearing. A comparison of Model 2 to Model 1 shows that experiences with education explain approximately 10% of the impact of career attitudes on premarital first-birth rates, and approximately 3% of the impact of luxury goods attitudes on premarital first-birth rates. In other words, one reason that young people with positive attitudes toward careers and luxury goods have lower premarital birth rates is that they are more likely to be enrolled in school throughout young adulthood.

The effects of attitudes toward careers and luxury goods are not explained by early adulthood experiences with union formation and work. In fact, the effects of these attitudes grow stronger with the inclusion of early adulthood experiences in the same model. This is mainly because of their association with cohabitation. Although positive attitudes toward careers and luxury spending overall *reduce* premarital childbearing rates, those attitudes are associated with increased likelihood of cohabitation, which in turn *raises* premarital childbearing rates (Loomis & Landale, 1996; Manning, 1995; Manning & Landale, 1996).

Table 5.4 explores the role of early adulthood experiences in explaining the impact of attitudes toward childbearing on marital childbearing behavior. Overall, comparing Models 2, 3, and 4 to Model 1 reveals that early adulthood experiences do not explain much of the impact of attitudes on marital childbearing behavior. Among women, experiences with both school and union formation explain a small portion of the impact of attitudes toward activities with children. That is, young women with strong positive attitudes toward activities with children are slightly less likely to be enrolled in school and tend to marry earlier than their peers, both of which lead to higher marital first-birth rates. Young women who believe that children cause a great deal of worry and strain to parents are somewhat more likely to be working full-time, which explains a small portion of the impact of those beliefs on marital childbearing behavior. Overall, however, Models 1–4 indicate that most of the impact of attitudes toward childbearing on marital childbearing behavior is net of experiences with school, cohabitation, marriage, and work.

Tables 5.3 and 5.4 show results that are consistent with the idea that early adulthood experiences with education, work, and union formation explain part of the impact of attitudes on childbearing behavior, but that attitudes have substantial independent effects as well. In fact, Tables 3 and 4 indicate that the impact of attitudes on premarital and marital childbearing behavior is *largely* independent of these early adult experiences. This means that, regardless of their educational attainment, union formation behavior, or work behavior, (a) young people with positive attitudes toward children and childbearing have higher rates of marital childbearing than their counterparts, and (b) young people with positive attitudes toward behaviors that compete with childbearing have lower rates of premarital childbearing than their counterparts.

Table 5.3.

Logistic Regression Estimates of Effects of Attitudes on Hazard of Premarital First Birth Net of Early Adulthood Experiences

	(1)	(2)	(3)	(4)
Attitudes Toward Competing Alternatives to Childbearing				
Educational Expectation	-.07 (.05)	.004 (.06)	.01 (.06)	.01 (.06)
Attitude Toward Careers	-.36** (.14)	-.34** (.14)	-.41** (.14)	-.41** (.14)
Attitude Toward Luxury Goods	-.33* (.16)	-.32* (.16)	-.36* (.17)	-.35* (.17)
Early Adulthood Experiences				
Education (previous month)				
Enrolled in School		-.56* (.29)	-.46 (.29)	-.40 (.30)
Accumulated Years of Schooling		-.17* (.10)	-.09 (.10)	-.09 (.10)
Union Status (previous month)				
Cohabiting [a]			1.50*** (.24)	1.47*** (.24)
Accumulated Years of Cohabitation			.06 (.09)	.06 (.09)
Accumulated Years of Marriage	—	—	—	—
Work Status (previous month)[b]				
Working Part-Time				-.33 (.46)
Working Full-Time * Man				.25 (.39)
Working Full-Time * Woman				-.17 (.38)
Chi-Square Value	102.13	109.79	196.08	197.19
Degrees of Freedom	21	23	25	28
Number of Person Months	70,879	70,879	70,879	70,879

Notes:
[a] $p < .10$, * $p < .05$, ** $p < .01$, *** $p < .001$, one-tailed tests.
All chi-square values are significant at the .001 level.
Coefficients are additive effects on log-odds of first birth.
Standard errors in parentheses.
Models include the following control variables: mother's total number of children, mother's age at first childbearing, average early family income, average later family income, family income decline, family financial assets, parents' average education, mother Catholic, mother divorced and remarried + mother divorced and not remarried (mother continuously married is reference category), gender, and dichotomous measures of age: < age 20 (reference), $20 \le$ age < 22, $22 \le$ age < 24, $24 \le$ age < 26; $26 \le$ age < 28, and age ≥ 28.
Source: Barber, J. S. (2001). Ideational influences on the transition to parenthood: Attitudes toward childbearing and competing alternatives. *Social Psychological Quarterly, 64,* 101–127.

Table 5.4.

Logistic Regression Estimates of Effects of Attitudes on Hazard of Marital First Birth Net of Early Adulthood Experiences

	(1)	(2)	(3)	(4)
Attitudes Toward Childbearing				
Attitude Toward Activities with Children	-.02 (.04)	-.02 (.04)	-.02 (.04)	-.02 (.04)
Attitude Toward Activities with Children * Woman	.16** (.06)	.16** (.06)	.18** (.06)	.18** (.06)
Belief that Children Cause Worry and Strain to Parents	-.16* (.07)	-.15* (.07)	-.15* (.08)	-.16* (.08)
Family Size Preference	.04** (.02)	.04** (.02)	.04** (.02)	.04** (.02)
Early Adulthood Experiences				
Education (previous month):				
Enrolled in School		-.66*** (.18)	-.71*** (.18)	-.64*** (.19)
Accumulated Years of Schooling		-.002 (.04)	.04 (.04)	.04 (.04)
Union Status (previous month)				
Cohabiting [a]	—	—	—	—
Accumulated Years of Cohabitation			-.01 (.05)	-.01 (.05)
Accumulated Years of Marriage			.26*** (.02)	.26 (.02)
Work Status (previous month)[b]				
Working Part-Time				-.24 (.30)
Working Full-Time * Man				.87* (.38)
Working Full-Time * Woman				-.31 (.21)
Chi-Square Value	217.26	229.07	477.07	480.39
Degrees of Freedom	22	24	26	29
Number of Person Months	93,549	93,549	93,549	93,549

Notes:
[1] p < .10, * p < .05, ** p < .01, *** p < .001, one-tailed tests.
All chi-square values are significant at the .001 level.
Coefficients are additive effects on log-odds of first birth.
Standard errors in parentheses.
Models include the following control variables: mother's total number of children, mother's age at first childbearing, average early family income, average later family income, family income decline, family financial assets, parents' average education, mother Catholic, mother divorced and remarried + mother divorced and not remarried (mother continuously married is reference category), gender, and dichotomous measures of age: < age 20 (reference), 20 ≤ age < 22, 22 ≤ age < 24, 24 ≤ age < 26; 26 ≤ age < 28, and age ≥ 28.
Source: Barber, J. S. (2001). Ideational influences on the transition to parenthood: Attitudes toward childbearing and competing alternatives. *Social Psychological Quarterly, 64,* 101–127.

The Attitudes of Important "Others"

In this section, we describe how the attitudes of "others" may be important in shaping young adults' childbearing behavior. We begin with parents' attitudes, which are probably particularly important in predicting early childbearing, and then partners' attitudes, which are likely to be especially important determinants of marital (or couple) childbearing behavior. Again, we begin with the mechanisms that may produce these relationships, and then turn to a review of existing empirical evidence.

Socialization and social control are two important ways that parents influence their children's behavior. Through socialization, parents affect their children's behavior by influencing how their children *want* to behave. Parents' attitudes and preferences for their child shape the child's own attitudes and preferences. Parents and children also share similar attitudes and preferences because of their shared social positions, background, and experiences; children may behave in accordance with their parents' preferences simply because their parents' preferences and their own opportunities were shaped by the same social forces (Bengtson, 1975). Overall, children are socialized to evaluate behaviors similarly to their parents. Thus, by behaving in accordance with their own attitudes and preferences, children may be conforming to their parents' wishes as well.

In addition, however, parents influence their children's behavior *independent* of their offspring's attitudes. The influence of social control—either parents attempting to get their children to behave in ways they find appropriate, or children altering their behavior simply to please their parents—operates independently of how children themselves might prefer to behave. Social control affects children's behavior through mechanisms such as punishment or rewards (Gecas & Seff, 1990; Smith, 1988).

Of course, socialization and social control are not completely independent processes. For instance, some aspects of social control require socialization—a mother who shows her child that an action has hurt or disappointed her is employing a social control technique that assumes the existence of socialization (Coleman, 1990). If the child is not socialized to value his mother's love and approval, then the social control technique (hurt and disappointment) is meaningless. And, some socialization techniques could be considered social control mechanisms. For instance, parents who try to convince their child to re-form his or her attitudes are attempting to control the child independent of what the child might prefer.

Parental preferences are probably particularly important during the transition to adulthood, a time during which parents exert considerable influence over their children. In general, parents' preferences may become less relevant as children age and as their opportunities and constraints change over time. Adulthood is associated with new and often unanticipated opportunities, as well as new socialization forces such as marital partners (Thomson, 1997).

Partners are likely to influence childbearing behavior via mechanisms similar to those discussed above. First, partners probably select each other based on similar attitudes toward childbearing and family size preferences. Second, once partnered, they probably influence each other's attitudes and preferences. Third, if their attitudes and preferences remain discordant, they influence each other's intentions. And, finally, if their intentions do not match, they influence each other's behavior via negotiation.

Thomson (1997) describes multiple models that may be used in this negotiation process. A gendered power perspective suggests that because men's power tends to be greater than women's power, men may have more power in negotiating childbearing decisions. A family spheres of influence perspective, however, suggests that women may have more power when it comes to family and childbearing decisions. A corollary to this is that the more men participate in the housework and childcare, the more power they tend to have over childbearing decisions. Finally, Thomson suggests that inertia probably plays a role—when partners disagree, they are probably most likely to continue what they are doing rather than negotiate a change. For example, partners with different preferences for having children may simply continue their current contraceptive behavior—whether using or not using contraception—and through their inertia influence their probability of childbearing. Lundberg and Pollak (1996) provide more detailed descriptions of these and other marriage bargaining models.

Empirical Evidence

Parents' attitudes. Model 1 of Table 5.5 shows that young adults whose mothers (a) prefer that their children have later marriages, smaller families, and more education, and (b) prefer that their daughters (or daughters-in-law) have careers tend to have later first births than their counterparts. Note that these relationships do not differ by gender. Each additional year a mother prefers her son or daughter to wait before marriage results in a .14 decrease in the monthly first-birth rate; thus, young adults whose mothers prefer that they marry at age 27 have first births at only 50% (exp $(-.14)^5 = .50$) the rate of those whose mothers prefer that they marry at age 22. Young adults whose mothers prefer a large family (4 children) have first births at 1.5 times (exp$(.14)^3 = 1.5$) the rate of those whose mothers prefer only one child. Each additional year of education mothers prefer for their children results in a .09 decrease in first-birth rate. This translates into a 30% (exp$(-.09)^4 = .70$) lower first-birth rate among young adults whose mothers prefer at least a college education than among those whose mothers prefer a high school education. Lastly, daughters whose mothers prefer that they have a career, and sons whose mothers prefer that their wives have a career, have first-birth rates that are about 25% (exp$(-.27) = .76$) lower than those for young adults whose mothers prefer no careers for their daughters or daughters-in-law.

Table 5.5.

Logistic Regression Estimates of Effects of Mothers' Preferences on Hazard of First Birth

	Base	(1)	(2)
Mothers' Preferences			
Mother's marriage age preference for child		-.11*** (.03)	-.08** (.03)
Mother's family size preference for child		.13* (.07)	.10† (.07)
Mother's minimum education preference for child		-.07* (.03)	-.08* (.04)
Mother's career preference for daughter/daughter-in-law		-.21* (.10)	-.18* (.11)
Children's Preferences			
Child's marriage age preference			-.09*** (.02)
Child's family size preference			.05† (.04)
Child's maximum education expectation			.04 (.03)
Child's career preference			-.14 (.11)
Daughter	.24** (.10)	.12 (.11)	.04 (.12)
Π^2	133.30	195.48	215.64
Degrees of freedom	18	24	28
Person months	91,372	91,144	87,287

Notes:
† p < .10, * p < .05, ** p < .01, *** p < .001, one-tailed tests.
All chi-square values are significant at the .001 level.
Coefficients are additive effects on log-odds of first birth.
Standard errors in parentheses.

Comparing the coefficient for gender in Model 1 to the coefficient for gender in the base model suggests that mothers' preferences explain approximately half of the gender difference in first-birth timing. This is because mothers hold different preferences for their sons' and daughters' behavior (Barber, 2000). In other words, part of the reason that young women enter parenthood earlier than young men is because their mothers prefer that they marry earlier and attain less education.

Model 1 also shows that the effects of mothers' preferences for marriage timing, family size, educational attainment, and careers are independent; each preference has an effect on first-birth rates regardless of the other preferences a mother might hold. Model 1 also indicates that, in the aggregate, mothers' preferences have the potential to impact their children's first-birth timing tremendously. For example, young adults whose mothers prefer early marriage (age 22), a large family (3 children), a high school education, *and* a stay-at-home mother enter parenthood at a rate that is four times higher than that for young adults whose mothers prefer late marriage (age 27), a small family (1 child), a college education, and a working mother. Finally, comparing the chi-square value for Model 1 to the chi-square for the base model indicates that adding mothers' preferences to the base model of family background characteristics results in a significant improvement in model fit.

We tested interactions with multiple characteristics of the adult child and of the family of origin to investigate the social context in which adult children were most likely to behave according to their mothers' preferences (analyses not shown in tables). These analyses provided no evidence that offspring with closer relationships to their mothers (from the child's perspective) were more likely to behave as their mothers wished. Furthermore, none of the characteristics of families analyzed here are related to whether adult children behave in accordance with their mothers' preferences.

As described above, socialization is an important mechanism through which parents influence their children's behavior. Through socialization, parents impart their own values and the values of society to their children. Thus, it is possible that the observed associations between mother's preferences and children's behavior shown in Model 1 result from the similarity between parents' and children's preferences. Model 2 investigates this hypothesis by adding measures of children's preferences to the models of mothers' preferences presented in Model 1. Comparing the estimated influence of mothers' preferences with and without children's preferences in the model provides an indication of the extent to which mothers' preferences influence children's behavior indirectly via the intervening mechanism of socialization to similar preferences. Because children's own preferences are probably more proximate to their behavior, whatever influence of mothers' preferences remains once children's preferences are included can be interpreted as the portion of the effect of mothers' preferences that is *independent* of the children's own preferences (the direct effect). If mothers' preferences influence children's behavior mainly because they influence the children's own preferences (the indirect effect), then the estimated effect of mothers' preferences will decline sharply when children's own preferences are included in the same model.

Not surprisingly, Model 2 shows that children's own preferences are a strong gauge of their behavior. Similar to mothers' preferences, the influence of children's preferences on first-birth timing does not differ by gender. And children who prefer early marriage and large families enter parenthood earlier than their peers who do not. However, the effects of mothers' preferences remain statistically significant even after children's preferences are controlled. Thus, although young adults' preferences are important predictors of childbearing behavior, their mothers' preferences regarding marriage, childbearing, school, and career behavior help determine their entry into parenthood *independent* of their personal preferences. In other words, mothers' preferences have substantial direct effects on offspring behavior. This is consistent with the notion that parents use social control techniques to influence their children's behavior and that they are able to influence their children's childbearing behavior independent of what the children themselves prefer.

Model 2 is also consistent with the socialization perspective. Decreases in the magnitude of the influence of mothers' preferences for marriage timing and family size that result when measures of children's attitudes are added to the model indicate that a portion of the influence of mothers' preferences is indirect via the children's own preferences. Although the impact of mothers' preferences for education is not explained by children's own preferences, 27% of the impact of mothers' marriage age preferences is explained by children's own preferences for marriage timing; 23% of the impact of mothers' family size preferences is explained by children's own family size preferences; and 14% of the impact of mothers' career preferences is explained by children's own career preferences.

Partners' attitudes. As stated above, partners' attitudes are also likely to influence childbearing behavior, particularly among married couples. Using the relatively few U.S. surveys that include both men's and women's family size preferences, Thomson and colleagues have thoroughly investigated the relative role of the influence of wives' versus husbands' family size desires and intentions. They find that both wives' and husbands' family size desires have important, substantial effects on subsequent childbearing behavior (Thomson, 1997; Thomson & Hoem, 1998; Thomson, McDonald, & Bumpass, 1990). Furthermore, they found that when couples disagree about the desire for additional children, their behavior falls in between that of couples who agree they want more children and couples who agree they do not want more children (Thomson, 1997; Thomson, McDonald, & Bumpass, 1990).

Additional analyses investigated the role of intentions in mediating the relationship between childbearing desires and behavior. Thomson (1997) found that, similar to the disagreement pattern noted above for behavior, the intentions of couples whose desires for additional children did not match fell in-between those couples in which both members desired additional children and couples in which neither member desired additional children. Furthermore, intentions mediated the relationship between childbearing desires and behavior. This is consistent with the Reasoned Action and Planned Behavior frameworks described above (Fishbein & Ajzen, 1975).

Attitude Change Over the Past Fifty Years

With a strong relationship between attitudes and childbearing behavior established, it is useful to ask how these attitudes have been changing, how they are likely to change in the future, and what that means for the future of childbearing behavior. As described above, attitudes toward multiple domains of life are likely to influence childbearing behavior, including attitudes toward gender roles, marriage, divorce, childbearing, premarital sex, extramarital sex, cohabitation, education, and careers. In looking at trends, we follow the same approach as above, dividing attitudes into two groups: attitudes toward behaviors that facilitate childbearing and attitudes toward behaviors that compete with childbearing.

Attitudes Toward Behaviors That Facilitate Childbearing

Attitudes toward marriage have changed dramatically since the 1950s (Thornton & Young-DeMarco, 2001; Veroff, Douvan, & Kulka, 1981). Between the 1950s and the 1970s, negativity toward marriage increased dramatically—young people became more positive toward remaining single, more negative toward marrying, and more concerned about marriage being restrictive. However, this increased negativity toward marriage was accompanied by only very modest increases in the percent of high school seniors wanting to remain single. And, this negative trend did not extend into the 1980s.

The most consistent trend in attitudes toward marriage is the increasing ideal age at marriage, which has been increasing steadily since the 1950s (Thornton & Young-DeMarco, 2001). However, even in the late 1990s, only a small fraction of people felt that a good marriage and family life were not important, preferred to remain single, believed they would not marry, or expected to divorce (Thornton & Young-DeMarco, 2001). Thus, marriage remains centrally important in individuals' lives.

Childbearing also remains central, with approximately 75% of people viewing parenthood as fulfilling; approximately 75% feeling that having children is not overly restrictive of parents' freedom; and approximately 60% believing that they are very likely to want children if they marry (Thornton & Young-DeMarco, 2001). Although ideal family size preferences have declined dramatically since the 1950s, the number of people expecting to remain childless is "quite small and relatively stable" (Thornton & Young-DeMarco, 2001, p. 1030). Thornton and Young-DeMarco (2001, p. 1030) conclude that, "marriage and children are not only centrally significant and meaningful to the vast majority of Americans, but may have become more valued, desired, and expected in recent decades."

However, Thornton and Young-DeMarco also conclude that the meaning of marriage and childbearing has changed dramatically in recent years. They note that marriage has become less powerful as an institution regulating sex and childbearing, that tolerance toward premarital sex increased dramatically in the 1960s and 1970s and has continued to slowly increase since then, and that the imperative for married couples to have children has relaxed considerably (Pagnini & Rindfuss, 1993; Thornton & Young-DeMarco, 2001). Tolerance toward nonmarital childbearing has also increased, although that trend is smaller than the trend for unmarried sex, and may have declined or even stopped in the 1990s (Thornton & Young-DeMarco, 2001). Finally, tolerance for childlessness among others has increased, as well.

Attitudes Toward Behaviors That Compete With Childbearing

The past 50 years have also witnessed substantial changes in attitudes toward behaviors that compete with childbearing. Although we have little information about the degree to which attitudes toward education and consumer spending have changed over the past fifty years, we know that attitudes toward work, and particularly toward working mothers, have changed dramatically.

Americans continue to support, to some degree, a gendered division of labor (Thornton & Young-DeMarco, 2001). This is truer among men than women. And, although the proportion believing that children suffer if their mother works outside the home has declined substantially over the past five decades, many people continue to be concerned about the effects of working mothers, especially in terms of family life and children's well-being (Thornton & Youn-DeMarco, 2001). In 1997–98, for example, 53% of men and 40% of women in the General Social Survey agreed or strongly agreed that, "a preschool child is likely to suffer is his or her mother works" (Thornton & Young-DeMarco, 2001, Table 1, panel C; Rindfuss, Brewster, & Kavee, 1996, Table 3).

Implications for Childbearing

These dramatic attitudinal changes toward marriage age and family size, premarital sex, and unmarried childbearing are likely to have important consequences for childbearing. It is not clear whether changes in gender role attitudes, however, will affect childbearing behavior. If current trends continue, the ideal marriage age will continue to increase, which will likely lead to even further delays in marriage and first births. However, because ideal family size preferences have leveled off at approximately two children, delayed marriage and childbearing, even into the mid-30s, is not likely to hinder the majority of couples' ability to achieve their desired completed family size. Researchers disagree about whether family size preferences will continue to decline. Morgan (2003) posits that ideal family size preferences are not likely to decline to zero. First births, he notes, are motivated by different desires than higher parity births. That is, first births are motivated by the desire for a child to love and care for; second births are often motivated by the desire for a sibling to the first birth, or to balance gender ratios; and third and higher births more often have economic motivations, which have declined dramatically in importance over time. Morgan concludes that strong desires to parent (and thus very positive attitudes toward parenthood) are compatible with small families. Finally, the trend in tolerance toward premarital sex and unmarried childbearing, after having increased dramatically for decades, has apparently leveled off, which suggests the potential for a corresponding leveling-off of unmarried childbearing.

Factors That Shape Attitudes

Because attitudes and behaviors are closely linked through reciprocal causal relationships (Ajzen, 1988), it is useful to consider how attitudes themselves are formed. Attitudes are not randomly occurring phenomena; they are constructed over time, throughout the life course, in response to many different, potentially important influences. Theories of attitude formation point toward a wide range of factors likely to shape and change attitudes, including the aforementioned early childhood socialization, dynamics of the parental family, individual experiences, and elements of social context such as peers, schools, the mass media, religion, and local community settings (Alwin, Cohen, & Newcomb, 1991; Gamson, Croteau, & Hoynes, 1992; Harris, 1995; Heider, 1958; Mead, 1967/1934; Zajonc, 1968). Findings from some long-term studies indicate that many attitudes remain relatively stable for substantial portions of the life course (Alwin, Cohen, & Newcomb, 1991), motivating research into the early life experiences and social contexts that shape attitudes. Although a comprehensive presentation of the factors that shape attitudes is clearly beyond the scope of this chapter, in this section we briefly summarize some of the key findings in research on the determinants of attitudes toward childbearing and the determinants of other attitudes that may influence childbearing.

First, we know that the family of origin has an important influence on childbearing-related attitudes. Intergenerational similarity in family size is one of the longest documented findings in social demography (Anderton, Tsuya, & Bean, 1987; Duncan et al., 1965; Johnson & Stokes, 1976; Kahn & Anderson, 1992), and the relationship between parental family size and children's family size preferences is also well documented (Hendershot, 1969; Stolzenberg & Waite, 1977; Waite & Stolzenberg, 1976). In previous research using the Intergenerational Panel Study of Mothers and Children, we found that not only does parental family size predict family size preferences as young people enter adulthood, but it continues to affect *changes* in family size preference across the years of early adulthood (Axinn,

Clarkberg, & Thornton, 1994). That is, those from a large family experience a greater increase in family size preferences during the transition to adulthood than those from smaller families. Moreover, mothers' preferences for their child's family size explain a good deal of the total effect of mothers' childbearing experiences on children's family size preferences (Axinn, Clarkberg, & Thornton, 1994). Although genetic similarity is likely to be a key reason for the intergenerational similarity in childbearing behavior (Barber, 2001b), it is also clear that parental childbearing behavior and preferences influence their children's family size preferences.

Second, we know that the impact of the parental family is not limited to the parents' family size or other childbearing preferences. For example, strong evidence indicates that parental divorce reduces children's family size preferences, although post-divorce changes in parents' own family size preferences play an important role transmitting these effects (Axinn & Thornton, 1996). Equally interesting, parents' divorce and remarriage also has important consequences for their *children's* attitudes toward premarital sex, cohabitation, marriage, and divorce (Axinn & Thornton, 1996). As we argue above, although these attitudes do not directly pertain to childbearing, they have potentially important consequences for childbearing behavior.

Third, we have good reason to believe that the behavior of siblings has important consequences for childbearing-related attitudes. Young people with many nieces and nephews prefer larger families (Axinn, Clarkberg, & Thornton, 1994). A number of different mechanisms may be responsible for this relationship, but it is likely that older siblings provide particularly important role models for young people (East & Jacobson, 2001; East & Kiernan, 2001; Hogan & Kitagawa, 1985). Although the empirical evidence is less clear, it may be that peers also provide important role models for young people, and that peer behavior and preferences shape individuals' childbearing preferences (e.g., Harris, 1995, 1998).

Fourth, we know that the life experiences of young people making the transition to adulthood shape childbearing-related attitudes. For example, early life premarital cohabiting experiences are associated with changes toward smaller family size preferences and higher tolerance of divorce (Axinn & Barber, 1997; Axinn & Thornton, 1992). These effects are strongest for cohabitations that dissolve rather than those that transform into marriage, and longer periods of cohabitation have stronger effects on family size preferences than shorter periods of cohabitation (Axinn & Barber, 1997). Premarital cohabitation is a specific form of premarital non-family living, and non-family living in general also reduces family size preferences and influences other childbearing-related attitudes (Waite, Goldscheider, & Witsberger, 1986). These effects of non-family living are independent of the relationship between educational attainment and attitudes (Waite, Goldscheider, & Witsberger, 1986). This is important because early adult educational experiences have also been linked to significant changes in attitudes (e.g., Alwin, Cohen, & Newcomb, 1991; Newcomb, 1961). Given these findings, it is likely that a wide range of early adult experiences have the potential to change specific dimensions of childbearing-related attitudes.

Fifth, biological and genetic factors may also have a strong influence on childbearing attitudes, as well as subsequent childbearing behavior. Multiple studies have implicated hormones in decisions about whether to become a parent, when to become a parent, and whether/when to have sexual intercourse. Women with higher testosterone levels tend to have more sexual partners (Cashdan, 1995); are less likely to agree with the statement: "I would not want to have sex with a man unless I am convinced he is serious about long-term commitment" (Cashdan, 1995); and enjoy activities with children less than women with lower testosterone (Udry, Morris, & Kovenock, 1995). Evolutionary psychological perspectives posit that women are more selective about their sexual partners than men, to ensure fathers who will bring enough resources to the relationship to support the family (Daly & Wilson, 1983). Booth (2000) speculate that there may be a feedback loop––women with higher testosterone engage in more non-family activities, and non-family activities may in turn increase testosterone levels. The same may be true for attitudes—negative attitudes toward family may increase testosterone, which in turn lead to even more negative attitudes toward family.

Kohler, Rodgers, and Christensen (1999), using the Danish Twin Registry, provide substantial evidence for genetic influences on childbearing behavior. They posit that genetic factors have a stronger influence on the transition from zero to one birth than on higher parity transitions. This is an important reason that genetic influences have seemed to increase over time. As fertility has declined; the transition from zero to one is a larger part of completed fertility when fertility is low than when fertility is high. They also find interesting differences in genetic influence by gender, with genes influencing women's childbearing behavior more than men.

Most important for this review of attitudes and childbearing behavior, Kohler, Rodgers, and Christensen (1999) suggest that much of the influence of genes on childbearing behavior is mediated by attitudes. This is consistent with a great deal of other research, which also finds a substantial genetic component among the determinants of attitudes (e.g., Abrahamson, Baker, & Caspi, 2002; Bouchard et al., 2003; Cleveland, Udry, & Chantala, 2001; Jang, Livesley, & Vernon, 2002; Olson et al., 2001). Of course, other studies, as well as Kohler, Rodgers, and Christensen (1999), also suggest that much of what determines attitudes is *not* genetic.

Overall, the finding that hormones and genes influence childbearing behavior in part via attitudes is consistent with our position that attitudes influence childbearing, and that attitudes are formed via multiple experiences throughout the life course. These studies do *not* suggest that genes or hormones determine attitudes as well as childbearing behavior—an argument that would render the relationship between attitudes and childbearing behavior spurious. Rather, they argue for a biosocial influence on attitudes, which in turn influences childbearing behavior.

Sixth, the structure of opportunities and constraints within which individuals live their daily lives, or the social, economic, and institutional context, also impacts attitudes. Most research on contextual influences on childbearing behavior does not focus on ideational mechanisms that may link contextual change to childbearing. Instead, such research usually favors connections between context and the costs and benefits of childbearing. Nevertheless, a growing body of recent evidence is consistent with the conclusion that dramatic changes in the social, economic, and institutional contexts of daily life can strongly influence attitudes (Barber, 1999; Bond, 1988; Hofstede, 1980; Ingelhart, 1977, 1990; Inkeles & Smith, 1974; Yang, 1988). Thus, attitudes are probably an important part of the link between contextual changes and behavioral changes.

Although there are strong theoretical reasons for expecting that changes in contextual characteristics produce both cost/benefit and ideational influences on behavior (Alexander, 1988; Coleman, 1990; Giddens, 1984), clear empirical evidence of these simultaneous effects is rare. There are two key reasons. First, a clear reciprocal relationship makes it difficult to measure the influence of attitudes on behavior (Alwin, 1973; Alwin & Scott, 1996). Behavior is guided by attitudes, but also attitudes are determined, in part, by prior behavior. Longitudinal data are thus required to study the influence of *either* attitudes on behavior or behavior on attitudes, and even with longitudinal data, the direction of influence is not completely clear. Second, many factors influencing behavior, including childbearing behavior, have both cost/benefit and ideational consequences. Education provides a useful example. Although public education is explicitly designed to propagate new ideas and information, education also restructures the costs and benefits of specific behavioral choices (Axinn & Barber, 2001). Other dimensions of context are also likely to share both cost/benefit and ideational consequences. As a result, social scientists rarely have the opportunity to document a purely ideational factor. Although this general lack of measurement to distinguish between ideational and cost/benefit influences on childbearing behavior prevents clear documentation of the simultaneous impact of both forces, attitudes are likely to be an important mechanism linking contextual changes to childbearing behavior.

Many different dimensions of social, economic, and institutional context have been linked to childbearing behavior, including employment, poverty, health services, religion, and public policies. Some analyses have focused on public policies, particularly those related to economic conditions, such as welfare policies, as well as abortion and family planning policies (Ellwood & Bane, 1985; Hoffman & Foster, 2000; Lundberg & Plotnick, 1995; Rosenzweig, 1999). For example, Lundberg and Plotnick (1995) find that lower welfare benefits, state funding for abortions, a greater availability of abortion clinics, and liberal laws about the sale, licensing, and advertising of contraception all lead to lower premarital first-birth rates.

Do such dimensions of the social, economic, and institutional context affect childbearing via attitudes, are their effects independent of attitudes, or do they explain the relationship between attitudes and childbearing? The example of state policies about abortion and welfare provides a particularly interesting case. After all, public attitudes of voters and elected representatives determine policies. Social norms, which clearly vary over time and space, are likely to play an important role here. For example, social norms about teenage premarital pregnancy are likely to influence, in addition to policies about abortion and family planning, individual attitudes about behaviors related to teenage premarital pregnancy, as well as the behaviors themselves. Thus, changes over time in attitudes may, at least in part, shape key dimensions of the social, economic, or institutional context that we believe influences childbearing behavior. This is not to argue, of course, that state policies themselves do not have independent consequences—it is merely to suggest that the goal of disentangling the intertwined connections among changes in attitudes, changes in context, and changes in childbearing behavior is likely to be quite demanding.

Conclusion

Our review of previous research reveals both strong theoretical reasons and consistent empirical evidence that changes in attitudes influence changes in fertility behavior. These influences include attitudes toward childbearing, attitudes toward other behaviors that facilitate childbearing, and attitudes toward other behaviors that may compete with childbearing. These influences span individuals' own, parents', partners', and peers' attitudes. Positive attitudes toward childbearing, or behaviors such as marriage that facilitate childbearing, increase the pace of childbearing. Positive attitudes toward behaviors that compete with childbearing, such as educational attainment and consumer spending, slow the pace of childbearing.

Long-term shifts in attitudes in the United States are probably responsible for some of the decline in U.S. fertility. Positive attitudes toward higher education, women's labor force participation, consumer spending, and other behaviors that compete with childbearing delay childbearing, reducing overall fertility. Between 1950 and 2000, many attitudes in these domains changed in exactly this direction. These macro-level trends combined with micro-level evidence of strong connections between attitudes and subsequent fertility behavior lead us to conclude that these attitude changes probably produced part of the fertility decline.

Given what we know about the causes of attitude change, non-fertility behavioral changes in the second half of the 20th century probably exacerbated the change toward attitudes that reduce fertility. Increasing labor force participation among women, increasing educational attainment, later marriage, increased divorce, increased premarital cohabitation, and increased consumer spending each produce more positive attitudes toward these same behaviors, on average. These behavioral trends of the second half of the previous century, therefore, probably contributed greatly to the trends in attitudes that contributed to declining fertility. Thus, changing attitudes are probably an important link between multiple behavioral changes in the United States and declines in fertility.

Some may not accept the studies we review as evidence that attitude changes are a potentially important cause of changes in fertility behavior. But for those who do accept this conclusion, it casts concerns over the future of fertility in the United States in an optimistic light. The impact of attitudes on fertility behavior reflects the relationship between individuals' preferences and their family formation outcomes. To the extent these relationships are strong, individuals are able to achieve the outcomes they want. To the extent these relationships are weak, other factors are preventing individuals from achieving the outcomes they want. In a complex society filled with numerous behavioral choices, low fertility is, at least in part, a reflection of preferences for alternatives to childbearing and childrearing.

On the other hand, as discussed in the closing portions of the chapter by Morgan, circumstances that prevent individuals from achieving the outcomes they want merit more serious scientific and public policy attention. Within fertility behavior these include both unintended childbearing, on the one extreme, and infertility, or inability to conceive and bear intended children, on the other hand. The social, economic, biological, and public policy factors that constrain individuals from implementing their fertility preferences deserve our highest research priority. Understanding the relationships among attitudes, preferences, and behavioral outcomes is a necessary step toward understanding the constraints that prevent those preferences from being realized. The next step is a more precise understanding of the specific individual and contextual constraints that prevent a strong association among attitudes, preferences, and fertility outcomes.

References

Abma, J. C., Chandra, A., Mosher, W. D., Peterson, L. S., & Piccinino, L. J. (1997). Fertility, family planning and women's health: New data from the 1995 National Survey of Family Growth. *Vital Health Statistics, 23*(19), 1-114.

Abrahamson, A. C., Baker, L. A., & Caspi, A. (2002). Rebellious teens? Genetic and environmental influences on the social attitudes of adolescents. *Journal of Personality and Social Psychology, 83*(6), 1392–1408.

Ajzen, I. (1988). *Attitudes, personality, and behavior*. Chicago: Dorsey.

Ajzen, I., & Fishbein, M. (1980). *Understanding attitudes and predicting social behavior*. Englewood Cliffs, NJ: Prentice-Hall.

Alexander, J. C. 1988. *Action and its environments: Toward a new synthesis*. New York: Columbia University Press.

Alwin, D. F. (1973). Making inferences from attitude-behavior correlations. *Sociometry, 36*, 253–278.

Alwin, D. F. (1994). Aging, personality, and social change: The stability of individual differences over the adult life span. In D. L. Featherman, R. M. Lerner, & M. Perlmutter (Eds.), *Life-span development and behavior*. Hillsdale, NJ: Erlbaum.

Alwin, D. F., Cohen, R. L., & Newcomb, T. M. (1991). *Political attitudes over the life-span: The Bennington women after fifty years.* Madison: University of Wisconsin Press.Alwin, D. F., & Scott, J. (1996). Attitude change: Its measurement and interpretation using longitudinal surveys. In B. Taylor & K. Thomson (Eds.), *Understanding change in social attitudes* (pp. 75-106). Aldershot, Hants, England: Dartmouth.

Anderton, D. L., Tsuya, N. O., & Bean, L. L. (1987). Intergenerational transmission of relative fertility and life course patterns. *Demography, 24,* 467–480.

Axinn, W. G., & Barber, J. S. (1997). Living arrangements and family formation attitudes in early adulthood. *Journal of Marriage and the Family, 59*(3), 595–611.

Axinn, W. G., & Barber, J. S. (2001). Mass education and fertility transition. *American Sociological Review, 66*(4), 481–505.

Axinn, W. G., & Thornton, A. (1992). The relationship between cohabitation and divorce: Selectivity or causal influence? *Demography, 29*(3), 357–374.

Axinn, W. G., & Thornton, A. (1993). Mothers, children, and cohabitation: The intergenerational effects of attitudes and behavior. *American Sociological Review, 58*(2), 233–246.

Axinn, W. G., & Thornton, A. (1996). The influence of parents' marital dissolutions on children's attitudes toward family formation. *Demography, 33,* 66–81.

Axinn, W. G., & Yabiku, S. T. (2001). Social change, the social organization of families, and fertility limitation. *American Journal of Sociology, 106,* 1219–1261.

Axinn, W. G., Clarkberg, M., & Thornton, A. (1994). Family influences on family size preferences. *Demography, 31*(1), 65–79.

Barber, J. S. (1999, August). *Communities and attitudes: The influence of nonfamily institutions and experiences on dispositions toward marriage.* Paper presented at the meetings of the American Sociological Association, Chicago.

Barber, J. S. (2000). Intergenerational influences on the entry into parenthood: Mothers' preferences for family and nonfamily behavior. *Social Forces, 79*(1), 319–348.

Barber, J. S. (2001). Ideational influences on the transition to parenthood: Attitudes toward childbearing and competing alternatives. *Social Psychology Quarterly, 64*(2), 101–127.

Barber, J. S., & Axinn, W. G. (1998a). Gender role attitudes and marriage among young women. *Sociological Quarterly, 39*(1), 11–31.

Barber, J. S., & Axinn, W. G. (1998b). The impact of parental pressure for grandchildren on young people's entry into cohabitation and marriage. *Population Studies, 52*(2), 129–144.

Becker, G. S. (1981). *A treatise on the family.* Cambridge, MA: Harvard University Press.

Beckman, L. J., Aizenberg, R., Forsythe, A. B., & Day, T. (1983). A theoretical analysis of antecedents of young couples' fertility decision and outcomes. *Demography, 20*(4), 519–533.

Bengtson, V. L. (1975). Generation and family effects in value socialization. *American Sociological Review, 40,* 358–371.

Bond, M. H. (1988). *The cross-cultural challenge to social psychology.* Newbury Park, CA: Sage.

Booth, A. (2000). Biosocial perspectives on the family. *Journal of Marriage and the Family, 62,* 1018–1034.

Bouchard, T. J., Segal, N. L., Tellegen, A., McGue, M., Keyes, M., & Krueger, R. (2003). Evidence for the construct validity and heritability of the Wilson-Patterson Conservatism Scale: A reared-apart twins study of social attitudes. *Personality and Individual Difference, 34*(6), 959–964.

Brazzell J. F., & Acock, A. C. (1988). Influence of attitudes, significant others, and aspirations on how adolescents intend to resolve a premarital pregnancy (in premarital relations). *Journal of Marriage and the Family, 50*(2), 413–425.

Bulatao, R. A., & Lee, R. D. (Eds.). (1983). *Determinants of fertility in developing countries.* New York: Academic Press.

Burr, W. R., Leigh, G., Day, R., & Constantine, J. (1979). Symbolic interaction and the family. In W. R. Burr, R. Hill, F. I. Nye, & I. Reiss (Eds.), *Contemporary feelings about the family* (Vol. 2; pp. 42-111). New York: Free Press.

Caldwell, J. C. (1982). *Theory of fertility decline.* New York: Academic Press.

Cashdan, E. (1995). Hormones, sex, and status in women. *Hormones and Behavior, 29,* 354–366.

Chilman, C. S. (1980). Social and psychological research concerning adolescent childbearing: 1970–1980. *Journal of Marriage and the Family, 42*(4), 793–805.

Cleveland, H. H., Udry, J. R., & Chantala, K. (2001). Environmental and genetic influences on sex-typed behaviors and attitudes of male and female adolescents. *Personality and Social Psychology Bulletin, 27*(12), 1587–1598.

Coleman, J. S. (1990). *Foundations of social theory.* Cambridge, MA: Harvard University Press.

Coombs, L. C. (1974). The measurement of family size preferences and subsequent fertility. *Demography, 11*(4), 587–611.

Coombs, L. C. (1979). Reproductive goals and achieved fertility: A fifteen-year perspective. *Demography, 16,* 523–534.

Crimmins, E. M., Easterlin, R. A., & Saito, Y. (1991). Preference changes among American youth: Family, work, and goods aspirations, 1976–86. *Population and Development Review, 17*(1), 115–133.

Daly, M., & Wilson, M. (1983). *Sex, evolution, and behavior.* Boston: Willard Grant Press.

Dornbusch, S. (1989). The sociology of adolescents. *Annual Review of Sociology, 15,* 233–259.

Duncan, O. D., Freedman, R., Coble, J. M., & Slesinger, D. (1965). Marital fertility and family size of orientation. *Demography, 2,* 508–515.

East, P. L., & Jacobson, L. J. (2001). The younger siblings of teenage mothers: A follow-up of their pregnancy risk. *Developmental Psychology. 37*(2), 254–264.

East, P. L., & Kiernan, E. A. (2001). Risks among youths who have multiple sisters who were adolescent parents. *Family Planning Perspectives, 33*(2), 75–80.

Easterlin, R. A. (1980). *Birth and fortune.* New York: Basic Books.

Easterlin, R. A., & Crimmins, E. M. (1985). *The fertility revolution: A supply-demand analysis.* Chicago: University of Chicago Press.

Edwards, W. (1954). The theory of decision-making. *Psychological Bulletin, 51,* 380–417.

Ellwood, D., & Bane, M. J. (1985). The impact of AFDC on family structure and living arrangements. *Research in Labor Economics, 7,* 137.

Festinger, L. (1957). *A theory of cognitive dissonance.* Evanston, IL: Row-Peterson.

Fishbein, M., & Ajzen, I. (1975). *Belief, attitude, intention, and behavior: An introduction to theory and research*. Reading, MA: Addison-Wesley.

Freedman, R. (1979). Theories of fertility decline: A reappraisal. *Social Forces, 58*(1), 1–17.

Gamson, W. A., Croteau, D., & Hoynes, W. (1992). Media images and the social construction of reality. *Annual Review of Sociology, 18*, 373–393.

Gecas, V., & Seff, M. A. (1990). Families and adolescents: A review of the 1980's. *Journal of Marriage and the Family, 52*, 941–958.

Giddens, A. (1984). *The constitution of society: Outline of the theory of structuration*. Berkeley: University of California Press.

Goldscheider, F. K., & Waite, L. J. (1991). *New families, no families? The transformation of the American home*. Berkeley: University of California Press.

Goode, W. J. (1960). A theory of role strain. *American Sociological Review, 25*, 483–496.

Grube, J. W., & Morgan, M. (1990). Attitude-social support interactions: Contingent consistency effects in the prediction of adolescent smoking, drinking, and drug use. *Social Psychology Quarterly, 53*, 329–339.

Harris, J. R. (1995). Where is the child's environment? A group socialization theory of development. *Psychological Review, 102*(3), 458–489.

Harris, J. R. (1998). *The nurture assumption: Why children turn out the way they do*. New York: Free Press.

Heider, F. (1958). *The psychology of interpersonal relations*. New York: Wiley.

Hendershot, G. E. (1969). Familial satisfaction, birth order, and fertility values. *Journal of Marriage and the Family, 31*, 27–33.

Hochschild, A. R. (1989). *The second shift*. New York: Avon Books.

Hoffman, S. D. (1998). Teenage childbearing is not so bad after all...or is it? A review of the new literature. *Family Planning Perspectives, 30*(5), 236–240.

Hoffman, S. D., & Foster, E. M. (2000). AFDC benefits and nonmarital births to young women. *The Journal of Human Resources, 35*(2), 376–391.

Hofstede, G. H. (1980). *Culture's consequences: International differences in work-related values*. Beverly Hills, CA: Sage.

Hogan, D. P., & Kitagawa, E. M. (1985). The impact of social status, family structure, and neighborhood on the fertility of black adolescents. *The American Journal of Sociology, 90*(4), 825–855.

Inglehart, R. (1977). *The silent revolution: Changing values and political styles among western publics*. Princeton, NJ: Princeton University Press.

Inglehart, R. (1990). *Culture shift in advanced industrial society*. Princeton, NJ: Princeton University Press.

Inkeles, A., & Smith, D. H. (1974). *Becoming modern: Individual change in six developing countries*. Cambridge, MA: Harvard University Press.

Jang, K. L., Livesley, W. J., & Vernon, P. A. (2002). The etiology of personality function: the University of British Columbia Twin Project. *Twin Research, 5*(5), 342–346.

Johnson, N. E., & Stokes, C. S. (1976). Family size in successive generations: The effect of birth order, intergenerational change in lifestyle, and family satisfaction. *Demography, 13*(2), 175–187.

Kahn, J. R., & Anderson, K. E. (1992). Intergenerational patterns of teenage fertility. *Demography, 29*(1), 39–57.

Kasarda, J. D., Billy, J. O. G., & West, K. (1986). *Status enhancement and fertility: Reproductive responses to social mobility and educational opportunity*. New York: Academic Press.

Kohler, H., Rodgers, J. L., & Christensen, K. (1999). Is fertility behavior in our genes? Findings from a Danish twin study. *Population and Development Review, 25*(2), 253–288.

Lesthaeghe, R. (1998). On theory development: Applications to the study of family formation. *Population and Development Review, 24*(1), 1–14.

Lesthaeghe, R., & Surkyn, J. (1988). Cultural dynamics and economic theories of fertility change. *Population and Development Review, 14*, 1–45.

Lesthaeghe, R., & Willems, P. (1999). Is low fertility a temporary phenomenon in the European Union? *Population and Development Review, 25*(2), 211–228.

Lesthaeghe, R., & Wilson, C. (1986). Modes of production, secularization and the pace of fertility decline in Western Europe . In A. Coale & S. C. Watkins (Eds.), *The decline of fertility in Europe*. Princeton, NJ: Princeton University Press.

Loomis, L. L., & Landale, N. S. (1994). Nonmarital cohabitation and childbearing among black and white American women. *Journal of Marriage and the Family, 56*, 949–962.

Lundberg, S. J., & Plotnick, R. (1995). Adolescent premarital childbearing: Do economic incentives matter? *Journal of Labor Economics, 13*, 177–200.

Lundberg, S. J., & Pollak, R. A. (1996). Bargaining and distribution in marriage. *Journal of Economic Perspectives, 10*(4), 139–158.

Manning, W. D. (1993). Marriage and cohabitation following premarital conception. *Journal of Marriage and the Family, 55*, 839–850.

Manning, W. D. (1995). Cohabitation, marriage, and entry into motherhood. *Journal of Marriage and the Family, 57*(1), 191–200.

Manning, W. D., & Landale, N. S. (1996). Racial and ethnic differences in the role of cohabitation in premarital childbearing. *Journal of Marriage and the Family, 58*, 63–77.

Marini, M. M. (1978). The transition to adulthood: Sex differences in educational attainment and age at marriage. *American Sociological Review, 43*, 483–507.

Mead, G. H. (1967). *Mind, self, and society*. Chicago: University of Chicago Press. (Original work published 1934)

Morgan, S. P. (2003, May). *Is low fertility a 21st century demographic crisis?* Presidential address at the annual meetings of the Population Association of America, Minneapolis, MN.

Morgan, S. P., & Waite, L. J. (1987). Parenthood and the attitudes of young adults. *American Sociological Review, 52*, 541–547.

Newcomb, T. M. (1961). *The acquaintance process*. New York: Holt, Rinehart and Winston.

Notestein, F. W. (1953.) Economic problems of population change. In *Proceedings of the Eighth International Conference of Agricultural Economists*. London: Oxford University Press.

Olson, J. M.,Vernon, P. A., Harris, J. A., & Jang, K. L. (2001). The heritability of attitudes: A study of twins. *Journal of Personality and Social Psychology, 80*(6), 845–860.

Pagnini, D., & Rindfuss, R. R. (1993). The divorce of marriage and childbearing: Changing attitudes and behavior in the United States. *Population and Development Review, 19*, 331–347.

Plotnick, R. (1992). The effects of attitudes on teenage premarital pregnancy and its resolution. *American Sociological Review, 57*, 800–811.

Preston, S. H. (1986). Changing values and falling birth rates. *Population and Development Review, 12*, 176–196.

Rindfuss, R. R. (1991). The young adult years: Diversity, structural change, and fertility. *Demography, 28*(4), 493–512.

Rindfuss, R. R., & St. John, C. (1983). Social determinants of age at first birth. *Journal of Marriage and the Family, 45*, 553–565.

Rindfuss, R. R., Brewster, K. L., & Kavee, A. L. (1996). Women, work, and children: Behavioral and attitudinal change in the United States. *Population and Development Review, 22*(3), 457–482.

Rindfuss, R. R., Morgan, S. P., & Swicegood, G. (1988). *First births in America: Changes in the timing of parenthood.* Berkeley: University of California Press.

Rindfuss, R. R., Swicegood, C. G., & Rosenfeld, R. A. (1987). Disorder in the life course: How common and does it matter? *American Sociological Review, 52*, 785–801.

Rosenzweig, M. R. (1999). Welfare, marital prospects, and nonmarital childbearing. *Journal of Political Economy, 107*(6, pt. 2), S3–S32.

Rutenberg, N., & Watkins, S. C. (1997). The buzz outside the clinics: Conversations and contraception in Nyanza Province, Kenya. *Studies in Family Planning, 28*(4), 290–307.

Smith, T. E. (1988). Parental control techniques: Relative frequencies and relationships with situational factors. *Journal of Family Issues, 9*(2), 155–176.

Stolzenberg, R. M., & Waite, L. J. (1977). Age, fertility expectations and plans for employment. *American Sociological Review, 42*, 769–783.

Thomson, E. (1997). Couple childbearing desires, intentions, and births. *Demography, 34*(3), 343–354.

Thomson, E., & Hoem., J. M. (1998). Couple childbearing plans and births in Sweden. *Demography, 35*(3), 315–322.

Thomson, E., McDonald, E., & Bumpass, L. L. (1990). Fertility desires and fertility: Hers, his, and theirs. *Demography, 27*, 579–588.

Thornton, A. (1991). Influence of parents' marital history on the marital and cohabitational experiences of children. *American Journal of Sociology, 96*(4), 868–894.

Thornton, A., & Lin, H. (1994). *Social change and the family in Taiwan.* Chicago: University of Chicago Press.

Thornton, A., & Young-DeMarco, L. (2001). Four decades of trends in attitudes toward family issues in the United States: The 1960s through the 1990s. *Journal of Marriage and the Family, 63*(4), 1009–1037.

Thornton, A., Axinn, W. G., & Teachman, J. (1995). The influence of school enrollment and accumulation on cohabitation and marriage in early adulthood. *American Sociological Review, 60*(5), 762–774.

Udry, J. R., Morris, N., & Kovenock, J. (1995). Androgen effects on women's gendered behavior. *Journal of Biosocial Science, 27*, 359–369.

Valente, T. W., Watkins, S. C., Jato, M. N., Van Der Straten, A., & Tsitsol, L. M. (1997). Social network associations with contraceptive use among Cameroonian women in voluntary associations. *Social Science and Medicine, 45*, 677–687.

Veroff, J., Douvan, E., & Kulka, R. A. (1981). *The inner American: A self-portrait from 1957 to 1976.* New York: Basic Books.

Vinokur-Kaplan, D. (1978). To have — or not to have — another child: Family planning attitudes, intentions, and behavior. *Journal of Applied Social Psychology, 8,* 29–46.

Waite, L. J., Goldscheider, F. K., & Witsberger, C. (1986). Nonfamily living and the erosion of traditional family orientations among young adults. *American Sociological Review, 51*(4), 541–554.

Waite, L. J., & Stolzenberg, R. M. (1976). Intended childbearing and labor force participation of young women: Insights from nonrecursive models. *American Sociological Review, 41*(2), 235–251.

Watkins, S. C. (1995). Women's gossip and social change: Childbirth and fertility control among Italian and Jewish women in the United States 1920–1940. *Gender and Society, 9,* 469–490.

Yang, K. S. (1988). Will societal modernization eventually eliminate cross-cultural psychological differences? In M. H. Bond (Ed.), *The cross-cultural challenge to social psychology* (pp. 67–85). Newbury Park, CA: Sage. Zajonc, R. B. (1968). The attitudinal effects of mere exposure. *Journal of Personality and Social Psychology, 9*(pt. 2), 1–27.

6

CHILDBEARING DECISIONS: CAN ATTITUDE MEASURES PLAY A ROLE IN CAUSAL MODELING?

Shelly Lundberg
University of Washington

In their chapter, "How Do Attitudes Shape Childbearing in the United States?" Jennifer Barber and William Axinn argue that changes in attitudes, both towards childbearing and towards activities that might compete with childbearing, are responsible in part for the decline in U.S. fertility. They support this assertion with evidence that some measures of attitudes have a strong empirical relationship with transitions to married and unmarried parenthood, and that the patterns of these correlations are consistent with theories about the relationship between the cognitive/emotional processes that attitudes reflect and observed behavior.

How can we understand the role of attitudes in determining fertility, and can this understanding help us to predict future population growth in low-fertility societies such as the United States? This is a difficult issue for an economist to address since economics has produced, to my knowledge, no conceptual role for attitudes in determining behavior, and variables purporting to measure attitudes make only rare appearances in economic studies of demographic (or other) phenomena. Economic models of fertility focus on the constraints and opportunities that face households with desires for goods and leisure as well as children, and analyze changes in fertility in terms of changes in these constraints—incomes, prices, and contraceptive technology.[1] Preferences, in the form of a utility function whose arguments include the number and 'quality' of children, are assumed to be stable. Attitudes, as defined in the Barber/Axinn study, are either not addressed or are dismissed as rationalizations of intended behavior. As an economist, I perceive two tasks ahead of me: (1) to reinterpret this interesting discussion of attitudes and the attitude/fertility link in terms that I (and perhaps my students) can understand, and (2) to suggest some ways in which this reinterpretation might contribute modestly to the analysis of fertility.

Barber and Axinn argue that there is strong evidence (and a solid theoretical basis) to support a conclusion that attitudes influence childbearing behavior. That they have marshaled abundant evidence for a correlation between attitude measures and observed fertility is undeniable. They also note that changes in patterns of marriage, childbearing, and market work have probably, in turn, influenced attitudes.

---

[1] Hotz, Klerman, and Willis (1997) provide a recent survey.

There is clearly some element of circularity here, and the important (and difficult) questions we must ask are the following: Can we break out of this circle and establish a role for attitude measures in a causal model of fertility? To what extent have attitude changes driven fertility decline, rather than simply reflecting this decline?

The authors' second major point is that the attitude/behavior link is not limited to the agent's own attitudes towards the behavior of interest. Attitudes towards behaviors that compete with parenting, such as career ambitions, also affect childbearing, and the attitudes of parents, partners, and peers affect fertility timing and the number of children. This emphasis on the importance of competing behavior and conflicting roles is particularly salient for economists, raising as it does the important issue of opportunity cost: time and resources are limited and doing one thing means not doing something else.

What about the influence of others on fertility behavior? The effect of a spouse's attitudes towards children on fertility can be regarded as reassuring evidence that some sort of joint decision-making—in which the preferences of both partners affect actual childbearing—is occurring within marriage. The route through which a parent's attitudes affect her child's fertility, however, can be a bit more complex. Barber and Axinn note that parent's attitudes have both an indirect effect on fertility through the child's attitudes, which can be attributed to socialization, and a direct effect that indicates "they are able to influence their children's childbearing behavior independent of what the children themselves prefer." In this case, the child's behavior will depend not just on the parent's attitude, but also on her willingness and ability to exert control over the child's fertility decision.

Can we sort out these two effects empirically? The identification of the second (direct) effect requires that we can in fact observe the child's preferences. If the attitude measures available are incomplete or error-ridden measures, then remaining correlation between the parent's reported desires and the child's behavior may simply reflect the unobserved component of the child's preferences. Is this distinction important? Well yes, it is. If the parent's apparent influence on the birth of grandchildren is real, and exerted through social control, then fertility can be altered by policies that change the efficacy of this control, i.e., subsidized housing for young parents.[2] If the effect is spurious, and results from the intergenerational transmission of preferences, then external changes in constraints will not change behavior. On the other hand, if our measure of the child's attitudes towards childbearing is, for example, desired family size, this may already incorporate the anticipated inducements and punishments from parents, and so may over-control for the preferences of children.

---

[2] A recent study by Manacorda and Moretti (2002) argued that the high rate of parent-adult child co-residence in Italy is due to the parent's preference, and found that a social security reform that increased the wealth of one cohort of parents increased coresidence rates.

This example highlights my central point, which is that the interpretation of the empirical attitude/fertility relationship depends crucially upon whether we think that attitudes (or a particular indicator of attitudes) reflect the agent's preferences only, or whether they also incorporate perceived or expected constraints. To the extent that attitudes reflect constraints, and therefore mirror intended or desired outcomes, the coefficient on an attitude measure cannot be interpreted as "the effect" of this attitude on fertility. Barber and Axinn clearly recognize this point, and do discuss the determinants of attitudes and feedback effects of behavioral changes on attitudes, but I would argue that it deserves more emphasis, and suggests a more unified treatment of the determinants and effects of attitude and attitude changes. I am more sanguine than they appear to be about our ability to make progress in developing causal models.

Standard economic analysis begins with an individual or household with fixed preferences facing constraints that can change with market conditions, policy, or technological progress. I am capable of abandoning the fixed preference assumption and recognizing that preferences regarding childbearing may be subject to social and cultural influences, but I am not capable of abandoning the preference/constraint dichotomy.

Formally, your preferences are defined in terms of your ranking of alternative outcomes. For example, would you prefer two children plus a house in the mountains or one child and a house by the lake?[3] Your ranking of these alternatives can be expected to reveal much about your subjective evaluations of children and locational amenities, and thus be strongly correlated with relevant attitude measures. So something like the scale representing enjoyment of activities with children should be related to preferences for children, though preferences will also incorporate the individual's willingness to make tradeoffs between children and other 'goods.'

To explain behavior, we need to add constraints that specify which outcomes are feasible. The number of children I would choose if I were wealthy and possessed of unlimited energy would be more than I have now—though others might be willing, with greater wealth, to dispense with children altogether in favor of other, even more expensive and time-consuming activities. Choosing the preferred feasible outcome gives us 'demands,' 'intentions' (if in the future), or 'expectations' (if future behavior depends upon eventualities not perfectly foreseen).

Do the attitudes or attitude measures that influence fertility reflect individual preferences, or do they represent demands that also incorporate perceived constraints? Barber and Axinn provide a broad overview of relevant empirical studies, but the key points of the chapter are illustrated with empirical results from two interesting papers by Barber on the ideational and intergenerational influences on the transition to parenthood. A variety of attitude measures are employed in

---

[3] We will suppose that all other aspects of your life were held constant so that you need not think about property taxes or college costs.

these studies, and I will focus on them for illustrative purposes. These examples reveal that attitude measures are opportunistic (researchers use the measures that are available in surveys), diverse, and ambiguous in the degree to which they reflect perceived constraints, and therefore in the extent to which their coefficients in a behavioral equation represent causal effects of variations in preferences.

'Attitudes towards children and childbearing' is a vector that is significantly associated with the hazard of marital first birth for women (and thus with the joint outcome of marriage and first birth) and that includes three measures: a scale representing enjoyment of activities with children, a scale indicating agreement with a statement that children cause their parents worry and emotional strain, and preferred family size. Enjoyment of activities with children is the variable that most clearly reflects preferences, but perhaps not just preferences about parenthood. These sentiments are also likely to influence career choices and the willingness to baby-sit in high school. The ambiguity of the relationship between this measure and preferences for parenthood is apparent from the lack of predictive power for the transition to a marital first birth for men.

The belief that children cause parental worry and strain appears at first glance to be related to the information possessed by the individual, but it seems likely that much emotional weight is attached to such beliefs. However, this measure may also reflect the perceived constraints facing parents, and so may increase with actual environmental risks to children.

Are these measures representative of the attitudes that the authors believe have contributed to declining fertility in the United States? Barber and Axinn note that Americans continue to assert that marriage and children are very important to them. It seems unlikely that reported enjoyment of activities with children would show a distinct trend. If worries have increased over time, this is likely to reflect changing parenting conditions as much as changing preferences for children. The final attitude measure, preferred family size, is clearly an indicator of demand (or 'intentions' as Barber [2001] notes) and therefore should incorporate constraints such as the cost of children or the rewards to competing activities, such as market work. It is certainly not surprising that changes in preferred family size have tracked changes in fertility (surely it is the deviations from this pattern that are interesting) but it would be odd to assert that changes in fertility were 'caused' by changes in desired family size. These examples do not lead inexorably to the conclusion that shifts in attitudes have 'caused' declining fertility.

If we are looking for changes in attitudes that have caused fertility change, a better place to look may be in attitudes regarding competing behavior—cohabitation and delayed marriage, market work and consumption—and these are in fact the attitude changes emphasized by the authors. They report the interesting pattern of results in Barber (2001)—attitudes towards career and consumption affect the transition to premarital parenthood, but not the timing of marital birth. This finding is attributed to the interaction of social disapproval and personal attitudes, but a multitude of other explanations came to mind. For example, suppose that positive attitudes toward a career, as evidence of a forward-looking focus, are correlated with unobserved characteristics such as risk-aversion, or negatively correlated with impulsivity. These characteristics are likely to be stronger determinants of premarital than marital fertility. Recognizing that there are important individual attributes that we do not observe makes the interpretation of attitude 'effects' much more difficult.

Attitudes towards competing behaviors are hypothesized to affect fertility in a number of ways—one pathway is provided by cognitive consistency theory (which suggests that individuals find it distressing to hold positive attitudes towards two competing behaviors). Thus, a positive attitude towards a demanding career can cause an individual to moderate his or her enthusiasm for early parenthood. Barber and Axinn emphasize causal mechanisms again, in which attitudes shift fertility behavior through several different routes. However, if attitudes express intentions as well as preferences, then attitude measures may simply act as signals for other, unobserved determinants of behavior. If individuals who expect to earn high wages report positive attitudes towards a career, and expected wages are not observed, then part of the apparent effect of attitudes on fertility will be spurious. To the extent that attitudes towards competing behaviors are correlated with the true opportunity costs of fertility, attitudes are assigned too large a role in explaining individual differences, and changes in attitudes given credit for the impact of the cost/benefit wave they are riding.

What can be done to establish causal influence in a model with potentially endogenous attitude variables? There are a number of standard techniques. What they have in common is a focus on modeling variation or change in the variable of interest (attitudes) so that exogenous variation can be extracted. What is in some sense the reverse problem has been extensively studied by both economists and sociologists, and provides a useful example. The coefficient on 'number of children' in a women's wage regression is known to be a biased estimate of the 'effect' of children, since fertility is thought to be correlated with unobserved factors also correlated with low wages (such as attitudes towards career). In many empirical studies of the family gap in women's wages, attitudes and other unobserved determinants of wages are assumed to be constant over time, so that the difference in wages before and after children can be used to measure their effect.

Barber and Axinn mention the possible use of longitudinal data to sort out the effect of attitudes on fertility, presumably in a manner similar to the family gap analysis. However, they quite rightly note that the intertemporal interdependence of behavior and attitudes makes this approach problematic. If attitudes towards children are shifted by some unexpected shock, then such changes could also be used to construct a fixed-effect estimate of the effect of attitudes on fertility. Otherwise, instrumental variable or related methods could be used to exploit cross-section, rather than longitudinal, variance in attitudes. However, serious attention to the question, what causes attitudes? is required to make progress in this area.

Social scientists have studied the relationship between reported attitudes and many behaviors, but the analysis of attitudes would seem to be particularly important for explaining trends in fertility. The case to be made for believing that declining fertility is not just a consequence of change in constraints is a compelling one.[4] There is considerable evidence that fertility transitions have been sudden, sharp, and sometimes pervasive across socioeconomic groups facing different constraints, and there is evidence for the diffusion of innovations in fertility control, including, as Coale (1973) argued, the 'thinkability' of fertility control within marriage.

It seems clear that social and cultural influences have changed the role of children in contributing to the self-concept and satisfaction of their parents, and the distinction between preferences and constraints becomes admittedly murky when we consider behaviors in which stigma and the desire to conform to social norms are powerful motivators. For this reason, studies of the diffusion of norms and attitudes over space and time would seem to be key components of an attempt to sort out the mutual dependence of behavior and attitudes.

I would agree with Barber and Axinn that attitude measures and other subjective indicators can help to illuminate the sources of behavioral trends by revealing something of the cognitive processes of the individuals caught up in them. However, I would add that we need to know more about how our history, our culture, and our opportunities affect the stories we tell and the desires we are willing to express before we can make serious progress in understanding the causal effects of these attitudes on choices.

References

Barber, J. S. (2001). Ideational influences on the transition to parenthood: Attitudes toward childbearing and competing alternatives. *Social Psychology Quarterly, 39*(1), 101–127.

Coale, A. J. (1973). The demographic transition reconsidered. In *International Population Conference, Liege, 1973, Vol. 1* (pp. 53–72). Liege, Belgium: International Union for the Scientific Study of Population.

Hotz, V. J., Klerman, J. A., & Willis, R. J. (1997). The economics of fertility in developed countries. In M. R. Rosenzweig & O. Stark (Eds.), *Handbook of population and family economics* (pp. 275–347). Amsterdam: Elsevier Science.

Manacorda, M., & Moretti, E. (2002). *Intergenerational transfers and household structure: Why do most Italian youths live with their parents?* (CEP Discussion Paper No. 0536). London: Centre for Economic Performance, London School of Economics.

Pollak, R. A., & Watkins, S. C. (1993). Cultural and economic approaches to fertility: Proper marriage or mesalliance? *Population and Development Review, 19*(3), 467–496.

---

[4] See Pollak and Watkins (1993) for a discussion.

7
ATTITUDES AND LOW FERTILITY: REFLECTIONS BASED ON DANISH TWIN DATA

Hans-Peter Kohler
University of Pennsylvania

Introduction

Attitudes about childbearing clearly matter for fertility patterns in the United States. This relevance is convincingly demonstrated by Barber and Axinn (this volume) as they combine theoretical support from Fishbein and Ajzen's framework on "reasoned action and planned behavior" (Fishbein & Ajzen, 1975) with fascinating empirical findings based on the Detroit Intergenerational Panel Study of Parents and Children. Some of the key findings presented by Barber and Axinn include the following: (*a*) attitudes toward children and childbearing are strong predictors of first-birth timing, with positive attitudes increasing and negative attitudes decreasing birth rates; (*b*) the influence of attitudes towards children and childbearing is limited to maritally conceived first birth; (*c*) some attitudes seem to influence the first-birth rates of women, but not those of men; (*d*) positive attitudes towards behaviors that compete with childbearing reduce fertility, specifically premarital fertility; and (*e*) while education experiences explain part of the effect of attitudes on premarital fertility, early adulthood experiences do not seem to provide much of the impact of attitudes on marital childbearing behavior. Most of the impact of attitudes toward childbearing on marital childbearing is therefore net of experiences with school, cohabitation, marriage, and work.

These findings are consistent with other studies on attitudes, norms, and demographic behavior (e.g., Lesthaeghe, 2002). In addition, the analyses in Barber and Axinn provide a nice contrast to some of the ideational-change literature that argues that shifts towards postmodern family preferences (e.g., van de Kaa, 2001), or postmodern value orientation, primarily favor reductions in fertility. While Barber and Axinn acknowledge that changes in attitudes towards childbearing have contributed to the fertility decline in the United States in recent decades, they perceive changes in attitudes as being less unidirectional. Future trends may see a reversal of ideational change to more traditional value orientations (see also Lesthaeghe & Moors, 1995) as well as movements that discourage behaviors, such as premarital sexual activity, that are frequently seen as defining features of "modern" demographic behavior (e.g., Bearman & Brückner, 2002).

Barber and Axinn, as well as other studies in the literature, leave few doubts about the association of attitudes with variation in childbearing patterns. This association is particularly important during the demographically dense years in yearly adulthood when formal education, partnerships formation, entry into the labor market, and children compete for the time and attention of young adults. These years during young adulthood have also been the focus of attempts to understand lowest-low fertility levels with total fertility rates below 1.3 (Kohler, Billari, & Ortega, 2002), where social interaction processes—in part related to the formation and transformation of norms and attitudes regarding the timing of childbearing—have been emphasized as a mechanism leading to the rapid delay in childbearing that occurs in many European and other developed countries. Similarly, Barber and Axinn argue that changes in the attitudes towards childbearing have been a relevant factor in the decline of fertility in the United States during the last decades. The dynamics of future changes in attitudes and preferences for childbearing may therefore be an important determinant of potential limits to the decline of fertility, and of variation in fertility levels across developed countries (for a related discussion, see Morgan & King, 2001). Understanding the variation in attitudes within populations and the transformation of attitudes over time and/ or across cohorts, therefore, has the potential to provide an important link towards understanding patterns of low fertility and their potential future developments. Barber and Axinn note several mechanisms that lead to this variation in attitudes across individuals or over time, including (a) the family of origin and specifically parent's attitudes regarding family, children, and the relevance of female career orientation, (b) the behavior of parents and siblings with respect to fertility, marriage, divorce, etc., (c) the attitudes and behaviors of peers, (d) the life experiences of young adults during the transition to adulthood, (e) the structure and opportunities of the social, economic, and institutional context, and (f) biological factors such as hormone levels or genetic dispositions.

Some obvious problems or concerns arise in the type of analyses discussed in Barber and Axinn, and these issues potentially complicate inferences about the relevance of attitudes and their long-term implications. As the authors are well aware, problems in assessing the role of attitudes in their analyses—as well as in many other studies—include, for instance, the difficulties of assessing (a) the causal contribution of attitudes on behavior, especially given the fact that some attitudes are likely to be affected by the socioeconomic context as well as past and/or anticipated experiences during the life-course, (b) the contribution of attitudes on fertility behavior net of other influences such as changes in female wages, the returns to human capital, or other socioeconomic determinants of fertility and related behavior, and (c) the determinants of past or future dynamics of attitude changes. Addressing these issues is very challenging, and Barber and Axinn can hardly be criticized for not resolving more empirical concerns. Their study is already based on a remarkable multi-generation longitudinal data set that has become a benchmark for other researchers interested in studying attitudes and demographic behavior. In Europe, for instance, where the concept of the Second Demographic Transition leading to a transformation of values towards more individualistic and post-materialistic orientations is often used to explain low fertility (Lesthaeghe & van de Kaa, 1986; van de Kaa, 1987), no comparable data exist to study the role of attitudes in similar detail. Future data collection as part of the Gender and Generations Program (GGP), which is strongly inspired by the Detroit Intergenerational Panel Study of Parents and Children, may overcome this limitation and provide possibilities for comparative cross-country research on attitudes and childbearing in low-fertility contexts.

Instead of providing additional reviews or empirical analyses on the connection between attitudes and fertility behavior, I present in these comments regarding the Barber and Axinn chapter some specific perspectives on low fertility and the potential role of attitudes that are based on my work using Danish twin data. The first set of analyses further investigates the mechanisms through which parents influence the fertility of their children, with a specific focus on the distinction between influences mediated by socialization in the household and influences due to genetic dispositions. While this study does not draw explicitly on attitudinal data, the underlying mechanisms of this intergenerational transmission are likely to be closely connected with the intergenerational transmission of attitudes, personality traits, and preferences. The second set of analyses focuses on the relation between subjective well-being and fertility behavior. On the one hand, subjective well-being is partially a relatively stable characteristic of individuals that is closely related to personality traits; on the other hand, subjective well-being is affected by the partnership and childbearing experiences during adulthood, and the fact that respondent's reports about happiness reflect differential experiences. The analyses can therefore reveal the extent to which children affect happiness at different parities, which in turn illuminates some of the underlining motivations to have children and the attitudes that may be supportive of childbearing at different parities.

The Institutional Conditioning of Parental Influences

Parents are an important factor contributing to the formation of norms and attitudes early in life, and the effect of these norms and attitudes exerts important influences on the demographic behavior during the transition to adulthood. The importance of parents in this context stems from two pathways of intergenerational transmission. First, the parental household contributes to the formation of attitudes through socialization and social control. The former refers to the fact that parents influence children's attitudes and preferences; that is, through socialization parents shape how children would like to behave. The latter refers to the fact that parents provide incentives and constraints for their children's behavior to make them behave in ways that parents find appropriate. Second, parents have an important influence on attitudes through biological inheritance. This biological pathway is clearly much less controlled by parents, but it may nevertheless be of considerable relevance. For instance, personality traits, childbearing motivation, and fertility expectations have been shown to have an important genetic etiology (e.g., Bouchard, 1994; Bouchard & McGue, 2003; Miller et al., 2000; Rodgers & Doughty, 2000), and personality traits have also been directly linked to childbearing motivations (Miller, 1992).

This dual influence of the parents on attitudes and demographic behavior immediately suggests the question of relative contributions: Which pathway, transmission through socialization in shared environments or transmission through genetic dispositions, is more important? Twins studies provide one possible way to address the relative importance of shared environments—including the effects of the shared socialization in the same household—and genetic dispositions on behavior. Some of our earlier research on this topic (e.g., Kohler, Rodgers, & Christensen, 1999) suggests that the answer to this question is, "it depends". The relative contribution of these pathways is contingent on the demographic context, and the changes in fertility and marriage behavior in recent decades in Denmark have been associated with a transformation of how nature and nurture contribute to variation in fertility. Our prior studies, however, have primarily focused on complete fertility. Since attitudes are an important determinant of fertility behavior in early adulthood, it is important to investigate separately the patterns of early fertility, that is, fertility behavior that is concentrated in the early-years of adulthood and occurs relatively soon after the separation from the parental household. In Kohler, Rodgers, and Christensen (2003), we therefore follow up on some of our earlier studies with a particular focus on early fertility. This focus matches the focus in Barber and Axinn about the first birth, and it is also important because early adulthood constitutes a period in which attitudes are particularly likely to influence fertility behaviors.[1]

---

[1]Unfortunately, our data do not contain explicit information about attitudes towards childbearing to address the formation of attitudes towards childbearing through social and genetic pathways in detail. Nevertheless, as argued above, it seems plausible that attitudes are an important mechanism in the parental influence of children's behavior.

The analyses use the female twins cohorts born 1945–1968 from the Danish Twin Register (Kyvik, Green, & Beck-Nielsen, 1995; Kyvik et al., 1996). Figure 7.1 present the results of the behavior genetic analyses about the *level of early fertility*, defined as the number of children at the age at which 25% of the cohort members have had a first child. Fertility in our analyses is therefore measured around age 21 for the female cohorts born in 1945, and around age 25 for the cohort born in 1968. This indicator of early fertility has the advantage of not being affected by the delay in childbearing and reflects the same notion of early fertility across cohorts: it indicates that a woman belongs to the first in her birth cohort who have any children.[2] The figure shows that a substantial fraction of the variation in early fertility among women, between 60% (cohorts 1945–1952) and 43% (cohorts 1961–1968), is due to individual-specific experiences of the twins. The remaining fraction is related to influences mediated by the parents, comprising both social and genetic pathways. This fraction attributed to parents has not changed substantially across the cohorts 1945–1968. Most importantly, however, the results in Figure 7.1 reveal a striking transformation in the relative contributions of social and genetic factors to the determinants of early fertility behavior: For female cohorts born in the years 1945–1952, shared environmental factors constitute the most important influence leading to within-cohort variation in the level of early fertility, and heritable factors are virtually absent. This pattern reverses for the female cohorts born in 1961–1968. Genetically mediated differences among individuals emerge as the most important determinant of within-cohort variation in the level of early fertility, and the influence of shared environmental factors vanishes almost completely.

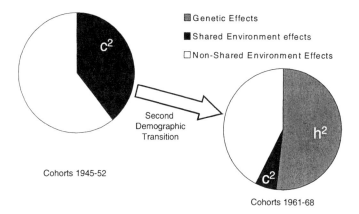

Figure 7.1. Results of Behavior Genetic Analyses About Level of Early Fertility

---

[2] Because this fertility measure is concentrated on 0, 1, 2 children, the standard methodology in twin studies for continuous outcomes is not optimally suited for our purpose. For this reason we chose a different methodology developed for the analysis of binary and ordered outcomes (Kohler & Rodgers, 1999) that is based on bivariate ordered probit models. The heritabilities and shared environmental effects therefore pertain to the latent propensity to have children.

The Danish female twin cohorts born 1945–1968, which underlie our investigation of early fertility as shown in Figure 7.1, attained early adulthood during a period in which the societal context of early demographic behavior was profoundly transformed as part of the Second Demographic Transition. For instance, from 1960–1995, the mean age at first birth in Denmark increased from 23.1 to 27.5 years, the proportion of out-of-wedlock births increased from 7.85 to 46.5%, and cohabitation prior to marriage became commonplace (Eurostat, 1998; Knudsen, 1993). The cohorts born around 1945 experienced merely the beginning of this transformation in early adulthood, as the youngest cohorts in our study (born 1968) faced a social and demographic context of early fertility that differed substantially from that experienced by their predecessors born 23 years earlier.

Thus, in the presence of strong social and normative influences of fertility and marriage behavior, as well as in the presence of tight economic conditions that restrict individuals' choices in early demographic behavior, genetic influences on fertility precursors may not translate to genetic influences on fertility outcomes. In these situations the socioeconomic and cultural context of early fertility is likely to dominate in demographic outcomes. This environmental pressure leaves little room for genetically mediated differences to express themselves in early fertility behavior. As a consequence, heritability h^2 is low, while shared environmental influences c^2 are of considerable relevance. This "constraint" on genetic influences exerted by the environment is likely to lessen during the second demographic transition and the trend towards low fertility. For instance, Udry (1996, p. 335) predicted this interaction between the importance of biological factors and the societal context, arguing that low-fertility societies are better suited for studying biological factors:

> Low-fertility societies provide wide behavior choice. Where behavior choice is broad and opportunities are egalitarian, biological variables, reflecting natural differences in behavioral dispositions, explain increasing variations in behavior. Applications of this principle to demographic research suggests that, increasingly, gendered behavior, fertility, contraception, abortion, nuptiality, occupational choice and other behaviors of interest to demographers will be influenced by biological choice.[3]

---

[3] Comparable analyses of the level of early fertility in male cohorts, which are not reported here, yield a statistically significant estimate of .30 for heritability. The results thus indicate that genetic influences on an early onset of fertility seem to be present also for males. At the same time, the analyses cannot conclusively support a time trend towards an increasing relevance of genetic factors. The main effect for shared environmental factors is not statistically significant in the different birth cohorts if we conduct the analyses in Figure 7.1 for males, nor are the differences between the heritability estimates h^2 in the three cohorts. The results for males therefore suggest the presence of genetic influences on an early onset of fertility, but they do not suggest that these genetic influences are subject to a clear trend across cohorts.

The findings in Figure 7.1 are consistent with a strong influence of parents on the early childbearing experiences of their children. The sum of shared-environmental and genetic influences on early fertility is substantial, and it is even larger in the younger cohorts as compared to the older cohorts. Although we cannot identify this in our study, an important aspect of this variation may be related to attitudes towards childbearing, attitudes towards competing behaviors such as professional careers, and fertility preferences. The above results, however, seem to suggest an important shift in the pathways through which this influence operates. Socialization has lost relevance in the younger cohorts born (1961–1968) as compared to the older cohorts (born 1945–1952), while genetic factors have increased in importance. Therefore, while the influence of parents on variation in early fertility in these Danish cohorts has not diminished, the extent to which parents consciously affect the early childbearing experiences of their children has diminished: biological pathways are mostly outside the conscious control of parents.[4] In terms of the research on attitudes, this finding suggests that attitudes that are closely linked to relatively stable personality traits, such as extraversion or agreeableness, gain in importance for childbearing behavior in young cohorts, while some attitudes that are more closely related to processes of socialization may lose relevance.

Attitudes and Low Fertility: Do Children Provide Happiness?

In this section we turn our attention from the variation in fertility across individuals to the determinants and consequences of fertility and its potential implications for subjective well-being. These analyses are linked to the studies in Barber and Axinn on the role of attitudes in childbearing, but they approach the issue from a different perspective. In particular, rather than investigating the role of attitudes on childbearing from the null-hypotheses that these influences are absent, one could equally ask the question of why the attitudes matter *so little* for childbearing. For instance, while period fertility started to drop significantly below replacement fertility during the 1970s and 1980s, most fertility surveys, value studies, and opinion polls have found that the number of children considered ideal for society or one's own family has remained above two, with declines in the desired fertility size noticeable only in the most recent data for some countries such as Germany and Austria (e.g., Goldstein, Lutz, & Testa, 2003). If the desired fertility stated in the surveys is—among other aspects—a reflection of attitudes towards childbearing, the question immediately arises of why individuals seem to fail to

---

[4] The selection of partners is probably the most important mechanism through which parents can influence the genetic dispositions of children, but is conditional on the current partner—without it, the influence is absent. Reproductive technologies may offers some further possibilities in the future.

achieve their desired family sizes, and in particular, why the achieved family size often falls substantially short of the stated intentions.

The unexpected obstacles of life, the coordination of couples, career surprises, health difficulties, and problems with conception are often cited as an explanation for populations on average rarely having as many children as their members say they would prefer. In other words, the attitudes towards childbearing and/or families are partially constrained by the social and institutional context, and these constraints may therefore weaken the relationship between attitudes and childbearing. Barber and Axinn, for instance, state:

> To the extent these relationships [between attitudes and childbearing] are strong, individuals are able to achieve the outcomes they want. To the extent these relationships are weak, other factors are preventing individuals from achieving the outcomes they want. In a complex society filled with numerous behavioral choices, low fertility is, at least in part, a reflection of preferences for alternatives to childbearing and childrearing (this volume, p. 85).

The empirical evidence presented in Barber and Axinn on the role of attitudes in childbearing pertains primarily to first births and marriage. First births are interesting since most women in the United States and elsewhere continue to have at least one child, and large differences in first-birth fertility pertain to the timing of the first child and the context (non-marital or marital) in which this first birth occurs. A large part of the evidence presented in Barber and Axinn, therefore, pertains to the timing of fertility, not necessarily the level of fertility. This fact makes it difficult to assess the extent to which changing attitudes towards childbearing or competing behaviors have contributed to the fertility decline in the United States or other developed countries, and Barber and Axinn are cautious about the extent to which they attribute fertility trends during the last decades to changes in attitudes. As a result, it is difficult to assess both the extent to which changes in attitudes have altered the motivations to have children, and the motivations to have children differ across parities.

In order to understand these motivations for children, including children in addition to the first child, Kohler and Behrman (2003) look at the consequences of partnerships and childbearing on subjective well-being. In particular, they argue that if individuals (a) do not have systematic misconceptions about the benefits of children and partnerships, and (b) make conscious and informed choices about the formation of partnerships and their level of fertility, the relationship exhibited by "Partner + Children = Happiness" should hold: individuals form unions or have children because these decisions increase—at least on average—their subjective well-being or "happiness".

The analyses in Kohler and Behrman are conducted using Danish twins aged 25–45 years who were interviewed in 2002 in an omnibus survey that included the question, "How satisfied are you with your life, all things considered?" Responses ranged from very satisfied to not satisfied at all. This question about subjective well-being, or "happiness", is interesting because it combines two different components. On the one hand, an important finding in the recent literature on subjective well-being is the remarkable stability of happiness over the life-course and the surprising insensitivity of subjective well-being with respect to variations in income, education, or occupation (e.g., Argyle, 2001). Related studies have therefore argued that "happiness" is much more similar to a trait than to a state (Lykken & Tellegen, 1996).[5] Moreover, happiness has been shown to be related to stable personality characteristics that have a substantial genetic etiology (Diener et al., 1999). A substantial fraction of variation in well-being and related personality traits across individuals is therefore due to unobserved genetic factors. Individuals' responses to the above question about the satisfaction with life, therefore, partially reflect variation in attitudes and personality characteristics: the responses in part distinguish between persons with an innately more optimistic or positive evaluation of life from those that have an innately more pessimistic or negative assessment.

Subjective well-being is therefore likely to be a cause and a consequence of fertility and related behaviors. It "causes" some fertility-related behaviors since it partially reflects a general attitude towards life that affects the transition into marriage (or cohabiting unions) and fertility behavior during the adult years; it is also a "consequence" of the life-experiences as differential fertility and partnership experiences are likely to leave footprints on respondents' evaluation of their lives. Kohler and Behrman (2003) attempt to disentangle this dual role of subjective well-being using data on monozygotic and dizygotic twin pairs that allow us to (a) estimate behavioral genetic models that decompose variation in outcomes/ behaviors within a population into variance consistent with genetic, shared-environmental and individual-specific factors, and (b) use within-MZ twin pair analyses, that is, fixed-effect analyses within identical monozygotic twin pairs, to control for unobserved social and/or genetic dispositions that affect both fertility/ partnership behavior and subjective well-being.

The bivariate behavior genetic analyses in Kohler and Behrman (2003) reveal for males a systematic positive association between the genetic components of variation in subjective well-being and of variation in fertility/partnership behaviors: genetic dispositions that tend to increase subjective well-being—say, dispositions towards a "happy personality"—are associated with a higher number of partnerships (particularly at ages 25–45), a higher probability of being currently in a partnership, and a larger number of children. For females, the correlations tend to be weaker and less uniform, and the correlations for closely related partnership behaviors—such as currently in partnership and the total number of partnerships— can even be in opposite directions.

---

[5] For example, Lykken and Tellegen (1996) report that variation in the well-being component of the Multidimensional Personality Questionnaire (MPQ) for twins in the Minnesota Twin Register in the 1980s is primarily associated with genetic variation, with neither socioeconomic status, schooling, family income, marital status, nor religious commitment accounting for more than 3% of the variance in well-being.

In the within-MZ twin pair analyses, Kohler and Behrman control for this stable long-term effect of satisfaction on fertility and partnership behavior by focusing on within-MZ twin pair differences in fertility behavior and well-being. These within-MZ analyses regress the difference in subjective well-being *within* a MZ twin pair on the difference in indicators of fertility behavior and union status.[6] Figure 7.2 shows these within-MZ estimates of the effect of fertility on a happiness index that is constructed as 0 = not satisfied or not particularly satisfied, 1 = rather satisfied and 2 = very satisfied. The bars in this figure represent the effect on happiness of the variables (*i*) whether a respondent has at least one child and the first child is a boy; (*ii*) whether a respondent has at least one child and the first child is a girl; and (*iii*) the number of remaining children. Standard OLS estimates, which do not control for endowments, are reported for comparison to our preferred within-MZ twin pair estimates.

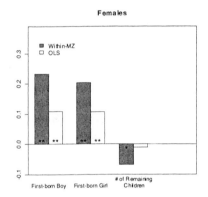 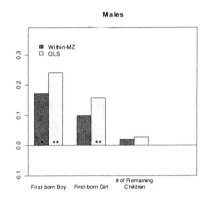

Figure 7.2. Within M-Z Estimates

---

[6] See Kohler and Behrman (2003) for details. The model assumes that happiness of twin i in pair j can be related to fertility and partnerships of twin i in pair j in the form

$$Happiness_{ij} = \beta_0 + \beta_1 \, 'partner_{ij} + \beta_2 \, 'fertility_{ij} + \beta_2 \, 'X_{ij} + \mu_j + \varepsilon_{ij}$$

where "$partner_{ij}$" is our representation of partnership behavior—for instance, currently married/cohabiting or the number of marriages or cohabitations—and "$fertility_{ij}$" is our representation of fertility behavior (e.g., at least one child, number of children, etc.). The term X_{ij} represents the influence of observed socioeconomic characteristics on happiness, and the term m_j represents the influence of unobserved endowments that are common to both twins in pair j. In MZ twin pairs, the term m_j thus captures the influence of *all* genetic dispositions as well as the influences of shared environments such as those associated with the parental household. The term ε_{ij} reflects additional unobserved influences on happiness that are specific to twin i in pair j. The within-MZ twin pair analyses eliminate (*a*) the influence of μ_j from the above relation for happiness, and (*b*) the influence of μ_j on the partnership and fertility indicators that are included on the right-hand-side of the regression. The within-MZ twin approach hence has the advantage of identifying the relevant coefficients, namely the coefficients β_1 and β_2, that reflect the influence of partnerships and fertility on subjective well-being, even if the unobserved endowments, μ_j, in this relation simultaneously affect partnership and fertility behavior. Standard analyses with survey data are biased in this context.

For females (left graph), the first-born child—independent of its sex—has a large positive effect on subjective well-being: having at least one child improves happiness by .20–.23, which is equivalent to 35–39% of one standard deviation. This effect of the first child is substantially underestimated by standard OLS regressions. In contrast to the large positive effect of the first child on well-being, additional children beyond the first child are not associated with higher levels of happiness. Instead, the within-MZ results for females in Figure 7.2 reveal that additional children beyond the first one tend to be associated with *lower* levels of happiness for females. Each child beyond the first decreases the happiness indicator by 13% of one standard deviation for females, and three children almost completely compensate for the positive effect resulting from the first child.

The corresponding analyses for males (right graph) result in a strikingly different pattern. First, there is an important sex difference associated with the happiness gains resulting from a first child: first-born boys have an effect on happiness equal to .172 (29% of one standard deviation of well-being) and almost twice as large as that of a first-born girl (.099 or 17% of one standard deviation). This effect is important since there is no revealed sex-preference in parity progression probabilities: the probability of having a second child as well as the overall number of children does not significantly differ between male twins having a boy or girl as their first child. While males therefore enjoy greater happiness from a first-born son than a first-born daughter, this does not translate into higher levels of fertility—perhaps because their female partners do not share the same sex-specific pattern of happiness gains derived from the first child. Second, additional children beyond the first child have virtually no effect on subjective well-being. Males therefore do not suffer the same declines in happiness with additional children as do females.

These findings are important because they are consistent with evidence from earlier studies of the costs and satisfactions associated with childbearing (e.g., Fawcett, 1983). In particular, respondents' motivation for the first child emphasizes family status, role, and emotional rewards for the parent, while the values motivating second births are strongly associated with providing companionship for the first child. Consistent with the focus on emotional rewards and family status, first children are associated with significant increases in parents' well-being, with males enjoying greater happiness gains from first-born boys than from first-born girls. The differential motivations for higher order children, which focuses on companionship for the first child, however, is also reflected in the results presented in Figure 7.2. For females, additional children beyond the first decrease well-being, and for males the effect of additional children is not distinguishable from zero. Hence, motivations other than subjective well-being seem to underpin the progression to additional children after the first child.

In addition, our results suggest that the attitudes influencing the progression to the first child may differ significantly from those affecting the progression to the second or higher-order children. The attitudes investigated in Barber and

Axinn primarily pertain to aspects that can be categorized under family status and emotional fulfillment, that is, attitudes are likely to matter most importantly for the first child. Attitudes that affect childbearing for the second and higher-order children may differ significantly. In addition, our findings on the happiness-gains due to children (as shown in Figure 7.2) are consistent with several studies in the literature that suggest that parents substantially value having at least one child, and that this continues to be the case even in contexts with low or lowest-low fertility. The happiness gains resulting from this first child may therefore limit the extent to which fertility declines are driven by reductions in first-birth fertility. Several studies, for instance, have shown that the declines to low or lowest-low fertility levels are primarily due to the combination of postponed first births and reductions in the parity progression probabilities to additional children (e.g., Kohler et al., 2002). The findings on subjective well-being also shed light on the potential intrinsic motivations for this pattern: The first child is clearly associated with large increases in well-being, and first children therefore seem to provide an important part of an individual's fulfillment in life. Second and higher-order children, on average, do not have this important role. If individual or couples behavior is constrained and childbearing is associated with important trade-offs in terms of competing goals, second and higher-order children may therefore be easier to forego than first children.

In additional analyses, not reported here in detail, Kohler and Behrman also show a male-female difference with respect to the role of children on well-being after controlling for the current partnership. Females derive happiness gains from children even after controlling for the current partnership status. The happiness of males, however, depends primarily on the partnership status; once the current partnership status is controlled for, men's happiness does not vary systematically with fertility. These findings suggest a somewhat provocative interpretation about the motivations of men and women to engage in partnerships: in particular, the results can be interpreted to suggest that women are in partnerships, among other reasons, in order to have children that increase their subjective well-being. Males, on the other hand, have children in order to remain in the partnerships that strongly affect their happiness. Having children is a strong predictor of currently being in partnerships for males (as well as for females). However, conditional on the current partnership status, children do not contribute to men's subjective well-being. This differentiation may also explain why attitudes towards children seem to be primarily relevant for the marital first-birth rates for females and not for males. Conditional on a current partnership, it is primarily women in our data who derive additional happiness gains from having children.

Conclusion

Barber and Axinn provide a fascinating review of the role of attitudes in childbearing behavior. One of the challenges ahead in this research, as well as in the research on low fertility more generally, is to understand how variation in attitudes about fertility emerges, and how attitudes towards childbearing change over time and matter differently for first and higher-order children. In these comments, I have used some of my research on the fertility of Danish twins to shed some light on these questions from a different perspective, as in the analyses by Barber and Axinn. While explicit measures of attitudes are lacking in these investigations, the processes underlying the results are closely related to the attitudes and preferences emphasized in Barber and Axinn.

The first set of analyses is based on behavior genetic models that decompose the components leading to variation in early fertility, that is, fertility behavior that is likely to be strongly affected by attitudes. The important results from these analyses are that the influence of parents on variation in early fertility has not changed markedly—between 40–57% of the variation is related to parents—but the pathways through which parents influence their children has changed markedly. In cohorts born 1945–1952, the variation is primarily related to differential social experiences of individuals in the parental household, while for cohorts born in 1961–1968, the influence operates primarily through genetic pathways. While the analyses cannot provide direct evidence, this may suggest important changes in the attitudes that matter most for early childbearing. In the older cohorts it is more likely to be related to attitudes shaped by parents through socialization, while in younger cohorts it may be more related to attitudes that are linked to different personality characteristics, innate abilities, or fixed preferences.

In the second set of analyses, we focus on the interaction between subjective well-being and fertility behavior. Subjective well-being is interesting in the context of attitudes because it is a cause as well as a consequence of fertility and related behaviors. In part, it reflects personality traits and stable personal attitudes that affect the probability of forming unions and having children, and it also is affected by an individual's experiences over the life-course. On the one hand, Kohler and Behrman show that unobserved endowments that affect well-being exert important influences on the probability of forming partnerships and having children, consistent with the results presented in Barber and Axinn. On the other hand, Kohler and Behrman also show that the motivation for having first and higher-order children differ substantially. First births are clearly associated with substantial increases in well-being for both males and females, while additional children have negative effects for women and no effect for males on happiness. This is consistent with the finding that self-realization is an important motivation for having at least one child, while concerns for children, other considerations than parents' subjective well-being provide the motivation for additional children.

In addition, the analyses discussed in these comments emphasize the role of endowments, including processes of socialization in the parental household and genetic dispositions, as an important consideration in addressing the role of attitudes and/or personality factors for childbearing in low-fertility contexts. Personality traits, and potentially also attitudes, are importantly related to these endowments. The presence of these unobserved factors can distort inferences about the relevance of attitudes or personality characteristics for childbearing, and the interaction among endowments, attitudes, and fertility behavior may constitute an important field of future research.

References

Argyle, M. (2001). *The psychology of happiness* (2nd ed.). London: Routledge.

Bearman, P. S., & Brückner, H. (2002). Promising the future: Virginity pledges and first intercourse. *American Journal of Sociology, 106*(4), 859–912.

Bouchard, T. J. (1994). Genes, environment and personality. *Science, 264*(5166), 1700–1701.

Bouchard, T. J., & McGue, M. (2003). Genetic and environmental influences on human psychological differences. *Journal of Neurobiology, 54*(1), 4–45.

Diener, E., Suh, E. M., Lucas, R. E., & Smith, H. L. (1999). Subjective well-being: Three decades of progress. *Psychological Bulletin, 125*, 276–303.

Eurostat. (1998). *New Cronos Database: Population and social conditions.* Brussels: Author.

Fawcett, J. T. (1983). Perceptions of the value of children: Satisfactions and costs. In R. A. Bulatao & R. D. Lee (Eds.), *Determinants of fertility in developing countries: Supply and demand for children* (pp. 429–457). New York: Academic Press.

Fishbein, M., & Ajzen, I. (1975). *Belief, attitude, intention and behavior: An introduction to theory and research.* Reading: Addison Wesley.

Goldstein, J. R., Lutz, W., & Testa, M. T. (2003). The emergence of sub-replacement family size ideals in Europe. *Population Research and Policy Review, 22*(5–6), 479–496.

Knudsen, L. B. (1993). *Fertility trends in Denmark in the 1980s: A register based socio-demographic analysis of fertility trends.* Copenhagen: Statistics Denmark.

Kohler, H.-P., & Behrman, J. R. (2003). *Partner + children = happiness? An assessment of the effect of fertility and partnerships on subjective well-being in Danish twins.* Unpublished manuscript, University of Pennsylvania.

Kohler, H.-P., & Rodgers, J. L. (1999). DF-like analyses of binary, ordered and censored variables using Probit and Tobit approaches. *Behavior Genetics, 29*(4), 221–232.

Kohler, H.-P., Billari, F. C., & Ortega, J. A. (2002). The emergence of lowest-low fertility in Europe during the 1990s. *Population and Development Review, 28*(4), 641–681.

Kohler, H.-P., Rodgers, J. L., & Christensen, K. (1999). Is fertility behavior in our genes: Findings from a Danish twin study. *Population and Development Review, 25*(2), 253–288.

Kohler, H.-P., Rodgers, J. L., & Christensen, K. (2003). Between nurture and nature: The shifting determinants of female fertility in Danish twin cohorts 1870–1968. *Social Biology, 49*(1–2), 76–106.

Kyvik, K. O., Christensen, K., Skytthe, A., Harvald, B. & Holm, N. V. (1996). The Danish twin register. *Danish Medical Bulletin, 43*(5), 465–470.

Kyvik, K. O., Green, A., & Beck-Nielsen, H. (1995). The new Danish twin register: Establishment and analysis of twinning rates. *International Journal of Epidemiology, 24*, 589–596.

Lesthaeghe, R. (Ed.). (2002). *Meaning and choice: Value orientations and life course decisions.* The Hague, Netherlands: NIDI.

Lesthaeghe, R., & Moors, G. (1995). *Is there a new conservativism that will bring back the old family? Ideational trends and the stages of family formation in Germany, France, Belgium and the Netherlands, 1981–1990* (IPD-Working Paper No. 1995-1). Brussels: Vrije Universiteit.

Lesthaeghe, R., & van de Kaa, D. (1986). Twee demografische transities? In R. Lesthaeghe & D. van de Kaa (Eds.), *Bevolking: Groei en krimp* (pp. 9–24). Deventer: Van Loghum Slaterus.

Lykken, D. T., & Tellegen, A. (1996). Happiness is a stochastic phenomenon. *Psychological Science, 7*(3), 186–189.

Miller, W. B. (1992). Personality traits and developmental experiences as antecedents of childbearing motivation. *Demography, 29*(2), 265–285.

Miller, W. B., Pasta, D. J., MacMurray, J., Muhleman, D., & Comings, D. E. (2000). Genetic influence on childbearing motivation: Further testing a theoretical framework. In J. L. Rodgers, D. C. Rowe, & W. B. Miller (Eds.), *Genetic influences on fertility and sexuality* (pp. 35–66). Boston: Kluwer Academic.

Morgan, S. P., & King, R. B. (2001). Why have children in the 21st century? Biological predispositions, social coercion, rational choice. *European Journal of Population, 17*(1), 3–20.

Rodgers, J. L., & Doughty, D. (2000). Genetic and environmental influences on fertility expectations and outcomes using NLSY kinship data. In J. L. Rodgers, D. C. Rowe, & W. B. Miller (Eds.), *Genetic influences on human fertility and sexuality* (pp. 85–106). Boston: Kluwer Academic.

Udry, J. R. (1996). Biosocial models of low-fertility societies. *Population and Development Review, 22*(Suppl.), 325–336.

van de Kaa, D. J. (1987). Europe's second demographic transition. *Population Bulletin, 42*(1), 1–59.

van de Kaa, D. J. (2001). Postmodern fertility preferences: From changing value orientation to new behavior. In R. A. Bulatao & J. B. Casterline (Eds.), *Global fertility transition* (pp. 290–331). New York: Population Council.

8

ATTITUDES, BELIEFS, AND CHILDBEARING

Duane F. Alwin[1]

The Pennsylvania State University

Introduction

I agree with the conclusion stated by Jennifer Barber and Bill Axinn that social scientists who study childbearing would benefit from greater emphasis on social psychological explanations of behavior. They emphasize the role of *attitudes*—predispositions to behave—in the development of childbearing and related behavior, and they assess the role of "attitudes" in hazard-rate models of the timing of non-marital and marital first births (see also Barber, 2000, 2001). They argue in support of four conclusions: (1) that more positive attitudes toward childbearing are predictive of childbearing, (2) that positive attitudes toward activities that compete with childbearing predict reductions in childbearing, (3) that attitudes predict across generational lines, from mother to child, suggesting the importance of reference groups for the development of behavior, and (4) that given the influence of attitudes on behavior, social changes in attitudes can be expected to bring about changes in behavior.

In these comments I will make a general set of observations about the use of the social psychology variables in research on childbearing. Often the concept of *attitude* is used generally to refer to *any and all* subjective or ideational variables that might have a role in shaping childbearing behavior. This is an obvious over-simplification, and the Barber-Axinn chapter encourages greater recognition of the conceptual variegation among social psychological concepts.[2] Using a broader range of available concepts, in contrast, I argue that behavior often follows from stable preferences about what ends, including behavioral outcomes, are desirable, as well as about the desirable means of achieving them. I return to what I mean by the concept of preferences, but suffice it to say at this point that preferences are a type of belief, distinct from attitudes, that order choices among behavioral options.

---

[1] The author acknowledges the assistance of Paula Tufis and Pauline Mitchell in the preparation of tables for this chapter.

[2] I use the term "attitude" (in quotes) when I follow the common practice of referring to any and all subjective variables that might shape childbearing behavior, but drop the quotes when I use the term attitudes to refer more narrowly to the concept as it is used in the social psychological literature as "latent predispositions to respond or behave in particular ways toward attitude objects" (see Alwin, 1973; Alwin & Scott, 1996).

A Conceptual Framework

In keeping with my agreement with the Barber-Axinn emphasis on social psychological explanations of childbearing, let me first introduce a general "social psychological" framework that attempts to include an array of different concepts that inevitably arise when we talk about "attitudes" exerting an influence on childbearing. I then focus on certain specific concepts contained in this framework and evaluate how useful they are to understanding childbearing, particularly concepts of beliefs, values, and preferences.

Table 8.1 presents the array of conceptual "buckets" that come up in discussions of social psychological factors that contribute to childbearing and related events. This conceptual scheme organizes these concepts, first, by distinguishing those referring to *ideas* from those referring to *behavior*, and second, by separating them by level of analysis—from the macro-environment, through the micro-, meso-, and exo-systems, to the individual.

Table 8.1.

Conceptual Framework for the Discussion of Environmental and Individual-Level Factors Related to Childbearing Decisions and Events

Level of Analysis	Content of Analysis	
	Ideational	Behavior
Environmental		
Macro/Cultural	Cultural beliefs Social norms	Aggregations of events (e.g., TFR = IFS x F_u x F_r x F_g x F_t x F_i x F_c x E)
Environmental Micro-, Meso-, and Exo-systems (Families, Generations, Marriages/unions, Social institutions)	Subcultural/institutional beliefs and norms	Social structural constraints
Individual	*Belief systems* Existential beliefs (Beliefs about what is) Values/preferences (Beliefs about what should be)	*Behavior* Events Intentions/decisions Expectations Attitudes

This framework begins at the macro level where this volume begins (see Morgan and Hagewen, this volume). The beginning point (upper right cell of Table 8.1) involves the consideration of fertility rates—which are aggregations of human childbearing events—and their components (see Bongaarts, 2002). These macro-level indicators of behavior are presumed to be linked to other macro-level phenomena (upper left cell of Table 8.1) involving ideas embodied in social and cultural beliefs. My assumption is that some unknown set of dynamic processes relate these two macro-level phenomena, that is, rates of fertility are presumed to influence social norms and cultural beliefs and vice-versa. In order to begin to understand how the latter might happen we need to appreciate the rest of the picture, as crudely depicted in Table 8.1.

Commencing from the macro level, on the idea side of the ledger, the conceptual framework moves down to the individual through a series of sub-macro environments expressing beliefs that are relevant to childbearing, and ultimately focuses on individual-level beliefs, values, and preferences. The interstitial (shaded) area in Table 8.1 deserves much more attention than we can give it here, given limitations of space. The concepts referring to micro-, meso-, and exo-environments are defined in Bronfenbrenner's (1979, 1990) work, which clarifies how behavior settings (environments) in which humans live out their lives shape their behavior.

The immediate settings in which actors are embedded—what Bronfenbrenner calls a *micro-system*—contains four main elements: the physical attributes of the setting, molar activities, roles, and relationships. We return to a consideration of roles and relationships when we discuss social norms below, but suffice it to say that these are extremely important aspects of the environment because roles constrain behavior and carry with them prescriptions that set expectations for behavior. Similarly, we cannot assign enough importance to the concept of "relationships" in shaping childbearing decisions (see Presser, this volume). In addition to the micro-system, the environment is composed of several outer layers––meso-system, exo-system, and macro-system. The *meso-system* contains all micro-systems in which ego is an actor, and their interconnections. The *exo-system* contains all other micro-systems that affect the individual, but in which ego is not an actor. And the *macro-system* contains broad cultural values and norms that exist at the macro-level, which we have already discussed.

The various sub-macro environmental systems are also assumed to present opportunities and constraints via social structural constraints on behavior. Several of the papers in this volume refer to these structural systemic factors (e.g., chapters by Morgan and Hagewen, Raley, Tucker, Thomson, and Bianchi in this volume). Given the primary focus of the present discussion, we must abandon further consideration of these structural elements.

Beliefs and Values

Social psychologists define beliefs and values as central to other cognitive phenomena, and it is important for present purposes to clarify the relationship of values to other "ideational" or "subjective" phenomena. Beliefs are cognitive representations of "what is"—basic information that produce states of "expectancy" about the physical and social environment (Rokeach, 1970). The "subjects" of beliefs—what beliefs are about—include a wide variety of phenomena, including the physical world, the self, other persons, and society. Beliefs relate these objects to their attributes.

There is widespread use of the concepts of value and preferences by rational choice theory, which is at the basis of modern economics (Becker, 1981, 1996), but they are also employed outside of this framework (see Homans, 1974). Rational choice theory assumes that humans primarily act to maximize utility, or to maximize benefits relative to costs, and that choices among alternatives are made on the basis of a rational calculation of costs and benefits with respect to maximizing certain desired ends. One does not have to reject these assumptions in their entirety to also admit that values and preferences might arise from "irrational" considerations (see Lundberg, this volume). One must admit, in any event, that rationality, like beauty, must always be considered from the eye of the beholder.

Of course, beliefs may or may not be true. For that matter, there may be no way of verifying the truth-value of all that is believed. The point is that whatever is real to individuals is real in its consequences (Thomas & Znaniecki, 1927). If parents believe children are capable of learning and developing a wide variety of skills, they will likely behave in ways compatible with that belief, providing as many learning opportunities as possible. If, on the other hand, parents believe (for whatever reason) that their children are incapable of learning, this result may occur as a "self-fulfilling prophecy" (Rosenthal & Jacobson, 1968).

The acquisition of information about the characteristics of objects in the physical and social environment or the relation among such characteristics is thought to be formed and developed relatively early in life. As the child develops, she "learns that there are certain (things) that virtually all others believe, other (things) that are true for her even though no one else believes them, other important beliefs about which (people) differ, and other beliefs that are arbitrary matters of taste" (Rokeach, 1970, p. 11). Some beliefs are acquired through direct experience, while others are derived from authority (e.g. parents, teachers, priests, rabbis or ministers). Beliefs about the desirability of children are undoubtedly to some extent dependent upon all or most of these factors. Whatever their source, beliefs become a relatively stable part of the individual's cognitive organization (see Alwin, Cohen, & Newcomb, 1991; Glenn, 1980). Of course, beliefs also change, and given their dependence on need and experience, some aspects of the belief system do not develop until adulthood (e.g. the ideal number of children for a person/family to have).

Values and Preferences

Although they are often used to refer to the same things, a distinction should be drawn between "preferences" on the one hand and "values" on the other. *Preferences* are observed regularities in behavioral choices—sometimes these are inferred from behavior, and sometimes they are inferred from questions posed by survey researchers. Very often, preferences are expressed in terms of a relative ranking of behavioral choices or end-states of existence (Alwin & Jackson, 1981). As such, they reflect underlying latent dimensions that are less likely to be observed directly, but which are so basic to human life that they often escape our attention. These latent dimensions are what are normally referred to as *values*. In this sense, preferences are "observed" variables and values are the "latent" underlying standards on which preferences are ordered (see Williams, 1968).

The concept of preferences has recently become the explicit focus of attention in explaining fertility patterns. A newly emerging version of "preference theory" emphasizes the early development of lifestyle preferences and the long-term impact of values and personal goals (Hakim, 2003).

Attitudes

Another concept that is often confused with beliefs and values, and which is central to our present concerns, is the concept of *attitude*. Rokeach (1970, p. 112) defines *attitudes* as "a relatively enduring organization of beliefs around an object or situation predisposing one to respond in some preferential manner." Also, while *attitudes* are conceived of with respect to specific objects and situations, *values* can be thought of as "abstract ideals, positive or negative, not tied to any specific attitude object or situation, representing a person's beliefs about ideal modes of conduct and ideal terminal goals" (Rokeach, 1970, p. 124). This is consistent with the way the concept of attitude is used in the Barber and Axinn research (see, e.g., footnote 1 in their chapter).

The attitude concept is often described as "the most distinctive and indispensable concept in contemporary social psychology" (Allport, 1968, p. 59). Following the definition from Rokeach (given above), attitudes are predispositions to respond or behave in particular ways toward social objects, along a positive or negative dimension (e.g., approval vs. disapproval, approach vs. avoidance, satisfaction vs. dissatisfaction). Attitudes are often thought to have emotional, cognitive, and behavioral dimensions, all of which are "evaluative" in nature. Such evaluations are often easily manipulated and are subject to situational factors. Some researchers have concluded that there is little evidence that stable, underlying attitudes can be said to exist (e.g., Abelson, 1972; Wicker, 1969), and even those who accept the theoretical legitimacy of the attitude concept evince considerable skepticism that the concept applies to all members of the population (Converse, 1964).

To summarize, it is important for our present purposes that we distinguish "beliefs" from "attitudes". Beliefs and values may be considered types of "attitude" variables, but to confuse beliefs and values with attitudes would be substantially similar to referring to concepts like family background, social class, or occupation as "demographic" variables.

Attitudes Toward Childbearing

Returning to Table 8.1, and moving counterclockwise we can follow this conceptual scheme from individual-level beliefs and values on to intentions, decisions, expectations, and attitudes that are presumably the product of underlying beliefs, values, and preferences. Note that I have put attitudes, intentions, and expectations in the same cell as behavior (or behavioral events) at the individual level in order to emphasize that these are really precursors of behavior. Presumably they are rooted in "ideas" but they reflect behavioral emanations of ideas, not the ideas themselves. Thus, I have included the concepts of *beliefs* and *values* (or *preferences*) to represent the relevant ideational constructs to which attitudes, intentions, and expectations are presumably linked.

The Barber-Axinn paper argues that theoretical models of childbearing consistently include attitudes as central components in understanding this important behavior. In making this point they put a great deal of emphasis on the Fishbein and Ajzen (1975; see also Ajzen, 1988; Ajzen & Fishbein, 1980) theories of reasoned action and planned behavior. This model states that an *attitude toward a particular behavior*, along with subjective norms, predicts intentions, and intentions predict behavior. If one could capture the "attitude toward the act" prior to the formation of behavioral intentions and, similarly, if one could capture intentions prior to behavior, the potential for the successful prediction of behavior intentions and behavior would be high.[3] Attitudes are also dependent upon prior behaviors, however (see Bem, 1970) and the longer the period of time between the measurement of attitudes and behavior, the less likely it is that such prediction may be guaranteed (see Alwin, 1973). Furthermore, attitudes are often affected by situational factors and the less the situations in which they are expressed are governed by normative patterns, the less likely it is that one can predict behavior from attitudes (Schwartz & Alwin, 1971).

---

[3] As I argue elsewhere in this comment, although the Barber-Axinn theoretical formulation is based on the Fishbein-Ajzen model (see Barber, 2000, p. 103), none of their measures actually assess attitudes to childbearing, or behavior intentions with respect to childbearing.

Why Are Beliefs Important?

In this section I develop the argument for considering beliefs, values, and preferences in the understanding of childbearing. To answer this question we begin with the same assumption stated by Barber and Axinn, namely, that behavior entails making choices between alternative courses of action. Here we are concerned with childbearing, but elsewhere I have addressed this topic with respect to a general discussion of behavioral processes involving other aspects of the family (see Alwin, 2001, 2003). The Barber-Axinn paper does a nice job of illustrating the issue of competing behaviors (e.g., the competition between childbearing and the labor-force participation of women).

Hierarchies of need help individuals order their preferences. Understanding human needs helps understand the nature of many human activities. Indeed, it has long been known that activities, or actions, are the behavioral linkage between needs and values. Put simply, activities are engaged in to meet needs. In their general theory of action, Talcott Parsons and Edward Shils (1951) argued that activities represent the linkage between needs and their satisfaction, and social theorists have long recognized the importance of motivating the study of behavior by attempting to understand its relation to the satisfaction of human needs.

Social and economic scientists typically formulate the problem of value(s) in terms of their linkage to satisfying basic material needs, but they also recognize that human behavior is motivated by the satisfaction of other needs as well (e.g., Becker, 1996; Coleman, 1990). Although much human activity is organized around the satisfaction of basic biological needs, people are also highly motivated to obtain social goods that are symbolic of value, such as social acceptance, self-fulfillment, or power.

Clearly, some needs, such as for food, sleep, sex, clothing, and shelter, are more "basic" and must be satisfied before others can be pursued. Needs for acceptance by the social group, obtaining respect from others, and self-actualization are also important basic needs, which in some instances compete for satisfaction. Maslow (1954) argued that needs exist on a dimension of importance and that their satisfaction is governed by a basic "hierarchy of needs." This is now the accepted framework for understanding the primacy of some needs over others. According to the Maslowian framework, "physical needs" override all other basic needs when individuals experience physical deprivation.

The "social-affectional" needs, or the needs for love and affection, are second, but only to physical ones. The third is "self-esteem," or the need for dignity, which has considerable significance to the well-being of children and their families; the fourth are "self-actualization" needs, which are met only after satisfaction of those above in the hierarchy. In the case of childbearing, there is little question that the value of having children conflicts with other values, and it is important to consider the "need for children" within this framework.

Whatever one takes to be the relationship among the types of basic needs, most agree that needs help define the end-states that motivate human behavior, and therefore help govern behavioral choices. They play a strong role in shaping behavior; however, it would be tautological to argue that *all* behavior results from an effort to satisfy needs. Clearly people "want" things that may not be in service of basic needs, or they may want more than they need.

Cultural Beliefs and Social Norms

Stable patterns of activities, stability of environments, and stable sets of needs and goals for the social group all lead to the stability of individuals. While psychologists have tended to use the concept of *personality* to understand the stability of individual differences, sociologists with an interest in culture often rely on somewhat less 'trait-like' concepts like *values*. The concept of value(s) as it is applied to the understanding of human behavior is useful in considering both the individual and cultural levels of analysis.

We typically think of the cultural counterpart to individual-level values as "shared values." We refer to such shared values as "social norms." Norms are distinctively "social" in nature and as such are reflected in cultural or societal solutions to problems, rather than something that exists at the level of individuals, though individuals are influenced by norms and their behavior frequently embodies those norms.[4] This is not to say that individuals' values are not acquired from the society or culture, via the influence of social norms, or that individuals do not have some role in promoting social change through the creation and development of new normative frameworks.

As a concept, "social norm" has two distinct features that may at times seem incompatible with one another, depending upon one's reference point. One primary feature of norms is their "behavioral" component. This involves the regularity or patterning of behavior. It involves the "typical" or "modal" behavior, although there may be many competing norms in the sense conveyed by the concept of cultural pluralism. There are, for example, religious norms for Catholics, Moslems, Protestants, Jews, etc., which are distinctly different (e.g., with respect to childbearing). Thus, what is typical of one group or subgroup in no way implies what is normative for others. The other primary feature of norms involves their "moral" elements, that is, the component of norms that carry with them an "ought" character to behavior that makes the actor believe what s/he is doing is "right" or "correct". Thus, social norms play a major role in the development of individual-level values. The potential for the influence of both macro-level and submacro-level social norms is depicted in Table 8.1.

---

[4] Sometimes the concept of "personal norm" is used to refer to regularities in the behavior of an individual. We prefer to use the term "value" when considering the individual, and the term "social norm" to refer to the group level. Clearly, values and norms are linked, but one is conceptualized at the individual level and the other is conceptualized as existing at the "social" level.

Values and other beliefs are linked to behavior and intentions, but the nature of this linkage clearly involves a set of reciprocal influences. For example, to the extent that women's labor-force participation is a matter of choice, it is reasonable to assume that values about the desirability of women's employment are a factor influencing the labor force behavior of women. At the same time, regardless of values, employment experiences under a regime that defines women's labor force participation as necessary, may well change people's beliefs and attitudes about the desirability of women's employment and the compatibility of work and family life (see Braun, Scott, & Alwin, 1994). More importantly, people's own beliefs and those of their immediate family members help to determine whether work and family goals are viewed as being compatible. If people believe that employment is incompatible with "being a good mother," then mothers who work are likely to feel considerable role-conflict and strain, promoting a negative view of the desirability of juggling family and work (Scott, Braun, & Alwin, 1993).

Attitudes vs. Beliefs

Both attitudes and beliefs are valid concepts for the examination of behavior. They differ in their development and in a number of other ways (see Alwin, 1994). Three important aspects of cognitive phenomena are their centrality, their stability, and the extent to which they can predict behavior. Of course, cognitive phenomena are of interest in their own right and should not be evaluated solely in terms of their ability to predict behavior.

The *centrality* of cognitive variables refers to the extent to which they are linked to other cognitive elements—one whose change in other elements is more central to the cognitive organization than one whose change has no implications for changes in other cognitive elements. *Stability* refers to the degree of change in a phenomenon per unit of time. The stability of cognitive dispositions is an important focus for research because it can tell us a considerable amount about the dynamic stability of the inter-relation of the individual and the environment.

Attitudes are considered to be reflective of beliefs and values rather than the reverse. In contrast to beliefs, attitudes are often thought to be easily manipulated and are subject to situational factors. With respect to stability, attitudes are considered to be somewhat less stable than beliefs.

Despite the emphasis placed by Barber and Axinn on the role of attitudes in a manner consistent with Fishbein and Ajzen's models of "reasoned action and planned behavior," their analyses *do not include any measures of the attitude toward the behavior*, as those models do—"attitudes toward childbearing" in this case. One therefore is left to wonder what they had in mind in motivating their work in this way. In fact, for the most part their measures are assessments of beliefs, preferences, or expectations, which are demonstrably different conceptually from attitudes. None of them explicitly operationalizes the concepts in the principal social psychological theory they employ.

To be concrete, Barber's (2000, pp. 108–109) measures included the following: (1) a scale representing enjoyment of activities with children, (2) a question asking about beliefs in whether children cause their parents "worry and emotional strain," and (3) a measure of preferences for family size. None of these is actually a measure of *attitudes toward childbearing.* Similarly, the measures of "parallel" attitudes– –i.e., attitudes towards those behavioral choices thought to be competing with childbearing—are not measures of attitudes per se. Here Barber's (2000, pp. 109– 110) measures included: (1) educational expectations ("What is the highest amount of schooling you think you will ever complete?"), (2) career expectations (agreement with the statement, "I do not expect work to be a major source of satisfaction in my life"), and (3) future importance of consumer goods (rating of the importance of seven consumer goods for the respondent in the future ("… after you've either been married for a while or have been out of school and working for a few years.")[5] Thus, their results speak more to the role of beliefs, rather than attitudes, in shaping childbearing.

Conclusion

The chapter by Barber and Axinn encourages us not to ask *whether* "attitudes" influence childrearing behavior, but for whom do "attitudes" matter and under what conditions. We should be reminded that their analyses focus only on the first 12 years of adulthood (i.e., ages 18–30) and focus solely on the transition to first parity. They do not focus on completed family size, so they are aware that in many ways their conclusions about the ultimate impact of early childbearing preferences or related cognitive factors on childbearing are premature. Nor do they focus on other events relevant to childbearing, such as contraceptive behavior and abortion, which are also presumably affected by "attitudes." Again, then, they are exploring a relatively limited role of the consequences of "attitudes" for behavior.

I have argued here for a broader conceptualization of the role of social psychological explanations for childbearing behavior. I pointed out that while Barber and Axinn conceptualize the role of attitudes in a manner consistent with Fishbein and Ajzen's models of "reasoned action and planned behavior," their measures do not include any measures of "attitudes toward childbearing," and their results pertain more to the impact of beliefs, rather than attitudes, on childbearing.

Finally, although Barber and Axinn provide a strong evidentiary basis for their conclusions, it is important to understand, as they do, that there may be alternative explanations for their "attitudes cause behavior" results. There are several possible alternatives, and I cannot go into all of them here. One, however, deserves brief mention—namely, that both individual differences in attitudes and behaviors are

---

[5] In fairness to Barber (2000), she does acknowledge that "educational expectations" are not a direct measure of an individual's attitude toward education.

spuriously due to unmeasured personality factors involving *the ability to defer gratification.* I mentioned earlier the tendency of sociologists to give too little attention to the concept of *personality* and the role of the stable individual differences in behavioral tendencies in the understanding of differences in attitudes and behavior (see Alwin, 1994). In the present case, the explicit focus is on time to first birth—both nonmarital and marital births. It is natural to wonder whether some of the findings that relate to ideational factors predicting time to first parity might be interpreted in this manner. This may especially be true for the assessed relationship between educational expectations and consumption aspirations, on the one hand, and time to first parity, on the other.

References

Abelson, R. P. (1972). Are attitudes necessary? In B. T. King & E. McGinnies (Eds.), *Attitudes, conflict and social change* (pp. 19–32). New York: Academic Press.

Ajzen, I. (1988). *Attitudes, personality and behavior.* Chicago: Dorsey.

Ajzen, I., & Fishbein, M. (1980). *Understanding attitudes and predicting social behavior.* Englewood Cliffs, NJ: Prentice-Hall.

Allport, G. (1968). The historical background of modern social psychology. In G. Lindzey & E. Aronson (Eds.), *Handbook of social psychology* (2nd ed., pp. 1–80). Reading, MA: Addison-Wesley.

Alwin, D. F. (1973). Making inferences from attitude-behavior correlations. *Sociometry, 36,* 253–278.

Alwin, D. F. (1994). Aging, personality and social change: The stability of individual differences over the life-span. In D. L. Featherman, R. M. Lerner, & M. Perlmutter (Eds.), *Life-span development and behavior* (pp. 135–185). Hillsdale, NJ: Lawrence Erlbaum.

Alwin, D. F. (2001). Parental values, beliefs, and behavior: A review and promulga for research into the new century. In S. L. Hofferth & T. J. Owens (Eds.), *Children at the millennium: Where have we come from, where are we going?* (pp. 97-130). New York: Elsevier Science Ltd.

Alwin, D. F. (2003). *The disciplined self: Transformations of child-rearing over the 20th century.* Unpublished manuscript, The Pennsylvania State University, University Park.

Alwin, D. F., & Jackson, D. J. (1981). Adult values for children: An application of factor analysis to ranked preference data. In R. M. Hauser, D. Mechanic, A. O. Haller, & T. S. Hauser (Eds.), *Social structure and behavior: Essays in honor of William Hamilton Sewell* (pp. 311–329). New York: Academic Press.

Alwin, D.F., & Scott, J. (1996). Attitude change: Its measurement and interpretation using longitudinal surveys. In B. Taylor & K. Thomson (Eds.), *Understanding change in social attitudes.* Aldershot, UK: Dartmouth.

Alwin, D.F., Cohen, R.L., & Newcomb, T.M. (1991). *Political attitudes over the life span: The Bennington women after fifty years.* Madison, WI: University of Wisconsin Press.

Barber, J. S. (2000). Intergenerational influences on the entry into parenthood: Mothers' preferences for family and nonfamily behavior. *Social Forces, 79,* 319–348.

Barber, J. S. (2001). Ideational influences on the transition to parenthood: Attitudes toward childbearing and competing alternatives. *Social Psychology Quarterly, 39,* 11–31.

Becker, G. S. (1981). *A treatise on the family.* Cambridge, MA: Harvard University Press.

Becker, G. S. (1996). *Accounting for tastes.* Cambridge, MA: Harvard University Press.

Bem, D. (1970). *Beliefs, attitudes and human affairs.* Belmont, CA: Brooks/Cole Publishing Co.

Bongaarts, J. (2002). The end of fertility transition in the developed world. *Population and Development Review, 28,* 419–444.

Braun, M., Scott, J. L., & Alwin, D. F. (1994). Economic necessity or self-actualization? Attitudes toward women's labor-force participation in Germany, Great Britain and the United States. *European Sociological Review, 10,* 29–47.

Bronfenbrenner, U. (1979). *The ecology of human development.* Cambridge, MA: Harvard University Press.

Bronfenbrenner, U. (1990). Discovering what families do. In D. Blankenhorn, S. Bayme, & J. B. Elshtain (Eds.), *Rebuilding the nest: A new commitment to the American family* (pp. 27–51). Milwaukee, WI: Family Service America.

Coleman, J.S. (1990). *Foundations of social theory.* Cambridge, MA: Harvard University Press.

Converse, P.E. (1964). The nature of belief systems in the mass public. In D.E. Apter (Ed.), *Ideology and discontent* (pp. 206–261). New York: Free Press.

Fishbein, M., & Ajzen, I. (1975). *Belief, attitude, intention, and behavior: An introduction to theory and research.* Reading, MA: Addison-Wesley.

Glenn, N. D. (1980). Values, attitudes and beliefs. In O. G. Brim & J. Kagan (Eds.), *Constancy and change in human development* (pp. 596–640). Cambridge, MA: Harvard University Press.

Hakim, C. (2003). A new approach to explaining fertility patterns: Preference theory. *Population and Development Review, 29,* 349–374.

Homans, G. C. (1974). *Social behavior: Its elementary forms.* New York: Harcourt Brace.

Maslow, A.H. (1954). *Motivation and personality.* New York: Harper & Row.

Parsons, T., & Shils, E.A. (Eds.). (1951). *Toward a general theory of action.* Cambridge, MA: Harvard University Press.

Rokeach, M. (1970). *Beliefs, attitudes and values.* San Francisco: Jossey-Bass.

Rosenthal, R., & Jacobson, L. (1968). *Pygmalion in the classroom.* New York: Holt, Rinehart and Winston.

Schwartz, M., & D. F. Alwin. (1971). Evaluation of social action. In E. O. Smigel (Ed.), *Handbook on the study of social problems.* Chicago: Rand McNally.

Scott, J. L., Braun, M., & Alwin, D. F. (1993). The family way. In R. Jowell, L. Brook, & L. Dowds (Eds.), *British social attitudes: Special international report.* Aldershot, England: Gower.

Thomas, W. I., & Znaniecki, F. (1927). *The Polish peasant in Europe and America.* New York: Alfred A. Knopf.

Wicker, A. W. (1969). Attitudes versus actions: The relationship of verbal and overt behavioral responses to attitude objects. *Journal of Social Issues, 25,* 41–78.

Williams, R. (1968). Values. In D. E. Sills (Ed.), *International encyclopedia of the social sciences* (pp. 283-287). New York: Macmillan.

III

How and Why Is Fertility Tied to Marriage—Or Not?

9

PARTNERSHIPS & PARENTHOOD: A COMPARATIVE VIEW OF COHABITATION, MARRIAGE, AND CHILDBEARING

Elizabeth Thomson

University of Wisconsin-Madison

Until the latter part of the 20th century, almost all children in almost all places were born to married couples. Parents needed to be married in order to provide for their children and to enjoy the support of extended family members and communities. As extended family and community supports for childrearing were transferred to states and markets, the necessity of marriage—or even partnership—for childbearing and childrearing declined.

Of course, even with state and market resources, having a partner to share the day-in, day-out responsibilities of providing and caring for children is easier than rearing children alone. Two parents can divide tasks in a complementary fashion to produce greater efficiencies in household production, or they can develop parallel competencies that provide a safety net in case one or the other is incapacitated. Two parents can support each other emotionally when a child has difficulties and congratulate each other when a child does well. Two parents increase the number and perhaps the strength of a child's ties to extended family and community. Thus, it is no surprise that a stable partnership comes first in Hobcraft and Kiernan's (1995) list of preconditions for the optimal transition to parenthood.

Marriage provides even more advantages for parenthood. As a contract between two heterosexual partners and the state, marriage offers legal protections for parents and

children and may provide access to public resources. As in the past, marriage is also a social contract between families, and may increase the parents' and children's claims on the resources of their extended kin. As a legal contract, marriage is more difficult to dissolve than other forms of sexual partnerships, producing a more stable environment for childrearing. Stability removes some of the risks associated with an efficient division of labor and increases the gains to shared investments such as the bearing and rearing of children (Pollak, 2000; Willis, 1999; Willis & Haaga, 1996).

In spite of these advantages, nonmarital births have increased dramatically in several wealthy countries. In some countries, cohabitation has become an alternative to marriage as a context in which to bear children; in others, increasing proportions of children are born to mothers who do not live with their child's father. But the patterns are not uniform and do not appear to be converging.

Nonmarital Childbearing in the Late 20th Century

Figure 9.1 shows changes from 1960 through 2000 in the nonmarital birth ratio (percent of births out of marriage) for ten countries selected to show variation in the timing of increases in nonmarital childbearing and its most recent levels.[1] In 1960, the ratio ranged from a low of 1.2% in Japan to a high of 25.3% in Iceland. Between 1970 and 1975, dramatic increases occurred in Sweden (and Denmark, not shown), followed a decade later by Norway. Other countries followed a more gradual increase. The United States is about in the middle. By 2000, Iceland's percentage had risen to 62.4, and most countries had bypassed the Iceland extreme of 1960. Note, however, that in Japan (and Greece, not shown), nonmarital childbearing remained rare, and in several other countries, below 20%.

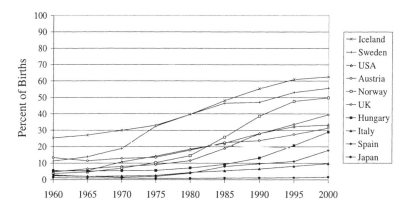

Figure 9.1. Nonmarital Birth Ratios, 1960-2000

Before exploring these variations; further, a methodological note is in order. The nonmarital birth ratio is comprised of several different components. It can increase when fewer women are married (with constant birth rates among married and unmarried women, respectively); when married women have fewer children; or when unmarried women have more children. Smith, Morgan, and Koropeckyj-Cox (1996) decomposed U.S. trends in the nonmarital birth ratio from 1960 to 1992 into changes in these behavioral components as well as changes in the age distribution of women of reproductive age. They found that declines in marriage accounted for

---

[1] The former East and West Germany are treated as two separate countries, given their political and economic separation during most of the period of observation. Estimates for most countries are reported by national statistical offices via the Council of Europe (2000) and/or Demoscope (http://demoscope.ru/weekly/app/app4013.php). Estimates were produced for the United States by the National Center on Health Statistics (www.cdc.gov/nchs/) and for Japan by the National Institute of Population and Social Security Research (2003). Data for Canada (see later figures) were found in Preston (1987) and updated by Statistics Canada (personal communication, 2003).

most of the increase in the ratio among African=American women. Until 1975, increases for African =Americans could also be attributed to declining marital birth rates—after 1984, to increasing nonmarital rates. Among White women, increases in nonmarital birth rates and declines in marriage contributed to an increasing proportion of nonmarital births. Cooper (1991) shows for the United Kingdom that the 1980–1989 increase in the nonmarital birth ratio was due equally to an increasing proportion of unmarried women and an increase in the nonmarital birth rate. In countries with very low nonmarital birth *rates* (e.g., Spain), increases in the nonmarital birth *ratio* have been associated with dramatic declines in marital birth rates (Cantisani & Dalla Zuanna, 1991).

From a behavioral perspective, both nonmarriage and nonmarital birth rates represent a shift of childbearing out of marriage. Postponement or avoidance of marriage without postponement or avoidance of parenthood produces high nonmarital birth ratios even if rates of nonmarital childbearing remain stable or decline. In any case, the correlation between the nonmarital birth ratio and the nonmarital birth rate across the 18 European countries studied by Cantisani and Dalla Zuanna (1991) is .97 for the mid--1990s (original analyses). Thus, it is reasonable to use the relatively plentiful data on nonmarital birth ratios to analyze cross-national differences in nonmarital childbearing.

Cohabitation as a Context for Childbearing

A more important measurement issue for analyses of nonmarital childbearing is the distinction between births to unmarried *couples* and births to unmarried *women* who are not living with the child's father. Because national vital registration systems rarely provide such data, we must rely on sample surveys to estimate the contribution of cohabitation to nonmarital births. Figure 9.2 presents life-table estimates of the proportion of births to unmarried couples or unpartnered women during the 1990s.[2] The countries are selected to show variation in the composition of nonmarital births and are ordered by the combined nonmarital birth ratio. In most countries, births to cohabiting couples comprise the majority of nonmarital births. This is true in countries where nonmarital childbearing is relatively rare (e.g., Italy and West Germany) and where it is quite common (e.g., Austria, France, and Sweden). In East Germany and the United States, however, large proportions of births occur to women living without a partner.

---

[2] Estimates for most of the countries are derived by Andersson (2002) from the Fertility and Family Surveys. He used six-year periods prior to each survey as the basis for life tables. Data for the United Kingdom are based on birth registrations in 1989 (Cooper, 1991). Heuveline, Timberlake and Furstenberg (2003) provided life-table estimates for Canada, New Zealand, and Switzerland used in subsequent figures. They used the three-year period before the survey for surveys conducted in the early 1990s, the period three to six years before the survey for surveys conducted after 1993. Because of the different methods and timing of observation of births, the sum of estimated births to cohabiters and to unpartnered women does not match exactly the nonmarital birth ratio reported by national statistical agencies.

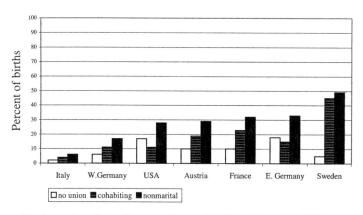

Figure 9.2. Nonunion, Cohabiting, and Nonmarital Birth Ratios, Mid-1990s

Does this mean that high rates of nonmarital childbearing are simply artifacts of our enumeration systems, having little meaning for our understanding of family life and reproduction? Not at all. Cohabitation offers many of the same advantages for parenting and for children as does marriage, but cohabiting unions are less stable than marriages, leaving children at higher risk of living with a single parent (Andersson, 2002; Andersson & Philipov, 2002; Heuveline, Timberlake, & Furstenberg, 2003). That risk is lower where cohabitation produces most of the nonmarital births and is likely less selective of troubled relationships. For example, U.S. and East German children experience high risks of living with a single mother early in life because so many of them are born to single mothers and, in the U.S., because of exceptionally high rates of separation and divorce (Andersson & Philipov, 2002). Although Sweden has a much higher nonmarital birth ratio, many fewer children live with a single mother before age 6. The difference can be attributed to very low proportions of nonunion births and more moderate separation rates, even for cohabiting parents.

To summarize, even though the connection between marriage and childbearing has loosened considerably in many wealthy countries of the world, marriage remains the most common venue for childbearing. In many countries, more than 90% of children are born in marriage. Births to cohabiting couples are increasingly common and account for most of the increase in nonmarital births. The implications of these changes for children's lives depend on the selectivity of couples into cohabitation or marriage, i.e., on the relative stability of cohabiting and marital unions as well as on the proportion of births to unpartnered women.

Explaining Nonmarital and Nonunion Childbearing

Explanations for cross-national variation in family formation patterns are roughly divided into economic and cultural forces, and most studies focus on one type of explanation or the other. Of course, economics and culture are interdependent. Pollak and Watkins (1993) point out that some cultural 'stories' are compatible with rational-actor economic theory, insofar as they accept the distinction between preferences and opportunities. Compatible theories specify culture as a source of variation in preferences and/or as a constraint on opportunities (i.e., the set of choices weighed by rational actors). Lesthaeghe and Surkyn (1988) claim that culture influences preferences and constraints not only directly but also by altering material conditions (e.g., employment policies, welfare regimes) that facilitate or inhibit childbearing.

Willis (Willis, 1999; Willis & Haaga, 1996) argues that nonmarital childbearing arises from the excess supply and relative self-sufficiency of women. 'Excess supply' is defined in terms of the number of men who are able to provide economically for the woman and her children. To the extent that cohabitation places fewer demands on men to provide economic support, the theoretical argument can be applied to childbearing in cohabitation rather than marriage. Positive effects of male wages and the male/female wage ratio on marriage (e.g., Moffitt, 2000; Oppenheimer, 2000) are consistent with the theory.[3]

Effects of employment markets and wages on marriage may, of course, be moderated by state redistribution of income or other resources to women, children, or parents. Considerable cross-national variation exists in the extent to which national welfare regimes provide support to parents, especially single parents (e.g., Gornick, Meyers, & Ross, 1997; Neyer, 2003). Studies of national policy effects on the number or timing of births produce mixed results (Neyer, 2003). None of this research considers policy effects on nonmarital childbearing.

In the United States, on the other hand, a large body of research exists on the potential effects of means-tested welfare programs on nonmarital fertility. Moffitt (1998) reports that a simple majority of studies find a significant relationship between welfare benefits and nonmarital childbearing or single motherhood. Welfare benefits do not, however, explain the increase in nonmarital childbearing over time and results are sensitive to data and model specification.

The second explanation for wide variation in nonmarital and nonunion childbearing is that citizens in different countries hold different norms or standards for family formation. Several studies have demonstrated an association at the aggregate level between fertility and abstract cultural values such as individualism, secularization, pragmatism, or postmaterialism (e.g., Lesthaeghe & Surkyn, 1988; Simons, 1999; Van de Kaa, 2001). Lesthaeghe (1995) showed that Protestant

---

[3] Positive effects of female wages on marriage (Sweeney, 2002) are not necessarily incompatible with the theory because the male/female wage ratio may be higher among those with the highest wages (Moffitt, 2000).

countries had much greater increases in nonmarital births (as a percentage of all births) between 1960 and 1975 than did other countries, net of a country's wealth, female education, and female employment. Pagnini and Rindfuss (1993) found parallels between trends in normative beliefs about nonmarital childbearing and the nonmarital birth ratio in the United States. At the individual level, quite strong effects of values, attitudes or norms and subsequent marriage or childbearing have been demonstrated (e.g., Barber & Axinn, this volume; Barber, Axinn, & Thornton, 2002; Moors, 2002; Thomson, 2002). In several European countries, Kiernan (2001) found substantial differences by religious attendance in the probability of having a first child in a first cohabiting union, and slightly smaller differences for births before a first union.

Both economic and cultural explanations implicate gender as an over-arching explanation for change and variation in childbearing patterns. McDonald (2000a) distinguishes between gender equity in individual-oriented institutions such as the labor markets and political systems of industrialized countries and family-oriented institutions (i.e., the household). He claims that fertility will be extraordinarily low when gender equity is high in individual-oriented institutions, but low in family-oriented institutions. Cross-national variation in fertility levels has been related to gender equality in the home, as well as in the public sphere (Chesnais, 1996, 1998; McDonald, 2000b). Within countries, policies designed to increase gender equity at home appear to increase childbearing (Duvander & Andersson, 2003; Oláh, 2001).

Cherlin (2000) argues that gender inequity at home has become a stumbling block for marriage. Women are seeking partners who will not only contribute to the household economy but also do a fair share of household work. In order to find such partners, Cherlin claims that women must cohabit; income potential can be observed through a potential mate's education, occupation, and employment, but household contributions can be assessed only through direct experience.

Of course, failure to find the dual-shift man could lead women to choose childlessness or nonmarital childbearing. Even the purely economic definition of male supply (Willis, 1999) begs the question—why would women choose to take on more responsibilities, economically and in the household, by having children without a partner or in a relatively unstable union? An implicit premise seems to be that women are more interested in motherhood than are men in fatherhood.

Jensen (2001) agrees, claiming that when children become primarily an emotional good, they are more valuable to women than to men. As a result, fertility is higher where "women can have and provide for children without being married. ... where this is not possible, men are the main obstacle for having children" (p. 1). Cherlin (2000) also asserts that women care more about 'emotional connections, altruism, & raising children' (p. 133), which limits their use of bargaining to obtain greater equity in the household (England & Farkas, 1986). Evidence for the stronger interest of women in children is mixed (Jenson 2001; Jones & Brayfield, 1997).

Perhaps gender ideologies and institutions make the costs of dual-shift parenthood higher for men than for women. Male-dominant gender ideologies have lost considerable power to restrict women's employment; but they continue to penalize men for doing 'women's work' (Brines, 1994). If men and women value parenthood equally, but men pay higher costs for taking on a full share of parental and household responsibilities, the net benefit of children to women would be greater.

Cross-National Patterns in Nonmarital Childbearing, Economics, Culture, and Gender

My goal in this section is to identify cross-national variation in economic, cultural, and gender indicators that should, according to theories discussed above, parallel variation in nonmarital childbearing. Nonmarital childbearing is represented by the percentage of nonmarital births in 1995 and in some cases by estimates for the 1990s of the percentage of births to cohabiting couples or unpartnered women. Indicators of economic and cultural contexts are drawn from the same general period. I use all countries for which data are available on the selected indicator of nonmarital childbearing and indicators of economic, cultural, or gender forces.

The analysis has two serious limitations. It ignores the complexity of variations in timing of union formation and births that can mislead us about the changing propensity of a particular population to have children in marriage or not. And it ignores the possibility that changing family behaviors lead to changes in economic conditions and/or cultural beliefs. But it's a start on the complex task of understanding the circumstances under which nonmarital and nonunion childbearing occur.

Economics

Figure 9.3 plots the nonmarital birth ratio in parallel with the percent of women economically active and women's wages as a percent of men's (United Nations, 2002). Employment opportunities for women provide the required self-sufficiency for unpartnered motherhood, and the female/male wage ratio is an indicator of women's excess supply, being inversely related to the supply of economically suitable fathers.

Across the 26 countries for which data are available, both indicators are positively associated with nonmarital births (r=.71, .57, respectively). Both associations are driven by the percentage of births to cohabiting couples (across a subset of 17 countries with appropriate data) rather than by the percentage of births to unpartnered women (analyses not shown). That is, employment and relatively high wages enable women to take the risk of having children in cohabitation and subsequently becoming single mothers, but do not appear to support childbearing without a partner.

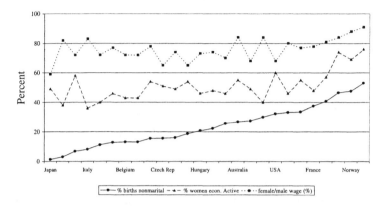

Figure 9.3. Nonmarital Births and Women's Economic Position

Figure 9.4 repeats the exercise for indicators of state support for parents: maternal leave benefits, measured as the proportion of a full year's salary (United Nations, 2000) and a scale of support for employment of mothers with children under age 6 (Gornick, Myers, & Ross, 1997). Both types of support may facilitate childbearing for all women, but they should be particularly important for unpartnered women or women in unstable (cohabiting) relationships. Although weak positive associations emerge, the number of countries is quite small (*n*=13). Analyses of the even smaller set of countries with estimates of nonunion and cohabiting births produced a stronger positive association with cohabiting births but a negative association with births to unpartnered women (not shown). These estimates may be particularly sensitive to outliers such as Sweden and the United States.

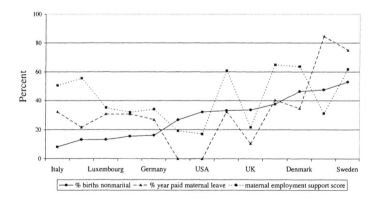

Figure 9.4. Nonmarital Births and Maternal Support Policies

Willis and others have argued that women's self-sufficiency and excess supply is particularly pronounced at lower levels of income (Moffitt, 2000; Willis, 1999; Willis & Haaga, 1996). As a result, we might expect the level of inequality to be associated with nonmarital childbearing, particularly childbearing without a partner. Figure 9.5 plots two indicators of inequality, the ratio of income above the 90th percentile to that below the 10th percentile, and the Gini Coefficient (Smeeding, 2002). Because no clear pattern was found for nonmarital childbearing, I plot here the proportion of births to cohabiting couples and to women living alone. Toward the right side of the figure, in countries where nonmarital births exceed a minimal threshold, a clear parallel can be observed between nonunion births and inequality. The association between inequality and nonunion births is consistent with research showing that the income penalty for single mothers after taxes and transfers was highest in the United States and United Kingdom where rates of nonunion births are relatively high, and much lower in countries such as Sweden and Italy where nonunion births are rare (Rake & Daly, 2002). While these results support economists' theoretical account of nonunion births, they could also arise from the contributions of single mothers' extreme poverty to overall levels of inequality.

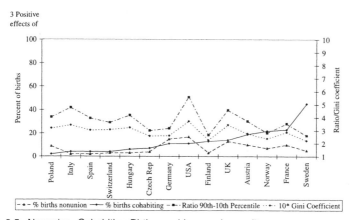

Figure 9.5. Nonunion, Cohabiting Births, and Income Inequality

Culture

Turning to the cultural explanation, I consider variation in norms specific to nonmarital childbearing in relation to a country's level of nonmarital childbearing. The International Social Survey Program (Zentralarchiv für Empirische Sozialforschung, 1997) presented respondents with two statements: *People who want children ought to get married; One parent can bring up a child as well as two parents.* Response options ranged from strongly disagree (1) to strongly agree (5). I use data for respondents under age 40 in order to capture the peer group for individuals in their childbearing years. Mean responses vary across countries, but are centered very closely around the midpoint, *neither agree nor disagree.*

Figure 9.6 shows that, even in countries with extremely low levels of nonmarital childbearing, respondents under 40 expressed considerable tolerance for having children outside of marriage or raising children as a single parent. With the exception of the extreme cases of Japan and Sweden, no clear relationship exists between either of these normative responses and the proportion of births that occur out of marriage. What this overall pattern masks, however, is a positive association (r=.60) between nonunion births and acceptance of one-parent families and a negative association (r=-.51) between cohabiting births and norms for marital childbearing (not shown).

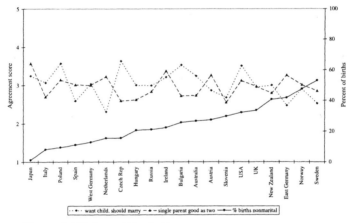

Figure 9.6. Nonmarital Births and Family Norms

The Eurobarometer Surveys (Reif & Melich, 1993) included an intriguing question about marriage, cohabitation, and singlehood as contexts for raising children. Respondents were asked whether they considered each of the following *to be a family: a married couple with child(ren), an unmarried couple with child(ren), a single parent with child(ren),* along with other household configurations. In every country, almost all respondents considered a married couple with children to be a family. Figure 9.7 shows the percentage of respondents under age 40 who defined cohabiting or single parents as living in a family. Although the pattern is not completely parallel, countries with high levels of nonmarital childbearing also have high proportions of respondents who define a cohabiting couple with children as a family (r=.84, *n*=16). The pattern arises for the most part from the proportion of cohabiting rather than nonunion births (data not shown). Stark contrasts are seen between the extremes of Greece and Sweden.

The definition of single parents as families is also associated with nonmarital childbearing (r=.65); oddly, however, respondents in Austria and East Germany— where unpartnered motherhood is quite common—were relatively much less likely to include single parents and children in their definition of 'family'.

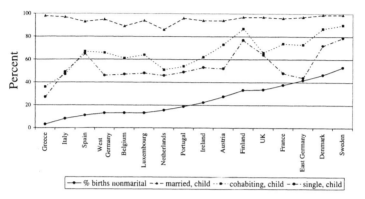

Figure 9.7. Nonmarital Births and Definition of Family

Not included in this analysis is the country with the lowest level of nonmarital childbearing, Japan. Data from the World Values Survey (Ingelehart et al., 2000) showed that Japanese respondents of childbearing age were only slightly less likely to agree that *A child needs a home with both mother and father* than were their counterparts in Sweden (not shown).

These results, taken together, are more consistent with normative adaptation to specific forms of family behavior—cohabitation versus nonunion childbearing––than with a general normative permissiveness as the source of behavioral variation. Furthermore, it is quite surprising that normative constraints are not strong in countries such as Japan, Italy, and Spain, where extremely low levels of nonmarital childbearing are found. Tolerance for a variety of family forms resulting from nonmarital and nonunion births appears to be quite widespread.

Gender

To identify potential relationships between gender equity in the home and nonmarital childbearing, I begin with one classic and one new question about norms for a couple's division of labor, both from the 1994 ISSP (Zentralarchiv für Empirische Sozialforschung, 1997). Respondents were presented with the following two statements: *A man's job is to earn money; a woman's job is to look after the home and family*; and *Both the man and the woman should contribute to the household income*. Responses were scored from 1 (*strongly disagree*) to 5 (*strongly agree*).

Figure 9.8 presents the mean response for respondents under 40, along with the nonmarital birth ratio, again all in the mid-1990s. At relatively high levels of nonmarital childbearing, we see a *negative* association between support of the single breadwinner model and nonmarital births, i.e., a *positive* association with marital childbearing. This result is inconsistent with the argument that women have children out of marriage where gender norms are most rigid. Rejection of the traditional division of labor is stronger where nonmarital births, particularly births to cohabiters, are especially high. No association was found between nonmarital childbearing and beliefs that both women and men should contribute to the household income. It is in fact rather astonishing that respondents in many of the most ideologically traditional countries agreed with this statement.

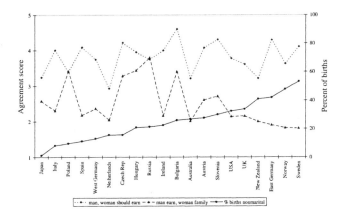

Figure 9.8. Nonmarital Births and Gender Role Norms

The 1998 Eurobarometer Survey provides data on norms for the allocation of childrearing. Respondents were presented with a list of childrearing tasks: *playing sport with the children, bringing the children to activities, changing the baby's nappies, dressing the children or choosing their clothes, taking the children to the doctor, helping the children with their schoolwork* and *going to parents' meetings, reading to the children, buying toys for the children, punishing the children, putting the children to bed, answering important questions raised by the child.* They were asked to indicate whether they thought each task *should be carried out mainly by the father, mainly by the mother or by both.* I constructed a scale from mean responses (1=father, 2=both, 3=mother) for all eleven tasks and for the four tasks involving physical care of children (nappies, clothing, doctor, bed). In every country, mean scores for both scales were at or just above the score for 'both'; not even a weak association can be discerned between normative childrearing tasks and nonmarital births (Figure 9.9). Among the smaller number of countries for which estimates of nonunion births were available, a positive association was discerned. Childrearing tasks were delegated more to mothers where high proportions of births were to unpartnered women (data not shown), supporting the hypothesized positive relationship between gender inequity and nonunion births.

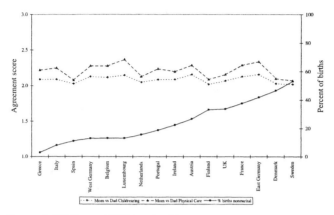

Figure 9.9. Nonmarital Births and Childrearing Norms

Finally, Figure 9.10 speaks to the question of fathering: Does men's willingness or ability to share childrearing foster marital births? The two indicators are a score representing policy support for father's involvement in childrearing and the percentage of child caregivers (14+ hours per week) who are men (Smith, 2001). With notable exceptions, and only at the higher levels of nonmarital childbearing, a positive association appears. Most of the association can be attributed to the higher rates of cohabiting births in countries with higher gender equity scores (data not shown). As with gender ideology, more gender-equitable institutions appear to be associated with *more* rather than less childbearing outside of marriage. This pattern presumably arises from greater gender equity in cohabiting than in marital unions.

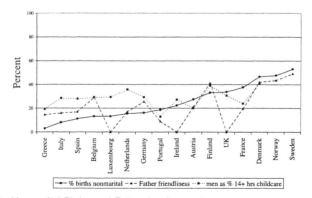

Figure 9.10. Nonmarital Births and Father Involvement

Discussion and Conclusion

Cross-national variation in nonmarital childbearing, in and out of cohabiting unions, is quite remarkable—from Japan, where virtually all children are born in marriage, to Iceland, where well over half are not. The composition of nonmarital births is also quite different, from the Nordic countries where births out of unions are rare and cohabitation is almost as common a context for childbearing as marriage, to the exceptional United States, United Kingdom, and East Germany, where the percentage of births to single women is astonishingly high.

The very broad-brush analyses presented above produced some support for economic explanations of nonmarital childbearing. Where nonmarital childbearing—especially childbearing in cohabitation—is relatively common, women's employment and relative wages appear to be associated with the proportion of nonmarital births. On the other hand, nonmarital childbearing was only weakly associated with state support for maternal employment or specific provisions for maternal leave, both of which could be equally important for marital childbearing. The fact that nonunion births are more common in countries with high income inequality and, in particular, where the income gap between single mothers and other parents is larger, is consistent with economic arguments about the lack of suitable fathers at low ends of the income scale. Whether inequality is driven by or produces higher levels of nonunion childbearing is not clear.

Patterns of association between normative beliefs and nonmarital childbearing suggest an adaptation of norms to behavior rather than the other way around (Lesthaeghe & Moors, 2002). For example, high levels of nonunion childbearing were associated with beliefs that one parent is as good as two, while high levels of childbearing in cohabitation were associated with rejection of marriage as a prerequisite for childbearing and with including cohabiting couples with children in definitions of 'family'. A cultural explanation requires a more general pattern of association in which both forms of nonmarital childbearing would be associated with norms for unconventional family behavior.

Perhaps another kind of cultural norm underlies low fertility in some settings, and high nonmarital fertility in others, i.e., standards for the quality of family life. Presser (2001) invokes an increasing sense of entitlement to leisure time as the source of lowest-low fertility, and class differences in the sense of entitlement as the source of differences in women's willingness to have children alone or in unstable unions. Barber (2001; Barber & Axinn, this volume) showed that preferences for luxury spending decreased the risk of nonmarital (but not marital) childbearing in the United States. Dalla Zuanna (2001) argues that Italian familism leads to delayed home-leaving and the acquisition of very high consumption standards based on the parents' level of living. Raymo and Ono (2003) explore a variant of this hypothesis for Japan where high proportions of young adults live with their parents. They found later marriage for women experiencing the highest "comforts of home"—having independent incomes but not contributing time or money as a condition of living with parents.

Studies of low-income parents in the United States also suggest that marriage is viewed as a luxury while cohabitation or 'visiting' relationships provide the budget alternative. Both mothers and fathers reported that they must achieve a strong financial as well as emotional basis for marriage (Furstenberg, 1996; Gibson, Edin, & McLanahan, 2003; Reed, 2003). Many respondents appeared to have unrealistic expectations about the quality and stability of any marital relationship.

Gender-equitable institutions and ideologies appear to support childbearing in cohabitation rather than in marriage, as hypothesized. Among countries with relatively high levels of nonmarital childbearing, father-friendly policies and men's participation in childcare were *higher* for countries with higher proportions of nonmarital births, most of which occurred in cohabitation. Similar patterns were observed for rejection of the single breadwinner model. These patterns could, of course, arise from the more common practice of gender equity in cohabiting than in marital unions. Supporting the gender equity hypothesis is the positive association between rigid views of maternal responsibility for childrearing and nonunion births.

Part of the problem in finding evidence for economic, cultural, or gender sources of nonmarital childbearing—particularly with regard to childbearing in cohabitation—may be differential selectivity of couples into cohabitation (with consequent differences in union stability) and differences across countries in legal and economic protections for dependent children and partners in cohabiting unions. Heuveline and Timberlake (2003) attempt to classify the institutional location of cohabitation on the basis of its incidence, duration, stability, and relation to childbearing in several low-fertility countries. They conclude that cohabitation is linked to marriage in all countries with moderate or high nonmarital birth ratios—except where the proportion of births to single women is also high (New Zealand, United States). Cohabitation is defined as equivalent to marriage in Sweden, an alternative to marriage in Canada and France, and a stage in the marriage process in Austria, Finland, Latvia, and Slovenia.[4] An implication of their analysis is that in countries with high proportions of births to single women, we should try to explain marital versus nonmarital childbearing; where births to single women are rare, the new demographic behavior to be explained is the proportion of births to couples who are cohabiting versus married.

Another reason for the lack of strong country-level associations with economic, cultural, or gender indicators is that unplanned pregnancies occur. A considerable proportion of births to single or cohabiting women are not planned (e.g., Kravdal, 1997; Musick, 2002; Toulemon 1995). This means that views of sexuality, contraception, and abortion, and access to the latter mediate and may interact with

---

[4] Because Heuveline and colleagues (2003) combine data for the two formerly separate parts of Germany, they cannot detect differences in the meaning of cohabitation related to very different patterns of nonmarital childbearing.

effects of preferences and opportunities on the risk of a nonmarital or nonunion birth. On the other hand, the set of decisions that do or do not result in a nonmarital or nonunion birth can also be viewed as simply the means to a goal that is economically or culturally driven (Willis & Haaga, 1996).

The fact that connections between economic or cultural supports for nonmarital childbearing were stronger among countries with relatively high levels of nonmarital childbearing suggests that different mechanisms produce the initiation of nonconforming family formation behavior than produce its spread throughout the population. Although births out of marriage have always occurred, small numbers of such births do not challenge and can even strengthen economic and cultural sanctions against them (Laslett, Oosterveen, & Smith, 1980). When a substantial minority of births occurs outside marriage, however, institutions and ideologies may be modified to accommodate them.

Finally, the level of analysis presented here may not be adequate for examining economic, cultural, or gender explanations for nonmarital and nonunion childbearing. Economic, cultural, and gender conditions vary considerably within as well as across countries. Even when a policy is the same for all citizens, its effects will depend on individual situations and characteristics. As mentioned above, economists predict greater economic gains to shared earnings for couples with more education (Moffitt, 2000; Oppenheimer, 2000) so that nonmarital and nonunion childbearing occur predominantly among the less well educated (Elwood & Jencks, 2001; Willis, 1999; Willis & Haaga, 1996). Welfare regimes also differ in the extent of their income redistribution and the degree to which policy supports for parents are means tested. As a result, market or policy effects may be discerned only for selected sub-groups (Gauthier & Hatzius, 1997). Kennedy (2003) finds, for example, that educational concentration of nonmarital births is greater in settings with less generous supports for parenthood (Italy, Spain) than in other, more family-friendly settings (East Germany, Norway).

Nonmarital childbearing has become a major component of fertility in many wealthy countries. The difference between "lowest low" fertility and close-to-replacement fertility depends to a great extent on the level of nonmarital childbearing (Coleman, 1999; Morgan & Hagewen, this volume). Furthermore, the implications of nonmarital childbearing—and whether it occurs out of unions or in cohabiting unions—for children's and parents' lives are enormous. For both reasons, connections between partnership and parenthood must remain at the forefront of fertility research.

Acknowledgments

This chapter is a revised version of the paper presented at the Conference on Creating the Next Generation: Social, Economic, and Psychological Processes Underlying Fertility in Developed Countries, The Pennsylvania State University, October 9–10 2003. The research was supported by a Vilas Fellowship from the University of Wisconsin-Madison and Center Grant HD98014 from the National Institute for Child Health and Human Development, National Institutes of Health. I am grateful to James Raymo and Statistics Canada for providing needed data and to Anat Yom-Tov for her able research assistance. Larry Bumpass and Sheela Kennedy provided insightful comments on a pre-conference draft. Of course, what remains is solely my responsibility.

References

Andersson, G. (2002, August 14). Children's experience of family disruption and family formation: Evidence from 16 FFS countries. *Demographic Research, 7,* Article 7. Retrieved from http://www.demographic-research.org/Volumes/Vol7/7/7-7.pdf

Andersson, G., & Philipov, D. (2002, August 2). Life-table representations of family dynamics in Sweden, Hungary, and 14 other FFS countries: A project of descriptions of demographic behavior. *Demographic Research, 7,* Article 4. Retrieved from http://www.demographic-research.org/Volumes/Vol7/4/7-4.pdf

Barber, J. S. (2001). Ideational influences on the transition to parenthood: Attitudes toward childbearing and competing alternatives. *Social Psychology Quarterly, 64,* 101-127.

Barber, J. S., Axinn, W. G., & Thornton, A. (2002). The influence of attitudes on family formation processes. In R. Lesthaeghe (Ed.), *Meaning and choice: Value orientations and life course decisions* (pp. 45–93). The Hague: Netherlands Interdisciplinary Demographic Institute.

Brines, J. (1994). Economic dependency, gender, and the division of labor at home. *American Journal of Sociology, 100,* 652–688.

Cantisani, G., & Dalla Zuanna, G. (1999). The new fertility transition in Europe. Have the gaps been bridged? In UASP-IUSSP (Ed.), *Proceedings of the Third African Population Conference: Vol. 3* (pp. 503–520). Liege, Belgium: IUSSP.

Cherlin, A. J. (2000). Toward a new home socioeconomics of union formation. In L. J. Waite & C. Bachrach (Eds.), *The ties that bind: Perspectives on marriage and cohabitation* (pp. 126–144). New York: Aldine de Gruyter.

Chesnais, J. (1996). Fertility, family, and social policy in contemporary Western Europe. *Population and Development Review, 22,* 729–739.

Chesnais, J. (1998). Below-replacement fertility in the European Union (EU-15): Facts and policies, 1960–1997. *Review of Population and Social Policy, 22,* 729–739.

Coleman, D. A. (1999). Reproduction and survival in an unknown world: What drives today's industrial populations and to what future? *Hofstee Lecture Series 5.* The Hague: Netherlands Interdisciplinary Demographic Institute.

Cooper, J. (1991). Births outside of marriage: Recent trends and associated demographic and social changes. *Population Trends, 63*, 8–18.

Council of Europe. (2000). *Recent demographic developments in Europe*. Strasbourg: Council of Europe Publishing.

Dalla Zuanna, G. (2001, May 8). The banquet of Aeolus: A familistic interpretation of Italy's lowest low fertility. *Demographic Research, 4*, Article 5. Retrieved from http://www.demographic-research.org/Volumes/Vol4/5/4-5.pdf

Demoscope. (2003). Retrieved from http://demoscope.ru/weekly/app/app4013.php

Duvander, A., & Andersson, G. (in press). *Gender equality and fertility in Sweden: An investigation of the impact of the father's use of parental leave on continued childbearing.* Rostock, Germany: Max Planck Institute for Demographic Research.

Ellwood, D. T., & Jencks, C. (2001). *The growing difference in family structure: What do we know? Where do we look for answers?* Cambridge, MA: John F. Kennedy School of Government, Harvard University.

England, P., & Farkas, G. (1986). *Households, employment, and gender.* New York: Aldine de Gruyter.

Furstenberg, F. F., Jr. (1996). The future of marriage. *American Demographics, 18*(6), 34–40.

Gauthier, A., & Hatzius, J. (1997). Family benefits and fertility: An econometric analysis. *Population Studies, 51*, 295–306.

Gibson, C., Edin, K., & McLanahan, S. (2003). *High hopes but even higher expectations: The retreat from marriage among low-income couples* (Working Paper 03-06-FF). Princeton, NJ: Center for Research on Child Wellbeing, Princeton University.

Gornick, J. C., Meyers, M. K., & Ross, K. E. (1997). Supporting the employment of mothers: Policy variation across fourteen welfare states. *Journal of European Social Policy, 7*, 45–70.

Heuveline, P., & Timberlake, J. M. (2003, May). *Cohabitation and family formation across Western nations.* Paper presented at the meetings of the Population Association of America, Minneapolis, MN.

Heuveline, P., Timberlake, J. M., & Furstenburg, F. F., Jr. (2003). Shifting childrearing to single mothers: Results from 17 Western countries. *Population and Development Review, 29*, 47–71.

Hobcraft, J., & Kiernan, K. (1995). Becoming a parent in Europe. In *Evolution or revolution in European population, Proceedings of the European Population Conference* (pp. 27–65). Milan: FrancoAngeli.

Ingelhart, R., et al. (2000). *World values surveys and European values surveys, 1981–1984, 1990–1993, and 1995–1997* (ICPSR version) [Data file]. Ann Arbor, MI: Inter-university Consortium for Political and Social Research.

National Institute of Population and Social Security. (2003). *Latest demographic statistics.* Tokyo: Institute of Population and Social Security.Jensen, A. (2001, June). *Are the roles of men and women being redefined?* Paper presented at the EuroConference on Family and Fertility Change in Modern European Societies: Explorations and Explanations of Recent Developments, Bad Herrenalb, Germany.

Jones, R. K., & Brayfield, A. (1997). Life's greatest joy? European attitudes toward the centrality of children. *Social Forces, 75*, 1239–1270.

Kennedy, S. (2003, August). *Converging patterns of family divergence? A comparative study of education differentials in the delay of marriage and childbearing and in the rise of nonmarital fertility.* Paper presented at the annual meetings of the American Sociological Association, Atlanta, GA.

Kiernan, K. (2001). European perspectives on nonmarital childbearing. In L. Wu & B. Wolfe (Eds.), *Out of wedlock: Causes and consequences of non-marital fertility* (pp. 77–108). New York: Russell Sage Foundation.

Kravdal, Ø. (1997). Wanting a child without a firm commitment to the partner: Interpretations and implications of a common behaviour pattern among Norwegian cohabitants. *European Journal of Population, 13,* 269–298.

Laslett, P., Oosterveen, K., & Smith, R. M. (Eds.). (1980). *Bastardy and its comparative history: Studies in the history of illegitimacy and marital nonconformism in Britain, France, Germany, Sweden, North America, Jamaica and Japan.* Cambridge, MA: Harvard University Press.

Lesthaeghe, R. (1995). The second demographic transition in Western countries: An interpretation. In K. O. Mason & A. Jensen (Eds.), *Gender and family change in industrialized countries* (pp. 17–62). Oxford: Clarendon Press.

Lesthaeghe, R., & Moors, G. (2002). Life course transitions and value orientations: Selection and adaptation. In R. Lesthaeghe (Ed.), *Meaning and choice: Value orientations and life course decisions* (pp. 1–44). The Hague: Netherlands Interdisciplinary Demographic Institute.

Lesthaeghe, R., & Surkyn, J. (1988). Cultural dynamics and economic theories of fertility change. *Population and Development Review, 14,* 1–45.

McDonald, P. (2000a). Gender equity in theories of fertility transition. *Population and Development Review, 26,* 427–439.

McDonald, P. (2000b). Gender equity, social institutions and the future of fertility. *Journal of Population Research, 17,* 1–16.

Moffitt, R. A. (1998). The effect of welfare on marriage and fertility. In R. A. Moffitt (Ed.), *Welfare, the family, and reproductive behavior* (pp. 50–97). Washington, DC: National Academy Press.

Moffitt, R. A. (2000). Female wages, male wages and the economic model of marriage: The basic evidence. In L. J. Waite & C. Bachrach (Eds.), *The ties that bind: Perspectives on marriage and cohabitation* (pp. 302–319). New York: Aldine de Gruyter.

Moors, G. (2002). Reciprocal relations between gender role values and family formation. In R. Lesthaeghe (Ed.), *Meaning and choice: Value orientations and life course decisions* (pp. 217–250). The Hague: Netherlands Interdisciplinary Demographic Institute.

Musick, K. (2002). Planned and unplanned childbearing among unmarried women. *Journal of Marriage and the Family, 64,* 915–929.

Neyer, G. (2003). *Family policies and low fertility in Western Europe.* (Working Paper 2003-021). Rostock, Germany: Max Planck Institute for Demographic Research.

Oláh, L. Sz. (2001). *Gendering family dynamics: The case of Sweden and Hungary.* Stockholm: Stockholm University Demographic Unit.

Oppenheimer, V. K. (2000). The continuing importance of men's economic position in marriage formation. In L. J. Waite & C. Bachrach (Eds.), *The ties that bind: Perspectives on marriage and cohabitation* (pp. 283–302). New York: Aldine de Gruyter.

Pagnini, D. L, & Rindfuss, R. R. (1993). The divorce of marriage and childbearing: Changing attitudes and behavior in the United States. *Population and Development Review, 19,* 331–347.

Pollak, R. A. (2000). Theorizing marriage. In L. J. Waite & C. Bachrach (Eds.), *The ties that bind: Perspectives on marriage and cohabitation* (pp. 111–125). New York: Aldine de Gruyter.

Pollak, R. A., & Watkins, S. C. (1993). Cultural and economic approaches to fertility: Proper marriage or *messaliance? Population and Development Review, 19,* 467–496.

Presser, H. B. (2001). Comment: A gender perspective for understanding low fertility in post-transitional societies. In R. A. Bulatao & J. B. Casterline (Eds.), *Global fertility transition* (pp. 177–183). New York: Population Council.

Preston, S. H. (1987). The decline of fertility in non-European industrialized countries. In *Below-replacement fertility in industrialized societies: Causes, consequences, policies* (pp. 26–47). New York: The Population Council.

Rake, K., & Daly, M. (2002). *Gender, household and individual income in France, Germany, Italy, the Netherlands, Sweden, the USA, and the UK* (Luxembourg Income Study Working Paper No. 332). Syracuse, NY: Maxwell School of Citizenship and Public Affairs, Syracuse University.

Raymo, J. M., & Ono, H. (2003). *Coresidence with parents, the "comforts of home", and the transition to marriage among Japanese women.* Unpublished manuscript, University of Wisconsin-Madison.

Reed, J. M. (2003, August). *How unmarried couples with children think about marriage.* Paper presented at the annual meetings of the American Sociological Association, Atlanta, GA.

Reif, K., & Melich, A. (1997). *Eurobarometer 39.0: European community policies and family life, March-April 1993* (4th ICPSR ed.) [computer file]. Conducted by INRA (Europe), Brussels. Ann Arbor, MI: Inter-University Consortium for Political and Social Research.

Simons, J. (1999). The cultural significance of Western fertility trends in the 1980s. In R. Leete (Ed.), *Dynamics of values in fertility change* (pp. 78–120). Oxford: Oxford University Press.

Smeeding, T. M. (2002). *Globalization, inequality and the rich countries of the G-20: Evidence from the Luxembourg Income Study (LIS)* (Luxembourg Income Study Working Paper No. 320). Syracuse, NY: Maxwell School of Citizenship and Public Affairs, Syracuse University.

Smith, A. J. (2001, June). *Parental leave: Supporting male parenting? A study using longitudinal data of policy variation across the European Union.* Paper presented at the EURESCO Second Demographic Transition in Europe Conference, Bad Herrenalb, Germany.

Smith, H. L., Morgan, S. P., & Koropeckyj-Cox, T. (1996). A decomposition of trends in the nonmarital fertility ratios of blacks and whites in the United States, 1960–1992. *Demography, 33,* 141–151.

Sweeney, M. M. (2002). Two decades of family change: The shifting economic foundations of marriage. *American Sociological Review, 64,* 132–147.

Thomson, E. (2002). Motherhood, fatherhood and family values. In R. Lesthaeghe (Ed.), *Meaning and choice: Value orientations and life course decisions* (pp. 251–271). The Hague: Netherlands Interdisciplinary Demographic Institute.

Toulemon, L. (1995). The place of children in the history of couples. *Population, 7,* 163–186.

United Nations. (2002). *The world's women 2000: Trends and statistics.* Retrieved from http://unstats.un.org/unsd/demographic/ww2000

Van de Kaa, D. J. (2001). Postmodern fertility preferences: From changing value orientation to new behavior. In R. A. Bulatao & J. B. Casterline (Eds.), *Global fertility transition* (pp. 290–331). New York: Population Council.

Willis, R. J. (1999). A theory of out-of-wedlock childbearing. *The Journal of Political Economy 107,* S33–S64.

Willis, R. J., & Haaga, J. G. (1996). Economic approaches to understanding nonmarital fertility. *Population and Development Review, 22*(Suppl.), 67–86.

Zentralarchiv für Empirische Sozialforschung. (1997). *International social survey programme: Family and changing gender roles II* (2nd ed.) [computer file]. Köln: Zentralarchiv für Empirische Sozialforschung.

10
PARTNERSHIP STABILITY AND MARITAL OUTCOMES IN A REPRESENTATIVE UK SAMPLE

Sara Jaffee

University of Pennsylvania

Stable partnerships, of which good marriages are the prototype, promote well-being in children and adults by facilitating economic security, stable employment, and adequate housing and social support (Waite & Gallagher, 2000). Thus, as Thomson notes in her chapter (this volume) on cross-national comparisons of nonmarital childbearing patterns, it matters whether children are born to single mothers, cohabiting couples, or married parents because these various family structures are differentially associated with access to material resources and social capital that promote positive human development. Theoretically, stable partnerships can include long-lasting cohabitations. However, as Thomson notes, although cohabitation is becoming increasingly common in western, developed nations, cohabitations tend to be less stable than marriages, even when cohabiting couples have children.

There is considerable debate about *why* stable partnerships promote well-being, with some research supporting the hypothesis that good marriages *cause* positive outcomes by increasing economic security and fostering social ties (Laub, Nagin, & Sampson, 1998; Waite et al., 2000; Wright, Caspi, Moffitt, & Silva, 2001). The alternative hypothesis is that the association between marriage and economic and psychological well-being is spurious and can be accounted for by the fact that physically and psychologically healthy individuals with good economic prospects are the very individuals who make stable marriages in the first place.

Just as nonmarital childbearing is a heterogeneous phenomenon that includes births to single mothers as well as births to couples who have been cohabiting for many years, marriages also vary widely with respect to the amount of human and social capital that couples bring to the relationship. The analyses presented in this chapter tackle the question of why marriage promotes positive outcomes by examining the stability and correlates of various family structures in two very different groups of women with very different backgrounds: those who first became mothers when they were in their teens and those who first became mothers when they were in their twenties and older. Compared to women who delay childbearing, teen mothers are disproportionately likely to come from poor families, to have a history of conduct problems, and to have lower cognitive abilities and educational attainment (e.g., Coley & Chase-Lansdale, 1998; Fergusson & Woodward, 2000;

151

Jaffee, 2002; Kalil & Kunz, 2002; Maynard, 1997). Moreover, given moderately high levels of assortative mating for personality characteristics (Caspi & Herbener, 1990) and high levels of assortative mating for antisocial behavior and socio-demographic characteristics (Krueger, Moffitt, Caspi, Bleske, & Silva, 1998; Blau & Duncan, 1967), teen mothers are likely to be in relationships with young men like themselves. Thus, teen mothers and their partners are likely to bring low levels of human and social capital to their relationships. If marriage confers benefits only among those who already have good socioeconomic prospects and psychosocial functioning going into the relationship, then, on average, marriage should not benefit teen mothers and they should be indistinguishable from their cohabiting and single counterparts with respect to poor economic, physical, and psychological outcomes. In contrast, if marriage has causal effects on economic, physical, and emotional well-being, then these positive outcomes should accrue to all married couples, regardless of what they bring into a marriage. In support of the latter hypothesis, Kalil and Kunz (2002) find that, regardless of age at first birth, women who were married when they had their first child reported fewer depressive symptoms in later life than did women who were unmarried at the birth of their first child. The analyses presented in this chapter were designed to answer two questions. First, are family structures as stable among women who were teenagers at the birth of their first child compared to women who were at least in their twenties when their first child was born? Second, does marriage confer benefits to all couples, regardless of the human and social capital they bring to that relationship?

Method

The E-Risk Study Sample

Participants are members of the Environmental Risk (E-Risk) Longitudinal Twin Study. Although the study was originally designed to investigate the development of children's problem behaviors, it affords the opportunity to study partnership formations over a five-year period in an epidemiological sample of 1,116 families with young children. The E-Risk sampling frame was two consecutive birth cohorts (1994 and 1995) of twins born in England and Wales (Trouton, Spinath, & Plomin, 2002). The probability sample of 1,116 families was drawn from the total birth cohort using a high-risk stratification sampling frame in which high-risk families were those in which the mother had her first birth when she was 20 years of age or younger. Younger mothers ($n = 562$) ranged in age from 13–20 years when they had their first child (median = 19 years) and older mothers ($n = 554$) ranged in age from 21–42 years when their first child was born (median = 28 years). For 35% of the families, the twins were the mother's first birth. Women's partnership transitions were recorded for a five-year window that extended from 1994–1995 until 1999–2000. A Life History Calendar (LHC) was used to assess various life events over the five-year observation period (e.g., housing and relationship transitions, the birth of a new child, episodes of depression) and in 1999–2000 mothers were questioned about (1) home economics (e.g., household income, benefit receipt), (2) housing conditions (e.g., lack of home ownership, crowded housing), (3) neighborhood conditions (e.g., noisy neighbors, inadequate public transport, neighborhood crime), and (4) relationship quality (e.g., intimacy, social support, partner violence), as well as other topics that are not relevant to the analyses presented in this chapter.

Results

What Is the Stability of Partnership Structures for Older Versus Younger Mothers?

Virtually all mothers who were not single at the start of the observation period were married to or cohabiting with their children's biological father (only three mothers were in a relationship with a man other than the children's biological father). Younger and older mothers differed, however, with respect to partnership status at the start of the observation period. The vast majority of older mothers (83%) compared to just under half (49%) of the younger mothers were married. Compared to the older mothers, a much higher proportion of younger mothers were in cohabiting relationships (14% older mothers vs. 35% younger mothers) or single (3% older mothers vs. 16% younger mothers).

Marriages were relatively stable across the five-year observation period, but they were less stable for younger than for older mothers. For younger and older mothers, transitions out of marriages tended to result in women becoming single rather than cohabiting with a new partner.[1] Ninety-three percent of older mothers who were married at the start of the observation period remained so five years later. An additional 6% became single and the remaining 1% entered a new cohabiting relationship. This pattern of transitions was similar for younger mothers. Eighty-two percent of younger mothers who were married at the start of the observation period were still married five years later, an additional 15% became single, and 2% entered new cohabiting relationships.

Cohabitations were far less stable than marriages for both younger and older mothers, but particularly so for younger mothers. Fifty-four percent of older mothers who were in a cohabiting relationship at the start of the observation period were still in a cohabiting relationship (with the same man) five years later. An additional 21% were newly single, 22% had married, and 3% were in a new cohabiting relationship. In contrast, 41% of younger mothers who were in a cohabiting

---

[1]This finding may be specific to mothers of young twins. In samples of singleton children, mothers tend to re-partner rather than remain single after the break-up of a marriage or a cohabiting relationship.

relationship at the start of the observation period were still in a cohabiting relationship (with the same man) five years later. An additional 25% were newly single, 24% had married, and 10% were in a new cohabiting relationship.

Sixty-three percent of older mothers and 61% of younger mothers who were single at the start of the observation period remained so five years later. The remainder transitioned into marriages or cohabiting relationships, although which one depended on the woman's age at first birth. Specifically, 26% of older mothers got married whereas 11% entered new cohabiting relationships. The pattern was reversed for younger mothers, with only 8% transitioning into marriages and 31% entering cohabiting relationships.

In summary, although marriages were highly stable, they were more stable for older than for younger mothers. Cohabiting relationships were much less stable than marriages, with only half of the older mothers and under half of the younger mothers remaining in the same cohabiting relationship over the five-year observation period. Younger mothers were more likely than older mothers to be in cohabiting relationships at the start of the observation period and were also more likely than older mothers to transition into cohabiting relationships from other partnership statuses.

Are Younger and Older Mothers Equally Advantaged by Marriage?

Analyses of variance (ANOVA) were conducted to test the effect of (1) age-at-first-birth (younger versus older), (2) partnership status at the start of the five-year observation period (single, cohabiting, or married), and (3) the interaction between the two on a range of socio-demographic and relationship outcomes. Socio-demographic outcomes included total pre-tax household income, benefit receipt (excluding sickness benefits), housing problems (e.g., damp or condensation, over-crowding), and neighborhood problems (e.g., noisy neighbors, homes broken into, quality of available schooling). Relationship outcomes included total social support (e.g., from friends and family), and partner violence, relationship intimacy, and quarreling (single mothers reported on relationship quality and conflict only if they had a romantic partner). Table 10.1 presents standardized mean scores for these outcomes as a function of mother's age at first birth and partnership status at the start of the observation period. For virtually all outcomes, younger mothers were significantly more disadvantaged compared to older mothers (Table 10.2).

Table 10.1.

Means (Standard Deviations) in Z-Scores as a Function of Mother's Age at First Birth and Partnership Status

Sociodemographic Outcomes

	Household Income	Benefit Receipt	Housing Problems	Neighborhood Problems
Older Mothers				
Married	.66 (.82)	-.54 (.51)	-.39 (.63)	-.31 (.73)
Cohabiting	-.10 (.89)	-.12 (.90)	-.19 (.73)	-.01 (.87)
Single	-.19 (1.10)	.52 (1.22)	-.27 (.64)	.39 (1.35)
Younger Mothers				
Married	-.26 (.85)	.09 (.97)	.32 (1.19)	.18 (1.13)
Cohabiting	-.62 (.69)	.55 (1.06)	.35 (1.08)	.22 (1.06)
Single	-1.07 (.58)	1.27 (.97)	.46 (1.19)	.46 (1.23)

Relationship Outcomes

	Social Support	Partner Violence	Intimacy Quality	Quarrelling
Older Mothers				
Married	.12 (.91)	-.31 (.59)	.11 (.87)	-.27 (.95)
Cohabiting	-.13 (.93)	.00 (.87)	-.31 (1.13)	.13 (.98)
Single	-.19 (.89)	-.30 (.87)	-.01 (.92)	-.87 (.86)
Younger Mothers				
Married	-.11 (1.08)	.03 (1.08)	-.06 (1.06)	.13 (1.01)
Cohabiting	.00 (1.06)	.45 (1.22)	-.03 (1.04)	.38 (.92)
Single	-.13 (1.10)	.60 (1.37)	-.13 (1.31)	.19 (1.00)

Note: Differences between groups can be interpreted in terms of standard deviation units (d), where d = .3 is considered a small effect size, d = .5 is a moderate effect size, and d = .8 is a large effect size.

Table 10.2.
Test Statistics for Analysis of Variance Main Effects and Interactions for Socio-demographic and Relationship Outcomes

	Household Income	Benefit Receipt	Housing Problems	Neighborhood Problems	Social Support	Intimacy Quality	Partner Violence	Quarreling w/ Partner
Age at 1ˢᵗBirth	60.60***	67.34***	1.56	8.88***	1.03	2.71±	13.32***	12.31***
PartnershipStatus	93.91***	69.69***	51.38***	7.60**	.01	.00	31.08***	29.96***
Age xPartnership	5.08**	.17	.71	2.44±	2.92*	3.56*	2.16	3.66*

***p ≤ .001, **p ≤ .01, *p ≤ .05, ±p ≤ .10

Regardless of the relative disadvantage associated with young age-at-first-birth, marriage did confer benefits to younger and older mothers for some outcomes (Table 10.2). Single, cohabiting, and married mothers differed significantly in their reports of benefit receipt, housing problems, and partner violence. Post-hoc contrast analyses were conducted to detect differences between (1) single versus cohabiting mothers and (2) cohabiting versus married mothers on these outcomes. The effect of partnership status on benefit receipt was linear, such that single mothers received the most benefits and married mothers received the fewest benefits. With respect to housing problems and partner violence, married mothers reported fewer problems than cohabiting mothers, but cohabiting and single mothers did not differ significantly on these outcomes (analyses available upon request).

In cases where there was a significant interaction between age at first birth and partnership status in predicting a given outcome, post-hoc contrast analyses were conducted separately in the older and younger mother groups to determine how the effect of partnership status differed in these groups. These analyses showed that for certain outcomes, the benefits of marriage accrued only to older mothers. For instance, married, older mothers reported significantly fewer neighborhood problems, lower levels of quarrelling with their partners, and higher levels of relationship intimacy and social support compared to their single or cohabiting counterparts. In contrast, single, cohabiting, and married younger mothers could not be distinguished on these outcomes. With respect to household income, mothers in cohabiting relationships reported significantly more income than single mothers, but only in the younger mother group. Married mothers reported higher household incomes compared to cohabiting mothers regardless of mother's age at first birth. Analyses are available upon request.

Whereas partnership status was measured at the start of the observation period, the socio-demographic and relationship outcomes were measured five years later. Because partnership formations were less stable among younger compared to older mothers, it is possible that marriage was not universally associated with positive outcomes for younger mothers because a higher proportion of them dissolved their marriages and began cohabiting with a new partner or became single mothers. Some evidence for this was found when the analyses were conducted on the subset of women who remained in the same partnership formation over the entire five-year observation period ($n = 836$). Although younger married mothers remained indistinguishable from their single and cohabiting counterparts with respect to relationship intimacy and quarrelling, the interaction between age at first birth and partnership status was no longer statistically significant with respect to social support and neighborhood problems. Thus, when the analyses was confined to mothers who remained in stable partnerships (or remained stably single) over the five-year observation period, married mothers, regardless of age at first birth, reported fewer neighborhood problems. Single, cohabiting, and married mothers reported equally high levels of social support (though younger mothers reported less social support than did older mothers).

Conclusion

Thomson suggests that we investigate why nonmarital childbearing rates differ between and within countries because stable partnerships are associated with children's and adults' physical, psychological, and economic well-being and cohabitations tend to be less stable partnerships than marriages. However, not all marriages are created equal, and the analyses presented in this chapter suggest that the qualities some individuals bring to a relationship may prevent them from fully realizing the positive outcomes that have been linked to marriage (Waite & Gallagher, 2000). This was particularly true with respect to the quality of the relationships mothers reported. Even when the analysis focused on women whose relationship status did not change over the five-year observation period, older married mothers reported being in more intimate and less quarrelsome relationships than did their cohabiting and single counterparts, whereas younger married mothers reported equally high levels of relationship problems regardless of partnership status (though, crucially, they reported lower levels of partner violence). In contrast, our data showed that all marriages, regardless of the mother's age at first birth, promoted positive socioeconomic outcomes. Moreover, younger mothers (but not older mothers) who were in cohabiting relationships had significantly more income than did their single counterparts. This finding is important given that cohabitations were relatively more common among younger versus older mothers during the five-year observation period.

One limitation of these analyses is that teen motherhood was presumed to be a marker for a range of individual characteristics that can limit a young couple's financial prospects and promote dysfunctional relationships. Indeed, other work in this sample has shown that, compared to older mothers, the younger mothers engaged in more antisocial behavior and had lower educational attainment and reading ability (Moffitt & E-Risk Study Team, 2002). However, because the study was not designed to investigate women's partnership transitions in conjunction with the transition to parenthood, mothers were first assessed after their children were born. Thus, it is not certain that these maternal characteristics predated their children's births, though it would be difficult to explain how poor reading ability and antisocial behavior could arise as a result of childbirth. These results must be replicated in studies that follow women prospectively through the period when they first form intimate relationships and first make the transition to parenthood.

As Thomson notes, nonmarital childbearing is a heterogeneous phenomenon encompassing births to mothers who do not have partners and births to mothers who are in cohabiting relationships. These analyses suggest that marriage is also a heterogeneous phenomenon. What two individuals bring to a relationship in terms of human and social capital interacts in complex ways to promote physical, psychological, and financial well-being in adults and children.

References

Blau, P. M. & Duncan, O. D. (1967). *The American occupational structure*. New York: Wiley.

Caspi, A. & Herbener, E. S. (1990). Continuity and change: Assortative marriage and the consistency of personality in adulthood. *Journal of Personality and Social Psychology, 58,* 250–258.

Coley, R. L. & Chase-Lansdale, P. L. (1998). Adolescent pregnancy and parenthood: Recent evidence and future directions. *American Psychologist, 53,* 152–166.

Fergusson, D. M. & Woodward, L. J. (2000). Teenage pregnancy and female educational underachievement: A prospective study of a New Zealand birth cohort. *Journal of Marriage and the Family, 62,* 147–161.

Jaffee, S. R. (2002). Pathways to adversity in young adulthood among early childbearers. *Journal of Family Psychology, 16,* 38–49.

Kalil, A. & Kunz, J. (2002). Teenage childbearing, marital status, and depressive symptoms in later life. *Child Development, 73,* 1748–1760.

Krueger, R. F., Moffitt, T. E., Caspi, A., Bleske, A., & Silva, P. A. (1998). Assortative mating for antisocial behavior: Developmental and methodological implications. *Behavior Genetics, 28,* 173–186.

Laub, J. H., Nagin, D. S., & Sampson, R. J. (1998). Trajectories of change in criminal offending: Good marriages and the desistance process. *American Sociological Review, 63,* 225–238.

Maynard, R. A. (1997). *Kids having kids: Economic costs and social consequences of teen pregnancy*. Washington, DC: Urban Institute Press.

Moffitt, T. E. & E-Risk Study Team (2002). Teen-aged mothers in contemporary Britain. *Journal of Child Psychology and Psychiatry and Allied Disciplines, 43,* 727–742.

Trouton, A., Spinath, F. M., & Plomin, R. (2002). Twins Early Development Study (TEDS): A multivariate, longitudinal genetic investigation of language, cognition, and behaviour problems in childhood. *Twin Research, 5,* 444–448.

Waite, L. & Gallagher, M. (2000). *The case for marriage: Why married people are happier, healthier, and better off financially*. New York: Doubleday.

Wright, B. R. E., Caspi, A., Moffitt, T. E., & Silva, P. A. (2001). The effects of social ties on crime vary by criminal propensity: A life-course model of interdependence. *Criminology, 39,* 321–351.

11

THE IMPORTANCE OF GENDER RELATIONS FOR UNDERSTANDING LOW FERTILITY AND SINGLE MOTHERHOOD

Harriet B. Presser
University of Maryland

We have an interesting situation in the United States, shared by some other highly developed countries: At the same time that women are generally postponing parenthood, they are increasingly having and rearing children as single mothers—neither cohabiting nor married. Although some women are postponing motherhood *and* becoming single mothers, most are having late births with a partner *or* earlier births without one.

These simultaneous trends have very different economic implications. I have long argued that late motherhood gives women more time to enhance their human capital—their educational and occupational achievements—and has a positive payoff as well for their children (Presser, 1971, 1973, 1986, 1995). On the other hand, single motherhood—in the absence of a partner—is generally regarded as economically irrational, again for both mothers and children. We all know that two incomes are better than one, and that children tend to do better when they do not live in low-income households.

Consider, then, a critical question raised in Elizabeth Thomson's chapter (this volume), "why would women choose to take on more responsibilities, economically and in the household, by having children without a partner or in a relatively unstable union?" (p. 134). In other words, why are women being so economically irrational?[1] These women are not mostly teenagers; in the United States, about 70% of all nonmarital births are to women aged 20 and over, and most are not cohabiting (National Center for Health Statistics, 2000). As Shelly Lundberg (2001) has noted, these are typically women old enough to fit the economic assumption of rational decision makers who seek to maximize their self-interest—and they are making the choice to raise children alone.

A basic thesis of this chapter is that economic rationality is not the interesting story here, with regard to either late childbearing or single motherhood. Money certainly matters, and it matters more the poorer one is, especially when it comes to the consequences of nonunion childbearing. But in highly industrialized countries,

---

[1] One can ask the same question with regard to divorce, which is initiated mostly by women. Given that women are seriously set back economically as a consequence of divorce, why do they seek it, especially when they have children?

social and psychological factors appear to be primary movers in the decision-making process for childbearing—and rearing—with and without a partner, and for unplanned as well as planned births. [2] I shall argue that a core underlying dynamic is the nature of male-female interaction when such decisions are made. This is what I mean by *gender relations*—a topic that gets minimal attention in demographic literature.

My comments interweave some of the literature and analysis Thomson presents in her thorough chapter with my own views about why there are countries such as the United States. with both low fertility and high noncohabiting and nonmarital childbearing, and why there are variations to this pattern in other countries—some with no association between the two.[3] Being a discussant offers the rare opportunity for a demographer to offer hypotheses without having to follow through with the data analysis!

Economics, Culture, and Gender: Macro Explanations

Let us consider first some of the economic and cultural explanations for low fertility and nonmarital fertility that Thomson reviews. These studies, although important, leave much to be desired from a gender perspective. It is not that the situation of women is ignored. For example, there is considerable theorizing and some research about how improved economic opportunities for women allow for more "economic self sufficiency," and this in turn contributes to higher levels of nonmarital childbearing. It is acknowledged that nonmarital childbearing is concentrated among women with low education and earnings in many countries, yet economic explanations of the reasons for this situation are lacking. Such women are surely not the most economically self-sufficient.

The discussion of cultural explanations also reveals a need for more exploration of gender and social stratification issues in cross-national analyses. Thomson defines culture as the norms and values that constrain choices about marriage and childbearing, and she refers to the existing literature on the growing impact of individualism, secularization, and pragmatism on fertility—but those giving such

---

[2] I regard almost all births to adult women in western countries today as "wanted", even if the pregnancy was not planned at the desired time, given the widespread availability of the pill and other modern contraceptive methods, and the fallback of legal abortion if necessary. Some women are constrained by their values, religious or otherwise, in using such methods, and access to abortion may be restricted in some geographical areas, particularly rural towns; financial considerations are also relevant. But the large majority of American women are able to control their fertility by some means if they strongly desire to do so. It is the degree of wantedness—or unwantedness—that I see as the salient issue for most women when deciding the outcome of an ill-timed pregnancy. We should be studying the *intensity* of wantedness in the context of gender relations.

[3] A recent study by the United Nations Population Division (2002) claims there is currently no association among countries between nonmarital births and overall level of fertility. The important distinction between nonmarital and noncohabiting fertility levels is not made in this report, confounding the issue—because it is the growth in truly single motherhood that is the more remarkable social phenomenon. But in any event, we are a long way from understanding variations among countries.

explanations typically stop there. Thomson demonstrates with her analysis of European and U.S. data that, with few exceptions, there is a clear positive relationship between the percentage with more liberal views about single parenthood and marriage and the country's level of nonmarital or nonunion childbearing. This analysis does not distinguish between men and women or by socioeconomic group (although it is limited to adults under age 40). And, interestingly, she notes from another data source that "normative constraints are not strong in countries with extremely low levels of nonmarital fertility, such as Japan, Italy, and, in particular, Spain. Tolerance for a variety of family forms resulting from nonmarital and nonunion births appears to be widespread" (p. 139). The fact that these countries, despite their tolerant views, have low levels of nonmarital births, even among the poor—and very low fertility levels overall—is intriguing and needs further exploration.

The gender section in Thomson's chapter includes McDonald's (2000) thesis that the greater gender equity in individual-oriented institutions (e.g., labor markets and political systems) as compared to family-oriented institutions (e.g., home life) explains very low fertility levels—but this does not adequately explain nonmarital childbearing, particularly among single mothers. His thesis has policy relevance, as it implies that more social support for families would increase fertility. Would it also increase nonmarital childbearing? (The evidence on the effectiveness of family policies as fertility incentives, particularly in increasing family size and not just earlier timing of births, is mixed; moreover, when effects are evident, they are small; Sleebos, in preparation) And although I am all for family support, this is clearly only part of the picture, and may be more relevant in some contexts than others. Indeed, during a recent visit to the Czech Republic—with a total fertility level in 1999 of only 1.12 (United Nations Population Division, 2002)—I was told that many publicly supported childcare centers were being closed because of lack of demand. Women were not having enough children to fill them all.

Let's return now to the issue of low fertility, which in some countries is concurrent with high levels of nonmarital fertility, and consider what a focus on gender relations in a socially stratified context has to offer.

Gender Relations

Gender relations operate at both the macro and micro levels, but I want to focus here on the importance of studies at the micro level while recognizing that we need good multi-level studies that take context into account. If we are to understand better how men and women—not necessarily cohabiting or married to one another— relate to one another on issues of sex, reproduction, and parenthood, as well as on singlehood, cohabitation, and marriage, we need more research from a couple perspective with data on both partners in order to assess interpersonal dynamics.[4] There has been some excellent research on the resolution of differences in fertility preferences between spouses, and Thomson has been at the forefront of it (Thomson, 1997; Thomson, McDonald, & Bumpass, 1990), but I would like to see the couple perspective extended to other gender-relevant issues that deal with power, commitment, and entitlement, and include weakly coupled people. A major limitation is that such analyses require the collection of new data rather than the secondary analyses we so often heavily rely on, and we are a long way from obtaining comparative international data in this regard.

A few efforts on the theoretical side about changes in gender relations concerning parenthood and commitment are worth noting. An-Magrit Jensen (2001) argues that as the value of children shifts from economic to emotional, as it has in western societies, men and women react differently. Emotionally, women want children more than men, and thus in countries where nonmarital fertility is widely accepted, they can more fully realize their fertility desires without being constrained by men's preferences. In countries that are less tolerant of nonmarital fertility, women's fertility preferences are not met.

This is an interesting hypothesis, but it calls for empirical testing—not just about whether women generally are more committed emotionally to having children than men (which I suspect is true), but whether they are less committed to marriage than men (which I doubt). In any case, it is critically important to know what men and women expect and obtain from each other when they have sex before or in lieu of a committed union, the power dynamics involved, and whether there are differences by socioeconomic status as well as between countries. To emphasize: *We need to invest more in studies of gender relations in noncommitted relationships that may or may not lead to childbearing.*

I recognize that asking people in noncommitted, or even committed, relationships about the gender dynamics of their sexual partnerships is a sensitive topic. But we were diffident about asking unmarried adults about their sexual activity and contraceptive use, we went ahead, and we made significant progress. I think researching both men and women in noncommitted relationships—as a dyad—is possible and necessary for understanding the gender dynamics of low fertility as well as single motherhood.

---

[4] There is some research and theorizing about gender, power, and household decision making (e.g., Bittman et al., 2003), but to my knowledge this literature does not address commitment or reproductive and parenthood decisions among the nonunioned. Moreover, we know little about what people are bargaining for when they enter unions. As Bittman et al. note, "Exchange-bargaining theories say nothing about the content of the conversational sequences through which bargaining occurs" (p. 189).

Parenthood

Another important aspect of gender relations is the extent to which young men and women, in a committed relationship or not, differ in what they expect of themselves and of their partners as mothers and fathers, should they have children. I am unaware of any body of literature that rigorously considers this issue from a couples' perspective. Young women's expectations about fatherhood may affect their decision to have a child on their own—either because women who want children have had difficulty meeting a man who meets their expectations of fatherhood, or men are viewed as not very helpful in childrearing, married or not. This is what Thomson refers to in her chapter as "failure to find the 'dual-shift' man" who both contributes to household finances and does a fair share of housework. And she cites Cherlin (2000), who claims that in order to find such partners women must cohabit, because only then can they assess through direct experience how men will actually behave.

But it is not always women who are doing the assessing and rejecting. Something clearly is changing with regard to what men want of women, and how heavy a commitment to long-term parenthood they are willing to make. With all the good things that are supposed to come from having children in stable partnerships, as reviewed by Thomson, why are so many men seemingly becoming less interested? Is it the growing pervasiveness of sexual access outside of marriage, and a declining interest in children among men, as Jensen proposes? Jones and Brayfield (1997) provide comparative European data indicating that in most European countries women are more likely than men to view children as central to their lives, but the reverse is true for the Netherlands and Great Britain. This finding is not well explained.

Frances Goldscheider and Gayle Kaufman (1996) cogently argue that our lack of knowledge about the level of commitment between men and women is a serious void in our study of fertility. The increasing substitution of cohabitation for marriage, they claim, reflects a lower commitment of women to men, but even more of men to women. They argue that the same is true with regard to the importance of parenthood: declining for both, but more for men. Their article concentrates on the need for more research on men; I would include both men and women, delve into their gender relations, and link this to fertility behavior.

The Timing of Parenthood

If the importance of parenthood is in fact declining for both men and women, this may be related to the fact that it is being postponed by several years in many countries—and particularly by people who are well educated. The influence may be in both directions: Being able to control first births effectively with contraception and legal abortion allows young adults to invest more time in education, and more education encourages the desire to postpone parenthood, as I noted earlier. But whatever the process for individual women, I have argued that the postponement of first births in its own right can significantly affect women's outlook about how they want to lead their lives, by giving them more child-free time in the critically important early adult years. Life is profoundly different if women spend them with or without children. As I wrote thirty years ago, when asked to speculate about what would happen if we had "perfect fertility control":

> [Having such control]…does not suggest that all young women will wish to continue their education and seek careers outside the home. Rather, it means that more women than ever before will have time to consider the options and to experiment with them without unplanned interruptions. Such experimentation will reveal to some women that there are alternative sources of fulfillment aside from motherhood. Others may feel, on the basis of experimentation or experience, that activities outside the home cannot be substitutes for the rewards of motherhood…. Differences in preference may be a function of the kinds of opportunities women are exposed to outside the home. Some jobs are intrinsically more satisfying than others and offer greater opportunities for advancement; moreover, particular jobs may be more appealing to some women than to others. Accordingly, women may regard some jobs as substitutes for the rewards of motherhood, and others, not….
>
> And just as the increase in child-free time permits women to experiment with alternative life styles, so too does the increase in "spouse-free" time. The growing acceptance of premarital and postdivorce sex and the ability to control fertility effectively may lead unmarried couples increasingly to experiment with alternative living arrangements (Presser, 1973, pp. 139, 141).

I think these words written three decades ago (then regarded by some demographers as radical feminism!) are appropriate for understanding why today—with near perfect ability to control fertility—women are having the children they do, when they do, and in what context, partnered or not. Substantial proportions of women in the United States are late childbearers; others find themselves postponing forever because they have not found the right person or the right time, they do not really want children, or the person they think is right does not feel the same way about them. And then there are women who find motherhood much more satisfying than their jobs, and opt to have children, even if they have to do it alone—at least for the time being. They may not realistically appreciate how difficult single motherhood may be, or they may feel that whatever the economic, social, and psychological costs, it is better than waiting for children or for the right man.[5]

---

[5] A longitudinal study of mothers in New York City in the early 1970s (Presser, 1980) revealed that many single mothers wished (soon after the fact) that they had postponed motherhood. It would be revealing to know whether such a view is widespread among women who have recently become single mothers today.

The latter view may be more characteristic of less educated women whose jobs are not very rewarding, or at least not satisfying enough, and who have not had good experiences with men. They may also be women who do not hold strong traditional views about marriage and parenthood. In sum, I do not see such women's decisions to have children on their own as socially irrational.

Entitlement to Time of One's Own

Recently I have been thinking about how having more spouse-free and child-free time, as a consequence of the postponement of marriage and motherhood, gives women a greater sense of entitlement to time of their own, and how this may relate to the timing and number of births they eventually have. The salient tradeoffs are increasingly becoming the desire for children versus the desire for leisure, and the desire for children versus the importance of childrearing with a father/husband present—and less so between employment and homemaking. I have raised the question: "what is the changing nature of gender relations when men feel no less entitled to having time of their own while women increasingly expect men to participate more in childrearing—at least women who have children within marriage?" (Presser, 2001, p. 180).[6] This is an issue concerning both the first birth and the decision to have a second. As I have also said:

> . . . it takes only one child to make us a "parent." We may "desire" two or more children, but the marginal social—as distinct from economic—cost of the second child compared to the first is for many women greater, not less, relative to the benefit. By social cost, I mean specifically the value of personal time: time for child-free leisure activities (e.g., travel, entertainment, reading, being with friends, being able to sleep late). I contend that women, who generally assume day-to-day childrearing responsibilities, are becoming more like men in their sense of entitlement to personal time, and this trend encourages many women to postpone, forever, second births—even in the absence of marital instability. We need to operationalize this sense of entitlement in our research, both for men and women, so that we can better understand the relationship between first birth timing and completed family size—as well as the growing tensions in gender negotiations over time use within families (Presser, 2001, p. 180).

---

[6] There is little research on the gender gap in leisure. A study of pooled data for ten OECD countries covering the period 1980–1999 and based on time diary data showed little gender difference in leisure time, defined as the time left after subtracting paid and unpaid work and self care (Bittman & Wajcman, 2000). But men had more hours of "pure leisure"—that is, leisure that is not in combination with unpaid work and that is less interrupted. Moreover, among parents, not only did mothers spend more time with children than fathers, but a greater share of fathers' time with children was play time. A 1998–1999 U.S. study, also based on time diaries, reported that men have more leisure than women as well as better quality free time, and that children exacerbate the gender gap (Mattingly & Bianchi, 2003). Although this study controls for the effects of education (and other socio-demographic variables), it does not examine educational differences in time use for men and women.

Class differences in this regard need to be explored. I suspect that there are marked educational differences in women's views about the need to have children in order to achieve a meaningful life and in their sense of entitlement to time of their own that play out in marital and fertility behavior, including the decision to have a child unpartnered and with low income. Issues of time entitlement and the desire to be in control of one's time (rather than always "on call" with a young child) relate also to discussions about the role of uncertainty or unexpected contingencies. In other words, the concept of time and the notion of birth timing are intertwined.

To conclude, I am fascinated by the very low fertility levels that some countries are experiencing. They direct us to focus on questions that are highly relevant to gender and the meaning of marriage and parenthood in the 21st century. Further, fear of population decline helps make these societal issues rather than "just" women's issues, lifting them from their low levels on the research agenda. If we want to better understand fertility dynamics, including the concurrent trends of lowering fertility and increasing single motherhood, we need to better understand gender relations at both the macro and micro levels, with concentrated study of men as well as women, and people in non-committed as well as committed sexual relationships.

Acknowledgments

This paper was written while the author was a 2003–04 Fellow at the Center for Advanced Study in the Behavioral Sciences in Stanford, California.

References

Bittman, M., & Wajcman, J. (2000). The rush hour: The character of leisure time and gender equity. *Social Forces, 79*(1), 165–185.

Bittman, M., England, P., Sayer, L., Folbre, N., & Matheson, G. (I2003). When does gender trump money? Bargaining and time in household work. *American Journal of Sociology 109* (1), 186–214.

Cherlin, A. J. (2000). Toward a new home economics of union formation. In L. J. Waite, C. Bachrach, M. Hardin, E. Thomson, & A. Thornton (Eds.), *The ties that bind: Perspectives on marriage and cohabitation.* New York: Aldine de Gruyter.

Goldscheider, F. K., & Kaufman, G. (1996). Fertility and commitment: Bringing men back in. *Population and Development Review, 22*(Suppl.), 87–99.

Jensen, A.-M. (2001). *Are the roles of men and women being redefined?* Paper presented to the EuroConference on Family and Fertility Change in Modern European Societies: Explorations and Explanations of Recent Developments, held in Bad Herranalb, Germany, June 23–28.

Jones, R. K., & Brayfield, A. (1997). Life's greatest joy? European attitudes toward the centrality of children. *Social Forces, 75*(4), 1239–1270.

Lundberg, S. (2001). Nonmarital fertility: Lessons for family economics. In L.L. Wu & B. Wolfe (Eds.), *Out of wedlock: Causes and consequences of nonmarital fertility* (pp. 383–402). New York: Russell Sage Foundation.

Mattingly, M. J., & Bianchi, S. (2003). Gender differences in the quantity and quality of free time: The U.S. experience. *Social Forces, 81*(3), 999–1030.

McDonald, P. (2000). Gender equity in theories of fertility transition. *Population and Development Review, 26*(3), 427–439.

National Center for Health Statistics. (2000). Nonmarital childbearing in the United States, 1940–99. *National Vital Statistics Reports, 48*(16), 1–38.

Presser, H. B. (1971). The timing of the first birth, female roles and black fertility. *Milbank Memorial Fund Quarterly, 49*, 329–361.

Presser, H. B. (1973). Perfect fertility control: Consequences for women and the family. In C. F. Westoff et al. (Eds.), *Toward the end of growth: Population in America* (pp. 133–144). Englewood Cliffs, NJ: Prentice Hall.

Presser, H. B. (1980). Sally's corner: Coping with unmarried motherhood. *Journal of Social Issues, 36*(1), 107–129.

Presser, H. B. (1986). Comment. *Population and Development Review, 12*(Suppl.), 196–200.

Presser, H.B. (2001). Comment: A gender perspective for understanding low fertility in post-transitional societies. *Population and Development Review, 27* (Suppl.), 177–183.

Presser, H. B. (1995). Are the interests of women inherently at odds with the interests of children or the family?: A viewpoint. In K. O. Mason & A. Jensen (Eds.), *Gender and family change in industrialized countries* (pp. 297–319). Oxford: Oxford University Press (Clarendon).

Sleebos, J. (in preparation). *Low fertility rates in OECD countries: Facts and policy responses* (OECD [Organisation for Economic Co-operation and Development] Social, Employment and Migration Working Paper No. 13). Paris: OECD Publications Service.

Thomson, E. (1997). Couple childbearing desires, intentions, and births. *Demography, 34*, 343–354.

Thomson, E., McDonald, E., & Bumpass, L. L. (1990). Fertility desires and fertility: Hers, his, and theirs. *Demography, 27*, 579–588.

United Nations Population Division. (2002, November). *Partnership and reproductive behavior in low-fertility countries* (ESA/P/WP.177). New York: Author.

12

THE CHANGING PARTNERSHIP CONTEXT OF PARENTHOOD: WHERE DO RESEARCHERS GO FROM HERE?

Nancy S. Landale
The Pennsylvania State University

The role of marriage in family formation has changed dramatically in Europe and the United States since the mid-1960s. Perhaps the most fundamental change has been the rise in the average age at marriage, which has occurred concurrently with growing acceptance of sex outside of marriage. As an outgrowth of these trends, both cohabitation and nonmarital childbearing have increased substantially in many countries.

Elizabeth Thomson's chapter (this volume) addresses the changing role of marriage in childbearing in 25 relatively wealthy countries during the 1960–2000 period.[1] Focusing on the nonmarital birth ratio—or the percent of births occurring outside of marriage—Thomson documents both a substantial increase in nonmarital childbearing across most of the countries examined and considerable cross-national variation in the percentage of births to unmarried women in 2000. The data illustrate clearly that in many countries (e.g., Estonia, Iceland, Norway, Sweden) childbearing is now only loosely linked to marriage, while in others (e.g., Greece, Italy, Poland) the connection remains strong. Thomson also considers the role of cohabitation in nonmarital childbearing, noting that "most of the increase in nonmarital fertility is associated with cohabitation" (p. 142). However, as she evaluates explanations for cross-national variation in family patterns, the nonmarital birth ratio is emphasized. In analyses in which cross-national variation in various indicators of economic conditions, cultural beliefs, and gender equity is compared with cross-national variation in the nonmarital birth ratio, little correspondence is found. In discussing potential reasons for the lack of correspondence, Thomson notes that one problem is that analyses of nonmarital births confound births occurring outside of any union with births to cohabiting couples.

---

[1] The study largely focuses on Europe and the United States, although data from Japan, Australia, and New Zealand are included.

Cohabitation and Nonmarital Births

The issue of whether and how to consider cohabitation in studies of fertility patterns is the focus of my comment. Specifically, I begin with the following questions: Given the rise of cohabitation as a setting for childbearing in Europe and the United States, is it useful to look at marital versus nonmarital childbearing without regard to distinctions by cohabitation status? Are patterns of nonmarital childbearing what need to be explained, or is the choice among singlehood, cohabitation, and marriage as contexts for family building a more appropriate focus of inquiry?

As Thomson notes, it is widely documented that the rise in nonmarital childbearing in European countries is driven primarily by the growth of cohabitation (Kiernan, 2001). In Europe, the vast majority of nonmarital births are to cohabiting parents. In the United States, the pattern varies by race/ethnicity, but among Whites the increase in the nonmarital birth ratio is almost completely due to an increase in births within cohabiting unions (Bumpass & Lu, 2000; Wu & Wolfe, 2001). Further, among non-Hispanic Whites (and Hispanics), roughly half of recent nonmarital births occurred within cohabitation (Bumpass & Lu, 2000).

The growing role of cohabitation in nonmarital childbearing has stimulated discontent among family scholars with the use of the simple distinction of marital versus nonmarital births. For example, Heuveline, Timberlake, and Furstenberg (2003) contend that, "The nonmarital fertility ratio (NMFR), perhaps the most closely watched indicator of changes in family structure, has become an increasingly blunt instrument in light of the share of nonmarital fertility accounted for by cohabitation" (p. 47). Similarly, Lundberg (2001) argues that, "...the marriage-sole parent dichotomy is no longer adequate for either theory or empirical analysis" (p. 384). And Bumpass and Lu (2000) conclude their discussion of the role of cohabitation in accounting for the increase in unmarried childbearing in the United States by stating that, "this, again, has implications for how we conceptualize 'families' on the one hand, and 'unmarried childbearing' on the other" (p. 35). As each of these scholars has suggested, it is increasingly problematic to focus on nonmarital fertility without distinguishing among births to women living without a partner, births to cohabiting women, and births to married women. While tracking trends and variation in the nonmarital birth ratio continues to be a useful starting point for understanding changing family formation patterns, researchers clearly need to dig deeper into the nature and meaning of recent changes in the union context of childbearing.

Unfortunately, efforts to incorporate cohabitation into studies of the changing union context of fertility are often thwarted by problems of data availability. Information on cohabitation is increasingly included in family surveys; however, many important data sources do not include cohabitation as a union status and do not collect cohabitation histories alongside marriage histories. In particular, information on the role of cohabitation in long-term trends in nonmarital fertility is scarce. For example, Thomson's chapter provides trend data on *nonmarital* birth ratios for 25 countries for the period between 1960 and 2000. Data with which to construct a comparable table for *nonunion* birth ratios (the proportion of births occurring outside of a marital or cohabiting union) are not available. Thus, while it would be very useful to provide a comprehensive cross-national analysis of the long-term trend in nonunion births (as opposed to nonmarital births), researchers must rely on data that are less complete.

In an effort to document in a more limited fashion the different conclusions one might draw from examining patterns of nonunion fertility versus nonmarital fertility, I use data from the Fertility and Family Surveys conducted in a number of European countries.[2] Figure 12.1a shows the percentage of first births occurring outside of marriage for two birth cohorts of women in 14 European countries. The black bars summarize the experience of women born in the early 1950s and the grey bars refer to women born in the late 1960s. Within each birth cohort, there is considerable cross-national variation in the percentage of first births occurring outside of marriage, with generally low percentages in Southern and Eastern European countries and generally high percentages in Northern and Central European countries. In addition, with only one exception (Greece), the nonmarital birth ratio is higher for the later birth cohort (late 1960s) than for the earlier birth cohort (early 1950s).[3] In Figure 12.1b, I provide comparable information for the percentage of first births occurring outside of any union (that is, to women not living with a cohabiting partner or spouse). It is evident from Figure 1b that nonunion childbearing is relatively rare in the countries examined; moreover, there is little cross-national variation in the percentage of births occurring outside of any union. Within countries, cohort differences in nonunion childbearing also are very small. A comparison of Figures 12.1a and 12.1b illustrates what is now a widely accepted perspective—that the declining role of marriage in childbearing cannot be understood without simultaneous consideration of the growing role of cohabitation in fertility.

---

[2] The Fertility and Family Surveys were developed by the United Nations Economic Commission for Europe (UNECE). Participating countries collected broadly comparable data on reproduction, partnership formation, and educational-occupational careers, including complete histories of cohabitation, marriage, and fertility. Most of the surveys were administered in the early 1990s. The data included in this chapter were drawn from the standard country reports from the participating countries reporting information from comparable birth cohorts.

[3] The differences between the birth cohorts must be interpreted with caution because of differences in their ages at the time they were surveyed: The women in the 1950s cohort were about 40–44 and the women in the 1960s cohort were about 25–29. The information in Figures 12.1a,b and 12.2 reflects all first births that had occurred by the survey date; thus, first births after ages 25–29 are only included in the data for the 1950s birth cohort.

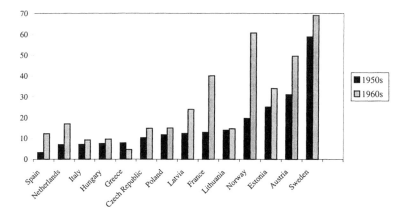

Figure 12.1a. Percent of First Births Occurring Outside of Marriage:
Mothers Born in Early 1950s and Late 1960s

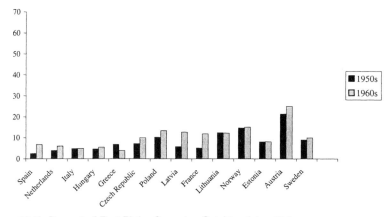

Figure 12.1b. Percent of First Births Occurring Outside of Any Union:
Mothers Born in Early 1950s and Late 1960s

Similarly, variation in the union context of fertility within countries often requires consideration of cohabitation. For example, racial/ethnic variation in the nonmarital birth ratio in the United States is well established. Figure 12.2a shows that in the early 1990s, about 18% of births to non-Hispanic Whites, 32% of births to Hispanics, and 72% of births to non-Hispanic Blacks occurred outside of marriage (Bumpass & Lu, 2000). However, as is shown in Figure 12.2b, a non-trivial share of births to unmarried women were to women who were living with a partner. When births to cohabiting women are re-classified as in-union births, Hispanics are more similar to non-Hispanic Whites and Blacks are more distinct from non-Hispanic Whites. About 9% of births to non-Hispanic White women and 15% of births to Hispanic women occurred outside of any (coresidential) union, compared to 56% of births to non-Hispanic Black women. Thus, to understand racial/ethnic differences in births outside of marriage, it is necessary to understand not only why Blacks are relatively less likely to bear their children in marriage, but also why they are relatively less likely to bear their children in cohabiting unions.

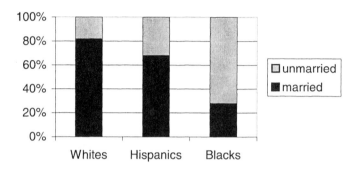

Figure 12.2a. Births by Mother's Marital Status and Race/Ethnicity, United States, 1990-1994

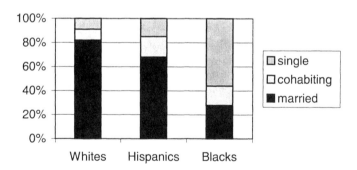

Figure 12.2b. Births by Mother's Union Status and Race/Ethnicity, United States, 1990-1994

Although Figure 12.2b illustrates the important role that cohabitation plays in family formation among Hispanics, cohabitation is especially common as a setting for childbearing in some Hispanic subgroups, such as Puerto Ricans. Among mainland Puerto Ricans, fully 37% of infants born in 1994–1995 had cohabiting parents, compared to 33% with married parents and 30% with parents who lived apart. Importantly, the financial contributions and involvement of the infants' fathers varied significantly by parental union status at the time of birth (Landale & Oropesa, 2001). Figure 12.3a shows the percent of fathers who made financial contributions to the mother and child about two years after the birth, by union status at birth. About 47% of fathers who did not live with the mother at the time of the child's birth made some financial contributions about two years later, compared to 85% of cohabiting fathers and 92% of married fathers. Similarly, cohabiting fathers had higher levels of participation in child care (when the child was roughly two years old) than fathers who lived apart from their infants at birth, but lower levels of participation than married fathers. For example, Figure 12.3b shows the percent of fathers who changed the baby's diaper at least once a week, by union status at birth. About 34% of single fathers, 58% of cohabiting fathers, and 75% of married fathers changed the baby's diaper at least once a week. Similar patters are found for infant feeding and for bathing the baby (Landale & Oropesa, 2001). These patterns make clear that, at least in some racial/ethnic groups, cohabiting fathers are very distinct from single fathers in terms of their level of involvement with the child.

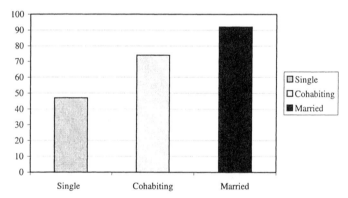

Figure 12.3a. Percent of Fathers Who Contributed Financially by Union Status at Birth, Puerto Ricans

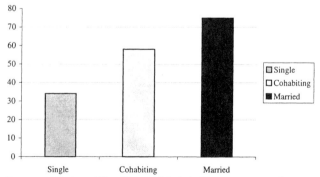

Figure 12.3b. Percent of Fathers Who Changed Baby's Diaper at Least Once a Week by Union Status at Birth, Puerto Ricans

Where Are We Going? Where Should We Go?

Heuveline, Timberlake, and Furstenberg, (2003) summarize the implications of recent changes in union patterns and their connections to fertility well: "It is abundantly clear from this and related research that we cannot continue to cling to the traditional categories for measuring change in marriage and childbearing. Accordingly, surveys must begin to produce data that are amenable to the family living arrangements that currently exist, rather than the forms observed in the past" (p. 66). Consistent with this assessment, one of the major recommendations of the Counting Couples Workshop (convened in 2001 to assess the adequacy of U.S. Federal statistics on marriage, divorce, remarriage, and cohabitation[4]) is that Federal surveys begin to collect more comprehensive information on cohabitation. Two basic recommendations regarding cohabitation were made: (1) basic questions on marital status should be supplemented with additional questions that ask unmarried persons their cohabitation status, and (2) complete marital, cohabitation, and fertility histories should be collected regularly in at least one Federal survey of a nationally representative sample of all adults in the United States. Consistent collection of these types of data in the United States and other countries will eliminate one obstacle to consideration of cohabitation in research on the union context of fertility. In addition, it will allow researchers to build on a growing body of scholarship that carefully describes the role of cohabitation throughout the life course (e.g., Bachrach, 1987; Brien, Lillard, & Waite, 1999; Bumpass & Raley, 1995; Bumpass & Lu, 2000; Graefe & Lichter, 1999; Heuveline, Timberlake, & Furstenberg, 2003; Landale & Forste, 1991; Manning, 2001; Manning & Landale, 1996; Smock, 2000).

At the same time, the analytic issues entailed in addressing the changing union context of fertility extend beyond the availability of data. Of course, the specific issues are numerous and depend on whether the research focuses on trends, variation across settings (e.g., cross-national variation), or individual-level differences in behavior. However, several issues cross-cut studies based on these various analytic strategies. The most fundamental of these issues—one that has been raised repeatedly and underlies much scholarship on cohabitation—pertains to the meaning of cohabitation in the family system. Specifically, should cohabitation be regarded as a form of singlehood, a form of marriage, or unique union type that is distinct from both marriage and singlehood (Rindfuss & VandenHeuvel, 1990)? The answer to this question has implications for how we treat cohabitation in research and, consequently, what we find out about the role of cohabitation in fertility. Thomson implicitly defines cohabitation as a form of singlehood by emphasizing the nonmarital fertility ratio in her analysis, but she recognizes the

---

[4] The Counting Couples Workshop was sponsored by the Data Collection Committee of the Federal Inter-agency Forum on Child and Family Statistics. It was held in December 2001 at the National Institutes of Health campus in Bethesda, Maryland.

dilemma. In discussing the findings of a recent study of cross-national variation in the role of cohabitation in children's lives (Heuveline, Timberlake, & Furstenberg, 2003), she notes that, "An implication of their analysis is that in countries with high proportions of births to single women, we should try to explain marital versus nonmarital childbearing; where births to single women are rare, the new demographic behavior to be explained is the proportion of births to couples who are cohabiting versus married" (pp. 22–23).

This suggestion is useful because it provides a strategy for dealing with the shifting role of cohabitation as the practice becomes better established. At the same time, continuing to conceptualize complex union/fertility patterns in terms of dichotomies sidesteps several key questions: (1) In what ways are the complexities entailed in current patterns of union formation related to fertility decisions and behaviors? (2) In what ways have the relationships between union patterns/ processes and fertility changed over time, and why? and (3) What considerations and motivations underlie the choices that individuals/couples make concerning the union context of childbearing?

Addressing the first two questions requires research that considers complexities, rather than simplifying them. For example, when the requisite data are available, it is desirable to classify births according to whether the mother is single, cohabiting, or married. In addition, there is still much to be learned from careful descriptions of the links between partnership formation and dissolution (including both cohabitation and marriage), shifts in union type (i.e., cohabitation to marriage), and childbearing from a life course perspective. Such an approach is increasingly utilized by family demographers concerned with understanding variation in children's family situations throughout childhood by maternal union status at birth (e.g., Bumpass & Lu, 2000; Graefe & Lichter, 1999; Heuveline, Timberlake, & Furstenberg, 2003; Landale & Hauan, 1992). In addition, further efforts to document the nature and stability of the roles played by parents in various union statuses might shed light on the meaning of cohabitation vis-a-vis marriage (e.g., Landale & Oropesa, 2001).

Studies to date have largely addressed the third question by inferring motivations from research on behaviors. For example, cohabitation is held to be a form of marriage if cohabitors behave more like married persons than like single persons, and a form of singlehood if the opposite holds. However, there is a case to be made for supplementing such an approach with qualitative research on how individuals perceive cohabitation and marriage—and how they make choices about union formation and childbearing within unions of various types. Smock and Manning (2001), for example, argue that qualitative approaches (e.g., in-depth interviews, focus groups, or ethnographic research) are potentially useful for understanding more about issues such as how roles in cohabiting unions are conceptualized and perceived (compared to roles in a dating relationship or a marriage); why cohabitors do or do not have (or expect to have) children, and what options men and women consider when deciding whether or not to cohabit (versus whether or not to remain single or marry). At the same time, marriage itself is changing, and such approaches might be used to better understand whether and in what ways individuals' perceptions of the changing long-term contract represented by marriage contribute to changes in union patterns and the union context of childbearing.

In summary, the family formation process is evolving in ways that require new approaches to understanding the union context of childbearing. As the long-term contract embodied in marriage has changed (Lundberg, 2001), so have the nature and prevalence of cohabitation. Even the meaning of singlehood has changed as nonmarital fertility has become more common. Given these complexities and the increasingly weak relationship between childbearing and legal marriage, research on the union context of fertility must at a minimum distinguish among births to married women, births to cohabiting women, and births to women who do not live without a partner. Recognition of this distinction and consideration of the union histories within which childbearing is embedded will require ongoing efforts to collect more complete data on cohabitation in both the United States and other countries.

References

Bachrach, C. A. (1987). Cohabitation and reproductive behavior in the United States. *Demography, 24*, 623–637.
Brien, M., Lillard, L., & Waite, L. (1999). Interrelated family-building behaviors: Cohabitation, marriage, and nonmarital conception. *Demography, 36*, 535–551.
Bumpass, L., & Lu, H. (2000). Trends in cohabitation and implications for children's family contexts in the United States. *Population Studies, 54*, 29–41.
Bumpass, L. L., & Raley, K. (1995). Redefining single-parent families: Cohabitation and changing family reality. *Demography, 32*, 97–109.
Graefe, D. R., & Lichter, D. T. (1999). Life course transitions of American children: Parental cohabitation, marriage, and single motherhood. *Demography, 36*, 205–217.
Heuveline, P., Timberlake, J. M., & Furstenberg, F. F. (2003). Shifting childrearing to single mothers: Results from 17 western countries. *Population and Development Review, 29*, 47–71.
Kiernan, K. (2001). European perspectives on nonmarital childbearing. In L. L. Wu & B. Wolfe (Eds.), *Out of wedlock: Causes and consequences of nonmarital fertility* (pp. 77–108). New York: Russell Sage Foundation.
Kiernan, K. (2002). Cohabitation in Western Europe: Trends, issues, and implications. In A. Booth & A. C. Crouter (Eds.), *Just living together: Implications of cohabitation on families, children, and social policy* (pp. 3–31). Mahwah, NJ: Lawrence Erlbaum Associates, Inc.
Landale, N. S., & Forste, R. (1991). Patterns of entry into cohabitation and marriage among mainland Puerto Rican women. *Demography, 28*, 587–607.
Landale, N. S., & Hauan, S. M. (1992). The family life course of Puerto Rican children. *Journal of Marriage and the Family, 54*(4), 912–924.

Landale, N. S., & Oropesa, R. S. (2001). Father involvement in the lives of mainland Puerto Rican children: Contributions of nonresident, cohabiting and married fathers. *Social Forces, 79*, 945–968.

Lundberg, S. (2001). Nonmarital fertility: Lessons for family economics. In L. L. Wu & B. Wolfe (Eds.), *Out of wedlock: Causes and consequences of nonmarital fertility* (pp. 383–389). New York: Russell Sage Foundation.

Manning, W. (2001). Childbearing in cohabiting unions: Racial and ethnic differences. *Family Planning Perspectives, 33*, 217–223.

Manning, W., & Landale, N. S. (1996). Racial and ethnic differences in the role of cohabitation in premarital childbearing. *Journal of Marriage and the Family, 58*, 63–77.

Rindfuss, R. R., & VandenHeuvel, A. (1990). Cohabitation: A precursor to marriage or an alternative to being single. *Population and Development Review, 16*, 703–726.

Smock, P. (2000). Cohabitation in the United States: An appraisal of research themes, findings and implications. *Annual Review of Sociology, 26*, 1–20.

Smock, P. J., & Manning, W. D. (2001). *A case for qualitative methods in U.S. family demography: Understanding the meaning of unmarried cohabitation* (Rep. No. 01-483). University of Michigan, Population Studies Center.

Wu, L. L., & Wolfe, B. (Eds.). (2001). *Out of wedlock: Causes and consequences of nonmarital fertility.* New York: Russell Sage Foundation.

IV

What Are the Long-Term Consequences of Current Fertility Trends for Individuals, Families, and Society?

13
CHILDREN AS PRIVATE AND PUBLIC GOODS: IMPLICATIONS OF FERTILITY TRENDS

Christine Bachrach
Rosalind King
National Institute of Child Health and Human Development

Anita Yuan
University of California, Los Angeles

In this paper, we explore three interrelated questions: (1) what resources do children provide for individuals and society; (2) what potential implications do three distinct aspects of current U.S. fertility patterns—small family size, delayed timing, and out-of-union births—have for access to resources typically provided by children; and (3) what potential societal responses could emerge as a result of these implications? We attempt to pull together and develop reasons why fertility is a "good" at both the individual and societal levels and, having reviewed explanations for the weakness of private incentives to invest in children, consider how social mechanisms might respond to address the problem of under-investment through either public or private means. The chapter is speculative, as any discussion of "implications" must be. It also borrows heavily from ideas in the past, but is undoubtedly incomplete in recognizing its debt to the many scholars who have addressed this issue.[1]

What Resources Do Children Provide?

We begin by asking a familiar and basic question: what good are children (and hence fertility) in the first place? Answers to this question derive from a number of different literatures, including research on the "value of children" conducted during the 1970s (Hoffman & Manis, 1979); the work of Schoen and his colleagues (1997), which suggests that children are a means of creating social capital; and that of Friedman, Hector and Kanazawa (1994), which proposes that children provide a means of "uncertainty reduction".

---

[1] Perhaps most notable is the 1986 publication of a volume of papers, *Below Replacement Fertility in Industrialized Societies: Causes, Consequences and Policies*, a *Population and Development Review* supplement. This volume contains many valuable contributions regarding the implications of low fertility.

We focus on three broad sets of "goods" provided by children to their parents. The first, social ties, encompasses all of the resources that children provide for parents through their social connection to them, including intangibles such as love, fun, and companionship; social capital; and instrumental supports such as help around the house and care-taking of the elderly. The second, social reproduction, encompasses the idea that by becoming a parent, adults can occupy and enact a valued social role that confers status as well as reproduce themselves in a new human being who will go on living after the adult has passed away.[2] The third, economic support, refers to financial transfers parents receive from their children.

Answering the question "what good are children?" requires that we consider not only what children provide for parents but also what they provide for the larger society. The production of children generates externalities (Haveman & Wolfe, 1993; White, this volume). Children eventually provide the productive workers and consumers that fuel the economy and fund pay-as-you-go pension systems (Lee, 1994). Furthermore, children are a means of social reproduction at the societal level: they are the next generation who will compose the voters, community leaders, and arbiters of public values in the future. Thus, we also focus on these two additional sets of "goods" provided by children.

Fertility Trends and Parents' Benefits From Children

How do current fertility patterns affect parents' access to resources such as social ties, social reproduction, and economic support? We consider three aspects of current fertility: small family size (including childlessness), delaying timing of births, and nonmarital fertility.

Social Ties

While childlessness may have some cost in access to social ties, variations in number of children within the small-family norm may have relatively little import for parents. Becoming a parent is associated with increased social integration among both men and women (Nomaguchi & Milkie, 2003). However, social ties with non-children provide ample sources of social ties for the childless. Older adults seeking instrumental help will turn to friends and neighbors if preferred sources (spouses, adult children, and other relatives, in that order) are not available (Cantor, 1979; Miner & Uhlenberg, 1997).

---

[2] Laslett and Brenner (1989) define social reproduction as the reproduction of "the activities and attitudes, behaviors and emotions, responsibilities and relationships directly involved in the maintenance of life", both from day to day and across generations.

Among parents, number of children appears to have little effect on access to social resources (Bachrach, 1980 Knodel, Chayovan, & Siriboon, 1992). Studies in North America and Thailand find that non-coresident children adjust the amount of material support they provide in response to how many other siblings are providing similar support (Checkovich & Stern, 2002; Connidis, Rosenthal, & McMullin, 1996; Knodel et al., 1992). Tradeoffs between the number of children and the intensity of parent-child bonds may be another factor: ties to children may be closer in small families, both because of the concentration of obligation in fewer children but also because of more intensive per-child investments of attention and care-giving by parents.

The effect of delayed birth timing on social ties is ambiguous. Delayed timing creates greater age differences across generations, which may reduce access to members of different generations[3] and decrease the chances that parents and children share common interests and values. On the other hand, delayed fertility permits the development of capital (human, social, and financial) prior to the arrival of the next generation. It allows time to form non-familial networks that may reduce dependence on children for social ties. Delayed childbearing may encourage richer networks of "weak ties" (Granovetter, 1973), contrasted with the strong kin networks of early childbearers, which may have less instrumental value.

The implications of nonmarital childbearing are very likely to differ by gender. Since females most often maintain control of the children they bear out-of-wedlock, their access to social ties via children may not be adversely affected by having a nonmarital birth. In the short run, social ties with kin may be intensified while "weaker" ties are reduced (Hofferth, 1984a). Fathers of children born out of wedlock, however, typically have much less contact with their children for much of their adult lives (Cooney & Uhlenberg, 1990). Little research has examined the effects of this on men's broader social integration, but Eggebeen and Knoester (2001) find that men living apart from children have higher levels of social contact than men with children at home. Wachter (1995) predicts that in 2030, non-Black U.S. elderly will have fewer biological kin, but more relationships with step-kin.

Social Reproduction

Smaller family sizes may offer fewer opportunities for social reproduction depending on how narrowly one defines the goal. One implication of the concept of "reproduction" is that parents do not just want to produce any child; they want one who is at least their equal in all respects. If each parent wants a child of the same sex, then a minimum of two children is required; if parents want a doctor or plumber, it may take more. Parents who simply want to continue their family line can make do with one child.

---

[3] Geronimus, Bound and Waidmann (1999) show how earlier childbearing in African American communities increases the probability that children grow up with access not only to healthy parents, but healthy grandparents as well.

Adoption provides an opportunity for social reproduction for biologically childless individuals by allowing them to legally assume the roles and statuses associated with parenthood.[4] Less formal mechanisms are also available. Collins (1991) describes the concept of "othermothers" in the African American community: women other than the biological mother of a child who share mothering responsibilities for that child. These relationships are often associated with recognition and status in family networks and the community.

Social reproduction implies some investment in producing a child with desired characteristics. Both smaller families and delayed childbearing may enhance social reproduction by allowing parents to invest more in their children. This is the classic tradeoff between quantity and quality. Parents with fewer children can make more intensive investments of time and money in rearing each child, presumably increasing the likelihood that children will "turn out well" in the parents' eyes. Parents who have delayed childbearing will presumably have acquired more capital in the interim and be better able to make investments. However, as the literature on the consequences of teen childbearing bears out, demonstrating such timing effects on child outcomes is difficult and controversial (Bachrach, Clogg, & Carter, 1993). The effects probably exist, but may not be as substantively important as previously imagined. Further, parental control over children's education and experience is limited by compulsory school attendance and the pervasive presence of the media. Parents, recognizing that child outcomes are not in their hands alone, may not be motivated to invest (Keyfitz, 1986). Even transmitting the interests and skills it takes to become a parent is harder in a small family, because parents make fewer demands on their children to care for each other.

Delayed fertility may also affect alternative paths to social reproduction. Delayed fertility provides time for developing other activities that provide satisfying avenues of social reproduction (e.g., community volunteer work, involvement with nieces and nephews). Delay also increases the chance that declining fecundity will make social reproduction through childbearing impossible.

Nonmarital fertility is likely to affect social reproduction differentially for men and women, for the reasons discussed previously. To the extent that social reproduction is dependent on not only on genetic relationship but also on social influence, men who are removed from their children's lives face important barriers to social reproduction. To the extent that parenthood outside of marriage is socially de-valued, nonmarital childbearing will be a less effective means of social reproduction than marital childbearing for both mothers and fathers. However, where alternative paths to socially valued roles are blocked, it may be the only viable means of social reproduction.

---

[4] However, uncertainties about child quality associated with adoption—relevant to the desire to have a child "equivalent" to them—deter adoption among many couples (Daly, 1988) and feed the demand for assisted reproductive technologies.

Economic Support

The declining economic value of children is a well-known staple in fertility theory (e.g., Caldwell, 1982; Coleman, 1990). Technological changes attending the industrial revolution increased the need for formal education and made it more difficult for children to contribute to household economies. Pension systems and other supports eliminated the need to rely on children for old-age security. In the mid-1970s, U.S. adults were highly unlikely to say they expected children to support them financially in old age or contribute to the education of their siblings. However, large majorities expected children to contribute money in family emergencies (Hoffman & Manis, 1979). Thus, even though children are not primary mechanisms for providing support, they are seen as a hedge against economic bad times.

Because of the long-standing decline in the economic value of children, number of children has little effect on the economic returns to childbearing. Having many children may increase the odds that at least one child *could* provide economic support, but still have little effect on the likelihood that parents *would* need or benefit from such support. The same argument undermines the importance of quality/quantity tradeoffs. Being able to invest more in each child's human capital may yield little actual economic return for the parent. Childless couples have no chance for economic support from a child, but lose relatively little compared to parents and, as discussed previously, are often able to call on substitutes (nieces and nephews, younger friends, neighbors, etc.) in times of need.[5]

Indeed, childbearing may, at the margin, increase the likelihood of needing to rely on others for economic support. Childless adults, who have not been subject to the motherhood penalty on wages during their working lives, may have greater financial independence. Reduced family size has been linked to long-term economic well-being among women (Hofferth, 1984b), while giving birth between ages 20 to 27 has been linked to lower wages through interruptions in career building (Taniguchi, 1999).

The logic governing the minimal impact of family size should also apply to the timing of children. Although early childbearing may be associated with lower lifetime earnings and a smaller capacity to save for retirement, the causal effect involved may be small. At the same time, early timing may reinforce the strength of kin obligations by bringing the generations closer together and permitting fewer opportunities to develop resources located outside the kin network. Indeed, expectations for financial support are higher among black Americans—among whom early childbearing is more often the norm—than among White Americans (Hoffman & Manis, 1979; Stack, 1974; Tienda & Angel, 1982).

---

[5] Research on living arrangements among older adults reflects a similar pattern. McGarry and Schoen (2000) demonstrate that smaller family size played a small role in the rise of independent living among widows during the period 1940–1990.

Nonmarital childbearing probably also has little effect on the likelihood that children provide economic support, although chances of having access to a child's resources in times of emergency may vary by gender in this case. If such "insurance" is important, then having a child out-of-wedlock may reduce its value because of lower investments in children, but only compared to having a marital birth, often not regarded as a viable alternative.

Fertility Trends and Benefits Children Provide to Society

Economic Growth and Public Transfers

Fertility is clearly relevant to economic growth at the societal level, although debates have raged regarding how it is relevant and how relevant it is. At the extreme, the case is difficult to dispute. If fertility fell to zero globally, humans would extinguish themselves as a species. Sustained zero fertility at the national level would leave immigration as the only means of providing productive workers, a solution rejected by many even with regard to more moderate scenarios (Bermingham, 2001; Meyerson, 2001). Although fertility rates have a direct theoretical link to economic growth, variations in fertility rates within a reasonable range of replacement levels may have little impact (Espenshade, 1978; McNicoll, 1986). This is largely because of the complexity of factors contributing to fluctuations in growth rates and the lead time in which to make adjustments for changing cohort sizes.

However, fertility has well-defined implications for the funding of pay-as-you-go public pension systems and other transfers that support elderly populations (Ricardo-Campbell, 1986). Both the timing and quantity of fertility affect the solvency of pension systems through their effects on the TFR, population growth rates, and dependency ratios. Higher period fertility increases the size of the generations charged with funding the system. If fertility is lower, productivity or tax rates must increase, or benefits must be reduced (Lee, 1994).

If lower fertility is accompanied by higher rates of investment in children, increased human capital, and higher productivity, this could offset the demographic effects of a smaller cohort size. In the United States, there is some evidence that children born since the early 1970s, the beginning of a sustained period of low fertility, do have marginally better proficiency in math, science, and, to a lesser extent, reading, at age 17 than earlier cohorts. Rates of college attendance and completion have also increased. (U.S. Department of Health and Human Services, 2001).[6] Despite massive increases in maternal employment, mothers are spending as much time with children as they did several decades ago (Bianchi, 2000). The

---

[6] See Preston (1984) and Coale (1986) for discussions of the potential negative effects of population aging on investments in education. We have not attempted a thorough analysis of trends in educational financing and educational outcomes here, and are agnostic as to whether meaningful improvements have been made.

implications of these trends for productivity, however, and their ability to offset the economic consequences of population aging seem highly uncertain.

Increased nonmarital childbearing has ambiguous implications for pension system solvency. High school graduation rates are lower among children born to unmarried parents (Haveman, Wolfe, & Pence, 2001). Although this literature is subject to the same uncertainties regarding causal inference as the birth timing literature, it is likely that some causal effect exists, probably owing to lower incomes and greater family stress. However, these effects would have an impact only on the productivity of future workers. Nonmarital childbearing should have a positive effect on the solvency of pension systems and other public transfer systems because it contributes to higher fertility, both through the number and earlier timing of births.

Societal Reproduction

A concern for societal reproduction implies a desire to ensure that the next generation embodies our values and reflects who we are. It implies a concern with the quality of the people who populate the next generation, a desire for people who understand and can enact American culture. Our shared understanding of what this means is at the heart of how we think about low fertility and define acceptable ways for creating the next generation. Number and timing of births are consequential for societal reproduction insofar as they affect the quality of children and the overall composition of the population.

Although greater investments in education may have produced marginal increments in educational outcomes in the low fertility cohorts born since the 1970s, there is little evidence that increased investments have produced better citizens. Voting in presidential elections by persons aged 18–24 declined from 50% in 1972 to 32% in 1996. The percentage of high school seniors reporting that "making a contribution to society" is an extremely important life goal remained almost unchanged between 1976 (18%) and 2000 (20%; U.S. Department of Health and Human Services, 2001).

Lower cohort sizes do change the age distribution of the population. If, as Ryder (1965) points out, the succession of cohorts provides the key to keeping society flexible and innovative, the older age structures implied by low fertility may change the character of society in important ways. Older people tend to be more conservative in their politics, and a predominance of older people implies better health for those parts of the economy that serve elders (Coale, 1986). Further, as birth cohorts shrink, immigration becomes the only way to maintain the size of succeeding generations. Indeed, shrinking cohort sizes may stimulate immigration by making jobs more available. Most Americans would like immigration into the country reduced (Espenshade & Hempstead, 1996), in part because of perceived economic competition but also because immigrants are seen as outsiders.[7,8] Very high levels of immigration would be necessary in order to change the age structure meaningfully (Coale, 1986).

Nonmarital fertility has ambiguous implications for social reproduction. Although children born to unmarried parents are more likely than children born within marriage to have poorer developmental trajectories and adolescent behavior and mental health problems, relatively little research has been done to identify causal relationships and pathways.[9] On the other hand, nonmarital fertility keeps fertility levels higher, reducing the need to draw on immigration to sustain cohort sizes.

Children as Private vs. Public Goods

As Nugent (1985) points out, private investments in children may be of little perceived benefit to individuals but may be essential to the availability of children as a public good and thus to society. The distinction between private and public goods was made by Samuelson (1954). Private goods can be clearly allocated to individuals and their use by one individual precludes use by another. On the other hand, one person's consumption of a public good does not detract from another person's consumption, and the other person cannot be excluded from consuming the good. Examples of public goods include clean air, good government, and safe neighborhoods.

Are children private or public goods? In some regards, children are clearly private goods. A particular child confers adult status only on its parents, not on others. If a child pays for medical care for an elderly parent, those same dollars cannot be used for other purposes. When children are young, it is fairly easy to "allocate" children to parents. Parents have legal rights regarding their children and children are intimately connected with their parents by proximity, time together, and emotional bonds, providing the opportunity for transfers of affection, companionship, stimulation, and fun. When a child is adopted by another family, these private resources are transferred to the new parents and cannot be enjoyed by the biological parent.

---

[7] Predictors of anti-immigration attitudes in the United States include not belonging to a ethnic minority group. and having "isolationist" attitudes that emphasized the U.S.'s difference and separation from other countries (Espenshade & Hampstead, 1996).

[8] The increasing diversity of the U.S. population, itself a consequence of high immigration levels, adds complexity to, and may contribute to redefining, the meaning of societal reproduction within this country.

[9] Two recent studies suggest such causal links may be weak. Korenman, Kaestner, and Joyce (2001) find little evidence of causal effects on outcomes related to infant health and child development once the family background of the mother was controlled, and Haveman et al. (2001) find no evidence of a causal effect on the likelihood of a teen birth, net of the mother's age at childbearing.

On the other hand, children do not stay children for long. The difficulty in classifying children as private vs. public goods lies largely in the fact that children grow up to be productive members of society and they leave their families. Even in childhood, the love that a child provides a parent can also be provided to others without diminishing the parent's consumption and parents' ability to exclude others from their child's circle of affection is limited. The "resources" that children produce expand dramatically as children grow into and through adulthood, and they benefit not only parents, but also friends, spouses, employers, communities, and governments.

A long tradition of research in economics and public finance deals with the problem of public goods (e.g., Barro & Sala-I-Martin, 1992; Hardin, 1968). Whereas individuals have incentives to invest in private goods because the investment is necessary to the enjoyment of the good, public goods can be enjoyed regardless of investment. This problem leads to the requirement that governments and other social entities be concerned with the creation and management of public goods.

In Table 13.1, we summarize our speculations about the impact of fertility patterns on resources provided by children. We argue that if smaller family sizes, delayed childbearing, and nonmarital childbearing have implications for the "goods" provided through fertility, the implications are most pronounced at the extremes (childlessness or fertility substantially below replacement) and are most consequential (and children least "substitutable") with respect to public goods such as the solvency of old age pension systems and societal reproduction. Put simply, low fertility is more of a problem for society than it is for individuals. To the extent that there is a problem, it requires a societal response.

Table 13.1.

Potential Effects of Fertility Patterns on "Goods" Provided by Children

	Small Family Size	Delayed Timing	Nonmarital Births
Goods for Parents			
Social ties	Childlessness has some cost; Number of children (within the small-family norm) may have little import	Negative effect via greater spacing of generations; Allows development of wider networks prior to childbearing	No (or +) effect for women; Negative for men
Social reproduction	At least one child necessary for family continuity; Substitute avenues available	Little impact; Potentially positive via child quality; Can reduce family size but permit effective substitution	Negative for men; Slight negative for women where status socially devalued
Economic support	Small cost to childlessness or few children because support provided through other means; "Stopgap" support may be important	Little impact; May reduce need for support by allowing capital accumulation	Negative effect, if any, confined to men
Goods for Society			
Economic growth	Extremely low population growth rates problematic; moderate variation around replacement probably not consequential		Depends on quality/quantity tradeoffs
Pension systems	Population growth rates directly related to ability to fund pension systems; both reduced numbers and delayed timing of children reduce growth rates; potential for quality/quantity tradeoffs →higher productivity		Depends on quality/quantity tradeoffs
Societal reproduction	Smaller cohort size requires more immigration for "replacement" of generations; Quality/quantity tradeoffs?		Depends on quality/quantity tradeoffs

Society's Response

Many observers of social policy and public opinion have noted that such a response is happening. Concern for the well-being, education, and development of children is on the rise in the United States (Haveman & Wolfe, 1993). Reports on the well-being of America's youth are produced annually (e.g., U.S. Department of Health and Human Services, 2001). Federal spending on children grew 246% between 1960 and 1997 (Clark, King, Spiro, & Steuerle, 2001). From "baby on board" signs to "No Child Left Behind" campaigns, the well-being of children has gained visibility and weight in public discourse.

Cultural values and institutional policies are two important ways that society can respond to changing economic realities and threats to the social fabric. Societal norms and cultures create a landscape of potentialities and constraints that form the context in which reproductive decisions are made (Morgan & King, 2001). Preston (1986) suggests that the value of "responsible parenthood" dominated the social construction of childbearing during the twentieth century, supporting norms for investment in children and the practice of birth control and abortion. Zelizer (1981) suggests a complementary theme in the development of strong norms against viewing children as economic assets and in favor of viewing them as "emotionally priceless" and "sacred". These shifts in values were deeply intertwined with the growth of industry and technology and the professionalization of physicians and other child care experts (Ehrenreich & English, 1978).

Public policies and programs go hand-in-hand with shifts in cultural values. A variety of public policy approaches have been employed to address societal problems caused by fertility patterns. In some cases, countries restrict the ability of couples to control fertility through birth control and abortion, usually on moral grounds. Most common among low-fertility countries are programs that support childbearing directly through financial incentives, and/or through implementing measures that reduce the cost of investing in children, such as subsidized child care, parental leave, health care, and education. The evidence from Europe suggests that these investments have been very costly relative to their effects (Demeny, 1986).

In the United States, most recent policies are aimed at influencing the quality, and not the quantity, of children.[10] Even when policies seek to alter fertility behavior (e.g., efforts to reduce nonmarital childbearing in the 1996 welfare legislation), their stated intent is to improve the circumstances of children, not the number of children born. Similar intent lies behind the many social programs aimed at improving the lot of poor children (Haveman & Wolfe, 1993).

---

[10] Recent efforts to restrict abortion are an exception, but are argued on moral, not demographic or economic, grounds.

Policies and programs to improve child quality can be framed in ways that provide positive support to parents, or in ways that make parents more accountable for their investments in children. The latter has a long history. Early on, compulsory school attendance and child protection laws gave teeth to the cultural values supporting responsible parenthood. Recently, we have seen increasing penalties for child neglect, failure to pay child support, and substance abuse by pregnant women. Haveman and Wolfe (1993, pp. 163–164) characterize public policies to improve child quality as largely directed at poor and unmarried families and grounded in a view of children as "innocent victims" whose upbringing "is seen as violating minimally acceptable standards." With the exception of the Earned Income Tax Credit, federal spending is increasingly channeled away from programs that leave spending on children to the parents' discretion (Clark et al., 2001).[11]

These pressures are reflected in broader cultural trends as well. The imperative to produce higher-quality children is reflected in the labeling of alcoholic beverages to discourage drinking by pregnant women, in consumer markets for educational toys, in the proliferation of programs that teach reading to preschoolers and SAT tests to high-schoolers, and, in general, in increased societal vigilance over children's safety, development, and health.

For the moment, the U.S. has unusually high fertility for an industrialized nation. However, this need not last. As societal norms supporting traditional family structures such as marriage and marital fertility weaken (Thornton & Young-DeMarco, 2001), the strength of cultural values undergirding childbearing may fade as well. If policy and normative pressures to ensure child quality raise the cost of childbearing further, the potential for significantly lower fertility could increase.

Acknowledgments

The authors gratefully acknowledge suggestions from Rebecca Clark and V. Jeffery Evans.

---

[11] The movement for school voucher programs is another recent exception.

References

Bachrach, C. (1980). Childlessness and social isolation among the elderly. *Journal of Marriage and Family, 42*, 627–637.

Bachrach, C., Clogg, C. C., & Carver, K. (1993). Outcomes of early childbearing: Summary of a conference. *Journal of Research on Adolescence, 3*, 337–348.

Barro, R. J.,& Sala-I-Martin, X. (1992). Public finance in models of economic growth. *The Review of Economic Studies, 59*, 645–661.

Bermingham, J. A. (2001). Immigration: Not a solution to problems of population decline and aging. *Population and Environment, 22*, 355–363.

Bianchi, S. (2000). Maternal employment and time with children: Dramatic change or surprising continuity? *Demography, 37*, 401–414.

Caldwell, J. (1982). *Theory of fertility decline*. New York: Academic Press.

Cantor, M. H. (1979). Neighbors and friends: An overlooked resource in the informal support system. *Research on Aging, 1*, 434–463.

Checkovich, T. J., & Stern, S. (2002). Shared caregiving responsibilities of adult siblings with elderly parents. *Journal of Human Resources, 37*, 441–478.

Clark, R. L., King, R. B., Spiro, C., & Steuerle, C. E. (2001). *Federal expenditures on children: 1960–1997* (Assessing the New Federalism Occasional Paper No. 45). Washington, DC: The Urban Institute.

Coale, A. (1986). Demographic effects of below-replacement fertility and their social implications. *Population and Development Review, 12*(Suppl.), 203–216.

Coleman, J. (1990). *Foundations of social theory*. Cambridge: Harvard University Press.

Collins, P. H. (1991). *Black feminist thought: Knowledge, consciousness, and the politics of empowerment*. New York: Routledge.

Connidis, I. A., Rosenthal, C. J., & McMullin, J. A. (1996). The impact of family composition on providing help to older parents – A study of employed adults. *Research on Aging, 18*, 402–429.

Cooney, T. M., & Uhlenberg, P. (1990). The role of divorce in men's relations with their adult children after mid-life. *Journal of Marriage and the Family, 52*, 677–688.

Daly, K. (1988). Reshaped parenthood identity: The transition to adoptive parenthood. *Journal of Contemporary Ethnography, 17*, 40–66.

Davis, K., Bernstam, M. S., &Ricardo-Campbell, R. (1986). Below replacement fertility in industrialized societies: Causes, consequences and policies. *Population and Development Review, 12*(Suppl.).

Demeny, P. (1986). Pronatalist policies in low-fertility countries: Patterns, performance, and prospects. *Population and Development Review, 12*(Suppl.), 335–358.

Eggebeen, D. J., & Knoester, C. (2001). Does fatherhood matter for men? *Journal of Marriage and Family, 63*, 381–393.

Ehrenreich, B., & English, D. (1978). *For her own good: 150 years of the experts' advice to women*. New York: Anchor Books.

Espenshade, T. J. (1978). Zero population growth and the economies of developed nations. *Population and Development Review, 4*, 645–680.

Espenshade, T. J., & Hempstead, K. (1996). Contemporary American attitudes toward U.S. immigration. *International Migration Review, 30*, 535–570.

Friedman, D., Hechter, M., & Kanazawa, S. (1994). A theory of the value of children. *Demography, 31*(3), 375–401.

Geronimus, A. T., Bound, J., & Waidmann, T. A. (1999). Health inequality and population variation in fertility-timing. *Social Science & Medicine, 49*, 1623–1636.

Granovetter, M. S. (1973). The strength of weak ties. *American Journal of Sociology, 78*, 1360–1380.

Hardin, G. (1968). The tragedy of the commons. *Science, 162*, 1243–1248. Haveman, R., & Wolfe, B. (1993). Children's prospects and children's policy. *Journal of Economic Perspectives, 7*, 153–174.

Haveman, R., Wolfe, B., & Pence, K. (2001). Intergenerational effects of nonmarital and early childbearing. In L. Wu & B. Wolfe (Eds.), *Out of wedlock: Causes and consequences of nonmarital fertility* (pp. 287–316). New York: Russell Sage.

Hofferth, S. L. (1984a). Kin networks, race, and family structure. *Journal of Marriage and the Family, 46*, 791–806.

Hofferth, S. L. (1984b). Long-term economic consequences for women of delayed childbearing and reduced family size. *Demography, 21*,141–155.

Hoffman, L. W., & Manis, J. D. (1979). The value of children in the United States: A new approach to the study of fertility. *Journal of Marriage and the Family, 41*, 583–596.

Keyfitz, N. (1986). The family that does not reproduce itself. *Population and Development Review, 12*(Suppl.), 139–154.

Knodel, J., Chayovan, N., & Siriboon, S. (1992). The impact of fertility decline on familial support for the elderly: An illustration from Thailand. *Population and Development Review, 18*, 79–103.

Korenman, S., Kaestner, R., & Joyce, T. J. (2001). Unintended pregnancy and the consequences of nomarital childbearing. In L. Wu & B. Wolfe (Eds.), *Out of wedlock: Causes and consequences of nonmarital fertility* (pp. 259–286). New York: Russell Sage.

Laslett, B., & Brenner, J. (1989). Gender and social reproduction: Historical perspectives. *Annual Review of Sociology, 15*, 381–404.

Lee, R. (1994). The formal demography of population aging, transfers, and the economic life cycle. In L. G. Martin & S. H. Preston (Eds.), *The demography of aging* (pp. 8–49). Washington, DC: National Academies Press.

McGarry, K., & Schoen, R. F., (2000). Social security, economic growth, and the rise in elderly widows' independence in the twentieth century. *Demography, 37*, 221–236.

McNicoll, G. (1986). Economic growth with below-replacement fertility. *Population and Development Review, 12*(Suppl.), 217–238.

Meyerson, F. A. B. (2001). Replacement migration: A questionable tactic for delaying the inevitable effects of fertility transition. *Population and Environment, 22*, 401–409.

Miner, S., & Uhlenberg, P. (1997). Intragenerational proximity and the social role of sibling neighbors after midlife. *Family Relations, 46*, 145–153.

Morgan, S. P., & King, R. B. (2001). Why have children in the 21st century? Biological predisposition, social coercion, rational choice. *European Journal of Population, 17*, 3–20.

Nomaguchi, K. M., & Milkie, M. A. (2003). Costs and rewards of children: The effects of becoming a parent on adults' lives. *Journal of Marriage and the Family, 65*, 356–374.

Nugent, J. B. (1985). The old-age security motive for fertility. *Population and Development Review, 11*, 75–97.

Preston, S. H. (1984). Children and the elderly: Divergent paths for America's dependents. *Demography, 21*, 435–457.

Preston, S. H. (1986). Changing values and falling birth rates. *Population and Development Review, 12*(Suppl.), 176–195.

Ricardo-Campbell, R. (1986). US Social Security under low fertility. *Population and Development Review, 12*(Suppl.), 296–312.

Ryder, N. B. (1965). The cohort as a concept in the study of social change. *American Sociological Review, 30*, 843–861.

Samuelson, P. A. (1954). The pure theory of public expenditure. *The Review of Economics and Statistics, 36*, 387–389.

Schoen, R., Kim, Y. J., Nathanson, C. A., Fields, J., & Astone, N. M. (1997). Why do Americans want children? *Population and Development Review, 23*, 333–358.

Stack, C. B. (1974). *All our kin: Strategies for survival in a black community.* New York: Harper & Row.

Taniguchi, H. (1999). The timing of childbearing and women's wages. *Journal of Marriage and the Family, 61*, 1008–1019.

Thornton, A., & Young-DeMarco, L. (2001). Four decades of trends in attitudes toward family issues in the United States: The 1960s through the 1990s. *Journal of Marriage and the Family, 63*, 1009–1037.

Tienda, M., & Angel, R. (1982). Headship and household composition among blacks, Hispanics, and other whites. *Social Forces, 61*, 508–531.

U.S. Department of Health and Human Services. (2001). *Trends in the well-being of America's children and youth.* Washington, DC: Author.

Wachter, K. (1995). *2030's seniors: Kin and step-kin* (Unpublished Working Paper). Retrieved from http://www.demog.berkeley.edu/~wachter/WorkingPapers/kinpaper.pdf

Zelizer, V. A. (1981). The price and value of children: The case of children's insurance. *American Journal of Sociology, 86*(5), 1036–1056.

14
CREATING THE NEXT GENERATION: WHOSE RESPONSIBILITY?

Lynn White
University of Nebraska

In 1994, Haveman and Wolfe published a monograph titled *Succeeding Generations*. This title cleverly and succinctly captures the issues I wish to raise in the final section of this symposium. Creating the next generation is concerned not just with reproducing numbers through fertility, but reproducing citizens who succeed—citizens who will produce goods and services, pay taxes, stay out of trouble, and contribute to the economic and social welfare of society. To produce succeeding generations, most men and women must be prepared not only to have babies but to parent, and societies must be prepared to provide an adequate level of resources.

As Morgan has demonstrated, producing adequate numbers has not been a problem in the United States and is unlikely to be in the foreseeable future. When we turn from the issue of quantity to issues of quality and equity, however, the picture is not so sanguine. The problem I wish to focus on is the systematic private and public underinvestment in children that reduces the likelihood of achieving gender or racial equity, reduces the likelihood of a succeeding generation, and may reduce women's willingness to undertake the responsibility of creating a new generation.

Private Investments in Children: A Growing Gender Imbalance

Surveys suggest that men are as likely as women to want children (Thornton & Young-DeMarco, 2001). Due to biological and institutional factors, men who want children have to marry and *stay* married. Permanent cohabiting relationships would have similar effects, but the bottom line is that one needs to live with children to parent them. Sending money helps, but a consistent body of research demonstrates that a support check does not have the same broad benefit for children as sharing a household and day-to-day interaction (Amato, 1998).

Research demonstrates that men in union with the mothers of their biological children are modestly more involved with day-to-day childcare than previous generations of fathers (LaRossa, 1988). Unfortunately, high rates of divorce and nonmarital births mean that a shrinking proportion of fathers are sharing households with their children—or any children—and thus many fathers are not available to share responsibility for children.

The net result is captured effectively in King's (1999) analysis of time spent in various parental statuses. Using a life table analysis of data from the National Survey of Families and Households, King shows strong racial and gender disparities in time spent as a custodial biological parent between the ages of 20 and 69. Table 14.1 demonstrates that White women spend 40% more time than White men as custodial biological parents, while African American women spend 50% more than White women and 300% more than African American men. Note that these estimates omit teenage parents, a phenomenon twice as likely among African Americans than Whites and more common among women than men, thus underestimating the actual gender and race gaps. A more striking comparison looks at what percentage of adults ages 30–34 are living with their biological children. Panel B shows that whereas approximately 75% of African American women are living with their biological children, only 20% of African American men are. Among Whites, the comparisons are 65% vs. 35%.

Table 14.1.
Parenting Experience by Gender and Race

Total Person Years as a Custodial Biological Parent

	Men	Women
African American	7	21
White	10	14

Percent Custodial Biological Parent at Ages 30–34		
African American	20	75
White	35	65

Total Person Years as a Custodial Parent (Step or Bio)		
African American	12	23
White	13	16

Source: King. R. B. (1999). Time spent in parenthood status among adults in the United States. *Demography, 36,* 377–385.

These data focus on biological parenting. Does stepparenting make up the difference? Are men parenting, just not their own children? One way to answer this is to expand the number of years spent as a parent to include custodial parenting of any sort, and panel C of Table 1 shows that such a definition reduces the gap somewhat. Among African American men, in particular, the expansion of parenthood to include living with others' children increases their role in parenting. Although gender gaps in parenting remain substantial, the data on stepparenting suggest a more equal gender division of parenting burdens.

Before accepting these data at face value, however, we should question whether stepfathers share the parenting burden with women as fully as biological fathers. In fact, we have a wide range of evidence to suggest that stepfathers are not equivalent to biological fathers in this regard. The parenting style of stepfathers is widely reported to be disengaged (Hetherington & Jodl, 1994). They do not and are not expected to share the emotional responsibility of caring for their partner's children. Recent data from Hofferth and Anderson (2003) indicate that stepfathers reported spending 5 fewer hours a week with their residential children than did married, biological fathers and reported feeling significantly less warm towards them. Stepfathers seldom have legal responsibility for the children and no long-term financial responsibility (Mahoney, 1994). Another large set of evidence suggests that on many child outcome measures, such as high school graduation, school achievement, and teen pregnancy, children from stepfamilies show almost identical disadvantage as children raised in single-parent families (McLanahan & Sandefur, 1994). Together, these bodies of research confirm McLanahan and Sandefur's (1994) conclusion that children living in stepfamilies are often living in single-*parent* families.

The data in King's study do not consider the marital status of parents, and thus cohabiting fathers are counted as living with their biological children. The large minority of nonmarital births that are born into nonmarital cohabiting unions— 40% is the figure Thomson (this volume) uses—is often used to suggest that rates of nonmarital childbearing exaggerate the extent to which fathers are missing from their children's lives at birth. Undoubtedly many of these children do have fathers in their lives, but a substantial amount of evidence suggests that cohabiting fathers do not share childrearing responsibility in the same way as married parents do. Cohabiting biological fathers spend less time with their children and express less warmth toward them than married biological fathers (Hofferth & Anderson, 2003). Cohabiting unions are more fragile and provide less long-term security (Graefe & Lichter, 1999). Further, there is reason to doubt whether cohabiting fathers' incomes are as available to children as are biological fathers' (Bauman, 1999; Heimdal & Houseknect, 2003). The same argument can be made with regard to stepfathers' incomes.

By including cohabiting fathers but excluding stepparents, information provided in Panel A of Table 14.1 both under- and over-estimates men's responsibility for children. Of course, the data also leave aside the marked gender differences that remain in married parents' day-to-day responsibility for childcare (Casper & Bianchi, 2002). On balance, I believe that we can regard Panel A in Table 14.1 as providing the closest approximation of the true gender and race difference in day-to-day parenting responsibility.

This gender imbalance in day-to-day responsibility for raising children is the result of relatively high divorce rates and high nonmarital fertility rates that have reduced men's involvement in childraising. What about the financial burden? As we know, significant policy efforts in the last decade have been aimed at increasing absent fathers' financial contributions to their children. A recent analysis suggests that the major effect of increased enforcement has been to maintain child support at historical levels despite the downward pressure associated with reductions in young men's earning capacity (Case, Lin, & McLanahan, 2003). The most recent data suggest that 52% of never-married mothers and 32% of divorced mothers do not have a child support award. Overall, only 29% of divorced mothers and 14% of never-married mothers receive a full child support amount from their children's fathers (U.S. Bureau of the Census, 2002). This income may well be viewed as a substantial contribution, especially to the lowest income families (Bartfeld & Meyer, 2001), and it may represent a substantial sacrifice on the part of some fathers. The bottom line, however, is that custodial mothers are supporting their children largely on their own incomes while fathers are far more likely to have disposable incomes.

As a result of these residential and marital patterns and these patterns of inter-household transfers, women and children face immediate hardship. Is the public sector ready to take up the slack?

Public Investments in Children

Nearly all societies give lip service to the idea that children are the future and thus deserving of public support. In the United States, however, the amount of money and programmatic effort put behind this rhetoric is both low and uncertain relative to the wealth of our country and the needs of its children. Although any measure of wealth puts the United States at or near the top of other industrialized countries, we rank near the bottom on most indicators of child welfare. Indicators such as infant mortality admit no quibbling about relative or absolute poverty, and on the infant mortality rate we rank close to the bottom. Using the same 14 industrialized countries that Thomson does, the U.S. ranks #1 in GNP and #12 in infant mortality.

Numbers such as these have caused dozens of well-designed comparative studies to conclude that the U.S. has made a low investment in children. To quote from just one, U.S. policies are:

... limited in scale, coverage, and generosity and are usually categorical and narrowly focused. They lack the comprehensiveness and universality of policies in other advanced industrialized countries.... The US has consistently invested a significantly smaller share of GDP in children and their families than almost all other such countries (Kamerman & Kahn, 2001, p. 70).

By definition, every society has children who are below average in income. A critical difference between the United States and other advanced industrialized nations is that they do something about it. A 1995 study by Rainwater and Smeeding demonstrated that U.S. children were 1.6 times more likely to be in poverty than the median of industrialized countries before government transfers. After considering government transfers, U.S. children were 3.2 times more likely to be in poverty. In short, our government does less than others to reduce the effect of child poverty.

Nearly 20 years ago, Sam Preston's presidential address to the Population Association of America (Preston, 1984) pointed to the rapidly falling poverty rates among the elderly juxtaposed to the rising poverty rates among children and asked about the age gap in public investment. In the years since then, the situation has not improved. Despite the development of several effective programs to make life better for poor families, the overall picture is not pretty.

On the positive side, several programs have made an important contribution to poor families. The Earned Income Tax Credit program has been an effective program in transferring income to low-income families, and 90% of the benefit goes to families so poor that they paid no taxes (Kamerman & Kahn, 2001). The Child Health Insurance Program (CHIP) has expanded Medicaid coverage to uninsured youngsters, so that Medicaid now covers 20% of American children. Head Start, which covers 900,000 poor youngsters, is another program that has made measurable improvements in the life chances of poor children (Kamerman & Kahn, 2001).

Despite these effective programs, the overall picture is a child welfare system that is underfunded and under siege. Despite the real strides made by CHIP, 12% of America's children still have no health insurance (www.kkf.org/). CHIP funding for children is a state-administered program with varying levels of federal support, depending on the state's overall economic level. This state support is on the cutting block in nearly every state legislature. The Head Start program has been under fire at the federal level, although it appears that it will maintain its current level of funding. While the federal budget deficit is soaring to pay for the war on Iraq and for tax cuts that seldom reach the poor, the majority of children's programs in the federal budget have experienced cut or frozen budgets (Children's Defense Fund, 2002).

Most telling, however, is the policy change embodied in the 1996 Personal Responsibility and Work Opportunity Reconciliation Act (PRWORA). In addition to reducing the amount of aid to poor families, this reform has withdrawn what modest responsibility the public sector had earlier assumed for children's economic well-being. The welfare reform policies of the 1996 Act clearly privatize responsibility for children's well-being by promoting marriage and work. The introduction to the law begins, "The congress makes these findings (1) Marriage is the foundation of a successful society (2) Marriage is an essential institution of a successful society which promotes the interests of children. . . " (cited in Curren & Abrams, 2000). Subsequent legislation has focused more on promoting marriage than on providing work.

It is widely accepted that children are a public good. That is, many of the benefits of raising productive children go to society as a whole rather than to their parents. As the baby boom generation gets ready to draw on the Social Security system and as rising tax deficits put more burden on the next generation to pay for our programs, public reliance on the next generation becomes increasingly plain. If children are an important public good, the public should bear some of the responsibility of raising children. In the United States, however, public policy continues to regard children as a consumer good with largely private utility. As a result, the family is the only structurally supported option for childraising in the United States. Despite the well-documented fragility of the contemporary family as an institution to provide for children, the public sector is determined to throw the burden for childraising back onto families.

Consequences

The private burden of raising the next generation has been shifted systematically to women and the public sector has been unwilling to take up the slack and has, in some ways, even reduced its claim to responsibility. What are the consequences of these trends?

Consequences for Women

Despite the changes in women's and especially mothers' labor force participation and the incremental improvements in women's wages compared to men's, a woman who wants to have children pretty much has to choose between penury and marriage. Only a very small proportion of women can support a family adequately on their own wages.

A large body of work demonstrates that children depress wages and opportunities for women at the same time as they elevate men's labor force efforts and rewards (Avellar & Smock, 2003). When you add to mothers' depressed wages the fact that mothers are more likely than fathers to have to spread this income among their children, gender differentials in income are striking. In an analysis of divorced mothers and fathers from the same marriages, Bianchi, Subaiya, and Kahn (1999) demonstrated that, considering both wages and interhousehold transfers, the average custodial mother household has nearly 74% of the total income as the non-custodial father's household but only 56% of the income-to-need as the father's household. It is no wonder that 25% of single-mother households were living below the poverty level in 2001 and that custodial mothers were nearly twice as likely to be poor as custodial fathers (Grall, 2003).

Less well documented are gender differentials in stress, worry, and role overload that result from women shouldering larger and larger proportions of the burden of caring for the next generation. A large literature demonstrates that children in the household are associated with greater distress and reduced well-being, especially for women (McLanahan & Adams, 1989; Savalainin, et al., 2000; Umberson & Gove, 1989). Few studies address how differential custody arrangements contribute to overall gender differences in well-being, but a large British study found that the prevalence of depressive episodes was three times higher for single mothers than for mothers in union or women without children (Targosz et al., 2003). The study found that these differentials are explained by differences in social isolation, stress, and material disadvantage.

These data about poverty and distress might lead theorists of rational behavior to conclude that women's taste for children must override their concern about poverty and stress. Such a conclusion overlooks the fact that one third of American children and the majority of children born to unmarried women were unintended pregnancies (Abma et al., 1997). Successful policy efforts have restricted access to abortion and contraception and even to information about birth control and increased cultural confusion by making abstinence a moral absolute in a culture that is increasingly sexualized. The result is that American girls have 10 times higher risk of giving birth than those in Sweden despite having almost identical rates of sexual behavior (Weinberg, Lottes, & Shaver, 1995). Women may be programmed biologically and socially to make more sacrifices for children than are men, but in the long run, only pro-natalist coercion created by limited access to abortion and contraception and confusing cultural messages are going to keep women having children in the face of such high, non-shared costs.

Consequences for Children

U.S. data on children's living arrangements are organized by parents' marital status rather than their biological relationship to the child, so that it is difficult to estimate what percent of children live with both parents. Recent data suggest that 69% of American children (38% of African American children) in 2002 lived in a household with two married adults, down from 77% in 1980 and 88% in 1960 (U.S. Bureau of the Census, 2003). After taking into consideration the proportion of these married couples that include stepparents, it appears that perhaps 60% of American children live with both biological parents.

Children who are not raised by their biological father are at higher risk for nearly every poor outcome studied by social scientists. Most of these differentials are characteristic of systematic disadvantage but are not dramatic (Cherlin, 1999). The exception is income. Children living in single-mother households are 4 to 5 times more likely to be poor than children living with two parents. Rank and Hirschl (1999) have estimated that 80% of children with a single parent will experience a spell in poverty before age 18 compared to 22% of children with two parents. More strikingly, 51% of children with an unmarried parent will spend a spell in deep poverty before age 18 compared to 10% of children with married parents. This means that half of children of unmarried parents have periods where their family income is below $7,500 for a family of three.

Being raised in a single-parent family does not necessarily doom children to poor outcomes, but it systematically raises the risk of sustained and deep poverty, reduced academic attainment, worse health, and greater likelihood of crime and antisocial behavior (Cherlin, 1999). The growing proportion of all children living in single-mother households means that these conditions affect a growing proportion of all U.S. children.

Consequences for Society

Because less is invested by fathers and by society, the next generation is less likely to be a 'succeeding generation.' Because poverty and single-parent families are disproportionately characteristic of minority children, these patterns have grave consequences for the likelihood that we will see the end to racial inequality in the next generation. Indeed, racial inequality is likely to be perpetuated and extended. Gender inequality is likely to be perpetuated as well, as unequal responsibility for children creates a sharply unequal playing field for men and women.

In the long run, these patterns may also have consequences for fertility rates, especially if we give young women access to contraceptive information and devices. Women's growing responsibility for the next generation is largely unappreciated and unsought. When they wise up, the supply line may be endangered (Folbre & Himmelweit, 2000).

Consequences for Men

In creating this session of the symposium, the organizers asked us to consider consequences for men as well as for women, children, and society. What are the consequences for men of this gender shift in childraising responsibilities? On the one hand, it means that they have more disposable income, more leisure time, and fewer worries. It is not all gravy, however. As Alice Rossi noted (1985), it means that they are less embedded in the 'caring institutions," with the result that they are subject, among other things, to higher risk of premature death and less social support in old age. They are also likely to spend part of their adult lives parenting other men's children, in a relationship arguably less satisfying than that of parenting their own children, while their relationships with their noncustodial children wither.

Public Policy Implications

What do we say to policy makers for whom gender and racial equality are not particularly important ends, who can send their own children to private schools rather than underfunded public schools, whose retirement income is not dependent on Social Security, and who can retire at night to gated communities? If they are not moved by the argument that children are public goods, can they be moved by the argument that children in whom too little is invested can become public bads—that the cost of policing and imprisoning them will outweigh the costs of providing decent schools?

This is a centuries-old public policy debate. Now, as in the time of Malthus, one side touts marriage and abstinence as the solution while the other side wants more public support and reduced inequality. Currently, programs aimed at abstinence and marriage are in the ascendency. Covenant Marriage programs, the Promise Keepers movement, the Million Man March, the Marriage Promotion programs associated with welfare reform, and new emphasis on child support programs—a variety of social movements or policy campaigns have been designed to get men to accept responsibility for their families.

It must be recognized, however, that not all of the disadvantage faced by women and children in single-mother households would be eliminated if the father was in the home. In many cases, this is 'reshuffled poverty" (McLanahan & Sandefur, 1994). Many of these unmarried women were poor before they got pregnant; many of these divorced women were poor when they were married and probably before they got married. As McLanahan and associates (2001) document in their study of fragile families, low education and low earning power are serious problems for the men and women who have nonmarital births. Although these young men may eventually earn enough to be able to make a difference in their children's lives, perhaps half have incomes inadequate to lift their young families out of poverty. A small but notable proportion of unmarried fathers have problems with substance abuse or violence that would do more to endanger than to support their families (McLanahan et al., 2001).

Yet, public programs are increasingly designed to privatize the costs of parenting. Alternative programs start with the premise that if society wants not just 2.0 births per woman but 2.0 citizens, society must assume more responsibility for childraising. This means more publicly supported programs for children, with society setting a firm floor for children's well-being below which we will not let them fall. This is exactly what we have done for the elderly.

Why don't we do it for children? Why is there so much public policy concern about prescription drugs for the insured elderly and so little concern about the 12% of children who are uninsured? Without a doubt, dollars spent on children are a better future investment than dollars spent on the elderly. Despite lip service to the idea that children are a public good, we continue to regard children as a private consumer good. By this logic, impoverished children without medical or dental care become a kind of private consumer debt that it would be bad policy to rescue improvident parents from, just as it would be bad policy to rescue them from the debt incurred by buying household electronics they could not afford.

Certainly parents have choices, but societies do, too (Haveman & Wolfe, 1994). In a recent piece, Karen Seccombe (2003) asks why some children do well despite disadvantaged backgrounds. She argues that resiliency is not merely an individual characteristic but also a structural one. Our European neighbors provide examples of dozens of programs and institutions that enhance the likelihood that children will flourish.

In a recent cross-national analysis, Pong and associates (2003) assess the efficacy of such programs in reducing children's disadvantage. They begin by establishing the gap in educational attainment between children of single-parent and two biological-parent families. Although nearly all societies have such a gap, family structure makes more difference in American children's achievement than it does in any other country. The authors introduce controls for various country-level public policies to see which ones are most effective in reducing family structure gaps. Far and away, the most effective policy was a universal child allowance.

Reluctantly, I agree with Danziger and Waldfogel (2000) that consideration of policy alternatives must begin with an awareness of U.S. political climate and what is possible here. Realistically, universal healthcare, much less a universal child allowance, is not likely to be enacted any time soon in the United States.

Policy analysts suggest that policies are more likely to be supported if they offer universal rather than narrow benefits, if they offer in-kind services rather than cash (that might be mis-spent), and if they extend current benefit programs rather than embark on something new. Research on poverty and child development suggests that early childhood is the most important time for intervention. Given these constraints, I think the most realistic policy option is to extend free, full-day public education down to one- year olds. Such a program would reduce the financial and other burdens that nearly all working parents face in arranging childcare for preschoolers, equalize the opportunities for children of all social statuses earlier in their lives when it matters the most, and shift some of the burden for childcare from custodial parents to the state. Obviously, there are real differences in the quality of public education that children receive in poor and wealthy neighborhoods, but my guess is that these differences are substantially smaller than the quality differences between cut-rate and expensive day-care programs.

The other requirement is to extend health insurance coverage to the 12% of America's children who still are uninsured. These are often the children of the working poor, the maids, nurse's assistants, and kitchen workers who have benefited least from recent tax changes. The establishment of the CHIP program suggests that there is broad public support for providing medical care to all children. However, major gaps remain in program provisions and cutbacks seem more likely than program extensions as state legislatures try to balance strained budgets. Without new federal legislation and tax support, the number of uninsured children is more likely to grow than to shrink.

Conclusion

In conclusion, I argue that the way we are creating the next generation reduces the likelihood that we will have a 'succeeding generation.' Changing culture and changing social structures, and in particular labor markets, have made families an increasingly fragile institution that is poorly situated to take growing responsibility for child-raising. Although more mothers are now returning to the labor force immediately after their children are born, they cannot realistically be expected to provide the sole support for their children. Because a well-educated and well-raised future generation is a public good that will benefit all of us, society as a whole needs to accept more responsibility for raising children. Such programs are indeed expensive, but less expensive than creating a new generation that spends more years in prison than in school. Public policy should recognize that, like the airline and the savings and loan industries, we cannot afford to let the next generation fail.

References

Abma, J., Chandra, A., Mosher, W., Peterson, L., & Piccininio, L. (1997). Fertility, family planning, and women's health: New data from the 1995 National Survey of Family Growth. *Vital and Health Statistics, 23*(19).

Amato, P. R. (1998). More than money? Men's contributions to their children's lives. In A. Booth & A. Crouter (Eds.), *Men in families: When do they get involved? What differences does it make* (pp. 241–278). Mahwah, NJ: Lawrence Erlbaum.

Avellar, S., & Smock, P. J. (2003). Has the price of motherhood declined over time? A cross-cohort comparison of the motherhood wage penalty. *Journal of Marriage and the Family, 65,* 597–607.

Bartfeld, J., & Meyer, D. R. (2001). The changing role of child support among never-married mothers. In L. Wu & B. Wolfe (Eds.), *Out of wedlock: Causes and consequences of nonmarital fertility* (pp. 229–255). New York: Russell Sage Foundation.

Bauman, K. J. (1999). Shifting family definitions: The effect of cohabitation and other nonfamily household relationships on measures of poverty. *Demography, 36,* 315–325.

Bianchi, S. M., Subaiya, L., & Kahn, J. R. (1999). The gender gap in the economic well-being of nonresident fathers and custodial mothers. *Demography, 36,* 195–203.

Case, A. C., Lin, I.-F., & McLanahan, S. (2003). Explaining trends in child support: Economic, demographic, and policy effects. *Demography, 40,* 171–189.

Casper, L. M., & Bianchi, S. M. (2002). *Continuity & change in the American family.* Thousand Oaks, CA: Sage.

Cherlin, A. (1999). Going to extremes: Family structure, children's well-being, and social science. *Demography, 36,* 421–428.

Children's Defense Fund. (2002). *The state of children in America's union.* Retrieved September 25, 2003 from www.childrensdefense.org/pdf/minigreenbook.pdf

Curran, L., & Abrams, L. S. (2000). Making men into dads: Fatherhood, the state, and welfare reform. *Gender & Society, 14*, 662–679.

Danziger, S., & Waldfogel, J. (2000). Investing in children: What do we know? What should we do? In S. Danziger & J. Waldfogel (Eds.), *Securing the future: Investing in children from birth to college* (pp. 1–15). New York: Russell Sage Foundation.

Folbre, N., & Himmelweit, S. (2000). Introduction: Children and family policy: A feminist issue. *Feminist Economics, 6*, 1–3.

Graefe, D. R., & Lichter, D. T. (1999). Life course transitions of American children: Parental cohabitation, marriage, and single motherhood. *Demography, 36*, 205–217.

Grall, T. S. (2003). Custodial mothers and fathers and their child support. U.S. Census Bureau, *Current Population Reports*, P60-225. Washington, DC: U.S. Government Printing Office.

Haveman, R., & Wolfe, B. (1994). *Succeeding generations: On the effects of investments in children*. New York: Russell Sage Foundation.

Heimdal, K. R., & Houseknecht, S. K. (2003). Cohabiting and married couples' income organization: Approaches in Sweden and the United States. *Journal of Marriage and the Family, 65*, 525–539.

Hetherington, E. M., & Jodl, K. M. (1994). Stepfamilies as settings for child development. In A. Booth & J. Dunn (Eds.), *Stepfamilies: Who benefit? Who does not?* (pp. 55–80). Hillsdale, NJ: Erlbaum.

Hofferth, S. L., & Anderson, K. G. (2003). Are all dads equal? Biology versus marriage as a basis for paternal investment. *Journal of Marriage and the Family, 65*, 213–232.

Kamerman, S. B., & Kahn, A. J. (2001). Child and family policies in the United States at the opening of the twenty-first century. *Social Policy and Administration, 35*, 69–84.

King, R. B. (1999). Time spent in parenthood status among adults in the United States. *Demography, 36*, 377–385.

LaRossa, R. (1988). The culture and conduct of fatherhood. *Family Relations, 37*, 451–457.

Mahoney, M. M.. (1994). Reformulating the legal definition of the stepparent-child relationship. In A. Booth & J. Dunn (Eds.), *Stepfamilies: Who benefits? Who does not?* (pp. 191–196). Hillsdale, NJ: Erlbaum.

McLanahan, S., & Adams, J. (1989). The effects of children on adults' psychological well-being: 1957–1976. *Social Forces, 68*, 124–146.

McLanahan, S., Garfinkel, I., Reichman, N. E., & Teitler, J. O. (2001). Unwed parents or fragile families? Implications for welfare and child support policy. In L. Wu & B. Wolfe (Eds.), *Out of wedlock: Causes and consequences of nonmarital fertility* (pp. 202–228). New York: Russell Sage Foundation.

McLanahan, S., & Sandefur, G. (1994). *Growing up with a single parent: What hurts, what helps*. Cambridge, MA: Harvard University Press.

Pong, S.-L., Dronkers, J., & Hampden-Thompson, G. (2003). Family policies and children's school achievement in single- versus two-parent families. *Journal of Marriage and the Family, 65*, 681–699.

Preston, S. (1984). Children and the elderly: Divergent paths for America's dependents. *Demography, 24*, 435–457.

Proctor, B. D., & Dalaker, J. (2002). Poverty in the United States. U.S. Census Bureau, Current Population Reports, P60-219. Washington, DC: U.S. Government Printing Office.

Rainwater, L., & Smeeding, T. M. (1995). *Doing poorly: The real income of American children in comparative perspective.* Luxembourg Income Study Working Paper. http://www.lisproject.org/publications/liswps/127.pdf

Rank, M. R., & Hirschl, T. A. (1999). The economic risk of childhood in America: Estimating the probability of poverty across the formative years. *Journal of Marriage and the Family, 61*, 1058–1067.

Rossi, A. (1985). Gender and parenthood. In A. Rossi (Ed.), *Gender and the life course* (pp. 161–191). NY: Aldine.

Savalainen, J., Lahelma, E., Silventionen, K., & Gautheir, A. H. (in press). Parenthood and psychological well-being in Finland: Does public policy make a differences? *Journal of Comparative Family Studies.*

Seccombe, K. (2002). 'Beating the odds' versus 'Changing the odds': Poverty, resilience, and family policy. *Journal of Marriage and the Family, 64*, 384–394.

Targosz, S., Bebbington, P., Lewis, G., Brugha, T., Jenkins, R., Farrell, M., et al. (2003). Lone mothers, social exclusion, and depression. *Psychological Medicine, 33*, 715–723.

Thornton, A., & Young-DeMarco, L. (2001). Four decades of trends in attitudes toward family issues in the United States: The 1960s through the 1990s. *Journal of Marriage and the Family, 63*, 1009–1037.

Umberson, D., & Gove, W. (1989). Parenthood and psychological wellbeing: Theory, measurement, and stage in the family life course. *Journal of Family Issues, 10*, 440–462.

United States Bureau of the Census. (2003). *Historical tables: Children's living arrangements 1960 to the present.* Retrieved from www.census.gov/population/socdemo/hh-fam/tabCH-1.pdf

Weinberg, M. S., Lottes, I. L., & Saver, F. M. (1995). Swedish or American heterosexual college youth: Who is more permissive? *Archives of Sexual Behavior, 24*, 404–437.

15

THE CONCENTRATION OF REPRODUCTION IN LOW-FERTILITY SOCIETIES: THE CASE OF THE UNITED STATES[1]

Daniel T. Lichter
Jillian Wooton
The Ohio State University

Introduction

Will women of childbearing age bear enough children to reproduce themselves and sustain population stability or growth in the long term? This is a question faced by 75% of the world's developed countries today and one that has serious social, political, and economic implications. Most post-transition developed countries, including the United States, have witnessed substantial declines in fertility over the past 40 years. The total fertility rate in many countries, such as Spain (1.2), Japan (1.5), and Germany (1.3), is well below replacement levels. And there are new forecasts that fertility declines have not yet bottomed out; indeed, they may fall below 1.0 in some countries (Golini, 1998). Others take a more cautious approach to alarmist rhetoric (Bongaarts, 2002; Morgan, 2003). Childbearing may be delayed but not forgone and delayed childbearing artificially places downward pressure on period fertility rates. Cohort fertility declines may therefore be much less extreme than period fertility declines (Bongaarts & Feeney, 1998). But such debates are mere distractions from the larger issue: Without significant increases in fertility or a massive infusion of immigrants, the current populations of many developed countries are not sustainable in the long term.

As noted in this volume by Morgan and Hagewen, the total fertility rate in the United States is extraordinarily high in comparison to that in other developed nations. In 2000, the total fertility rate moved above replacement levels (2.13) for the first time in 30 years (Martin et al., 2002). Coupled with a heavy influx of immigrants, a high fertility rate (even among native-born populations) ensures that the United States will sustain its current population size. In other developed countries, below-replacement fertility is associated with a host of potential problems: an older, less innovative population, economic stagnation and decline, and fewer educational and labor market opportunities for children and young adults, as their political interests are swamped by those of a burgeoning elderly population (Stark

[1] The authors acknowledge the helpful comments of Elizabeth Cooksey and Zhenchao Qian, and the useful discussion of participants at the Penn State Annual Family Symposium on "Creating the Next Generation," Pennsylvania State University, October 9–10, 2003.

& Kohler, 2002). The United States also faces challenges in the 21st century. Here the question is not whether population size is sustainable, but whether and how population composition (i.e., the characteristics of the population) will change over the next few decades. In fact, the answer will be partially determined by immigration policy (Espenshade, 2001), but it also depends on fertility differentials, including the changing concentration of reproduction among particular population subgroups.

Objectives

In this chapter, we examine recent changes in the *concentration of reproduction* in the United States, i.e., whether some population segments are shouldering a disproportionate burden of childbearing and childrearing. We have two central objectives. First, we measure the concentration of reproduction for five-year birth cohorts of women between 1896–1900 and 1951–1955. The 1951–1955 cohort was 45–49 in 2000 (and, presumably, finished with their childbearing). Second, we examine the changing share of births to particular population subgroups over the recent time period (e.g., 1970–2000). We focus primarily on the share of births contributed by historically disadvantaged groups: minorities, teenagers and young adults, single women, and the low educated. The reason is straightforward. If births are increasingly concentrated among disadvantaged groups, then in the absence of declines in inequality, America's next generation faces greater risk of economic hardship. The societal implications of low fertility depend on the changing concentration of reproduction, i.e., on which population segments actually bear and rear most of the children. A guiding hypothesis here is that inequality in reproduction today may be associated with many other dimensions of societal inequality tomorrow.

Unequal Childbearing in America

The Concentration of Reproduction

Has the burden of childbearing in America become more unequal over time? Surprisingly few studies have addressed this question. One exception is Vaupel and Goodwin (1987). They showed that, for the cohort of women born in 1930, 36% of the women (i.e., those bearing 4 or more children) accounted for 63% of all children born to this cohort. Moreover, 27% of these women accounted for one half of the offspring. Coined as women's "have-half," this measure summarizes the extent of unequal childbearing. Pullum, Tedrow, and Herting (1989) showed that the variance (as a measure of dispersion) in cohort parity declined significantly from the 1873 cohort to the 1933 cohort (10.2 to 3.7), a fact that suggests greater inter-individual equality in reproduction and a decline in the percent of women with very high fertility.[2] Such measures are not unrelated to those used to track the changing concentration of wealth or income over time. Indeed, the Gini index, and the Lorenz curve from which it is estimated, provide useful measures of inequality, including, as we argue here, inequality in the distribution of human reproduction.

A simple way to show the concentration of reproduction is to order women by parity, from lowest (0) to highest (7 or more), and then calculate the share of all births that can be attributed to women of a particular parity. The cumulative percentage of women by parity, plotted against the cumulative percentage of women's offspring, reveals the Lorenz curve. Equality is indicated by a Lorenz curve that is pitched at a (straight) 45° angle; this only happens if all women in the birth cohort have the same number of children. Deviations from the 45° line indicate inequality, that some women produce disproportionately large shares of children.

Using historical vital statistics data (National Center for Health Statistics, 2003), Figure 15.1 shows the concentration of reproduction curve for three birth cohorts: 1906–1910 (new century era), 1936–1940 (depression era), and 1951–1955 (baby boom era). These graphs suggest that the concentration of reproduction was highest at the turn of the 20th century and least concentrated for women born in the depression era. For the 1906–1910 cohort, roughly 20% of all women produced 50% of all babies. For the depression-born cohort, 28% of women produced 50% of the births (a pattern very similar to Vaupel and Goodwin [1987]). The most recent birth cohort reveals a slight shift toward greater concentration, although inequality in the burden of childbearing is not nearly as large as it was for the 1906–1910 cohort.

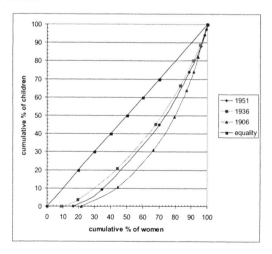

Figure 15.1 Concentration of Reproduction Curve for Three Birth Cohorts

---

[2] A large share (.56 of the .85) of the increase in mean parity between the 1908 and 1933 cohorts was due to declines in the share of women at parities 0 and 1.

To summarize inequality of childbearing, the Gini index measures the area between the Lorenz curve and the 45° line (that defines equality) as a ratio to the total area below the 45° line. The Gini index ranges hypothetically between 0 (complete equality) and 1 (complete inequality).[3] In Figure 15.2, we provide the Gini index for 5-year birth cohorts beginning in 1896–1900 and ending in 1951–1955. The results suggest quite high concentrations of reproduction at the turn of the 20th century, subsequent monotonic declines through the depression-born cohorts, and increases thereafter.

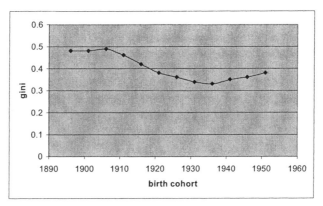

Figure 15.2 Gini Index for 5-Year Birth Cohorts

This cohort measure of fertility concentration closely tracks both period and cohort fertility rates surprisingly well, but in different directions. That is, reproduction is more highly concentrated when period fertility rates are high (when cohort size is large) and less highly concentrated when fertility is low (and cohort sizes are smaller) (data not shown). But a negative statistical association (r = -.52) between the concentration index and cohort fertility is evident in Figure 15.3, which plots the Gini indices against cohort fertility rates.[4] This means that the declines in fertility in the United States are associated with *more* inequality in human reproduction, as smaller shares of women produce larger shares of America's children.[5]

---

[3] The Gini index can be calculated as (Brown, 1994):

$$Gini = 1 - \sum_{i=0}^{k=1} (Y_{i+1} + Y_i)(X_{i+1} - X_i)$$

Where,

Y = Cumulative proportion of children
X = Cumulative proportion of women

[4] We do not want to overstate these results. We have only a small number of data points. Arbitrarily moving three or four of them could change this statistical relationship.

[5] The implication is that the negative relationship between the cohort fertility rate and the Gini index can be explained (at least in part) by the strong positive relationship between cohort childlessness and the Gini index. Indeed, additional analysis shows that the percent childless is strongly associated with the Gini (r = .94).

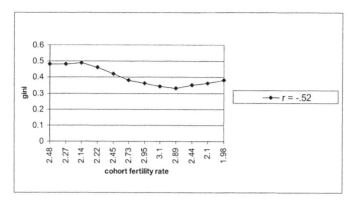

Figure 15.3 Gini Index Against Cohort Fertility Rates

Changes in the Shares of Births to Disadvantaged Groups

A limitation of any cohort measure of fertility, including our measure of within-cohort inequality in childbearing, is that it reveals little if anything about patterns among recent cohorts of women (i.e., 1956 and later), that is, those who have not yet completed childbearing. We have provided preliminary evidence that a declining share of America's women is shouldering a disproportionate burden (or experiencing a disproportionate share of the joy, depending upon your point of view) in reproducing the next generation. Any social and economic implications of this fact, however, rest heavily on whether some population groups, especially historically disadvantaged groups, are over-represented among the nation's newborns. As an illustration, Eggebeen and Lichter (1991) showed that about 25% of the 1980s rise in child poverty was due to growing fertility differentials between poor and nonpoor women. Changing poor-nonpoor fertility differentials placed upward pressure on child poverty rates.

For our purposes, we examine changes between 1970 and 2000 in the share of all newborns who are born to specific population groups: minorities, teenagers and young adults, unmarried women, and the least educated. Previous studies of children's development suggest that the children of these "at risk" groups are less likely to navigate childhood successfully (Lichter, 1997; McLanahan & Sandefur, 1995). This raises an obvious question: Is demographic momentum building for greater social and economic inequality, as larger proportions of "at risk" children today mature, often unsuccessfully, into adulthood?[6]

---

[6] From a demographic accounting framework, any changes in the proportion of children from disadvantaged groups reflect: (1) changes in the percentage of disadvantaged groups; (2) changes in fertility differentials between disadvantaged and advantaged groups; and (3) changes in the level of disadvantage among disadvantaged groups.

We begin by presenting the changing percentages of all births to different racial and ethnic groups in Table 15.1. Fertility differentials have both declined and converged across racial groups, but they still exist (Morgan et al., 1999). In 1994, for example, the total fertility rate was 2.3 among non-Hispanic Blacks and 3.0 among Hispanics. The fertility among non-Hispanic whites was below replacement level (1.8 births per woman). Despite large racial differentials in fertility, changes in the share of births across racial groups have been modest over the past 30 years (Table 1). For example, Whites contributed 83% of America's births in 1970 and 79% in 2000. For Hispanics, however, their share of all births increased by 136% over this time period. The relative stability in the share of all White births is due to growth in births to (largely White) Hispanics. In the absence of changes in racial or ethnic group equality among children, the future suggests more inequality, as growing shares of disadvantaged minorities (except African Americans) enter adulthood over the next 20 years.

Table 15.1.
Percent of All Births, by Race and Year

			Race			
Year	White	Black	Indian	Asian	Total	Hispanic
1970	83.3	15.1	0.6	—	—	—
1980	81.3	15.7	0.8	2.1	100	8.5
1990	79.1	16.5	0.9	3.4	100	14.3
2000	78.7	15.3	1.0	4.9	100	20.1

Studies show that the developmental trajectories of children of teen mothers suffer in comparison to those of children born to older mothers (see Martin, 2003 for an excellent discussion). But delayed childbearing is a signature feature of recent fertility trends in the United States (Martin, 2000; Rindfuss, Morgan, & Swicegood, 1996). How this translates into changing shares of births to teenagers is unclear. Table 15.2 provides several lessons in this regard. First and foremost, the share of all births to teenagers declined by about one third between 1970 and 2000, from 17.6% to 11.8%. From a developmental standpoint, this is positive news for America's newborns (and for America's future). Moreover, declining shares of teen births were evident for each racial and ethnic group considered here. Minorities (except for Asians) contribute disproportionately to all teen births, while Whites and Asians are underrepresented among the babies born to teenagers. Minority children are at less risk than in the past, but the share of births to teenagers among all minority births still greatly exceeds the corresponding share for Whites. All else being equal, this means that more minority children face the well-documented developmental disadvantages associated with having teen parents.

Table 15.2.
Percent of All Births to Teenagers, by Race and Year

	Race					
Year	White	Black	Indian	Asian	Total	Hispanic
1970	15.2	31.4	20.3	—	17.6	—
1980	13.5	27.0	24.0	5.4	15.6	19.0
1990	10.9	23.1	19.5	5.8	12.8	16.8
2000	10.6	19.7	19.7	4.5	11.8	16.2

For newborns, the risks associated with having teen parents are difficult to distinguish from risks associated with having unmarried parents. Indeed, over 90% of teen births are to born to unmarried teen mothers. As Thomson shows in this volume, nonmarital fertility also comprises a significant and growing share of the nation's births (i.e., 33% today, up from about 11% in 1970). To be sure, increasing numbers of children are raised by single parents. The good news, if there is any, is that a much larger share of them today are born to older women, who presumably are more prepared than teen mothers to be good providers and caretakers. This is shown in Table 15.3. In 1970, 50.1% of all children born outside of marriage were to teen mothers; a whopping 81% were born to mothers less than age 25. In 2000, only 28% of newborns had teen mothers, while over 33% had mothers over the age of 25, representing a significant increase from the 18.1% observed just 30 years earlier. Clearly, from a developmental standpoint, a smaller share of newborns today may face the developmental challenges associated with having young parents. If the concentration of reproduction is increasing in America, older mothers are now shouldering a larger burden in producing and shaping the next generation.

Table 15. 3.
Percent of All Births to Unwed Mothers, by Maternal Age and Year

		Age of Mother			
Year	%of unwed births	Under 20	20-24	25+	Total
1970	10.7	50.1	31.1	18.1	100
1980	18.4	40.8	35.6	23.5	100
1990	28.0	30.9	34.7	34.4	100
2000	33.2	28.0	37.4	34.6	100

Finally, we consider whether newborns have better educated mothers than in the past. A common perception is that the burden of childbearing is shouldered mostly by America's disadvantaged, while affluent and highly educated couples remain childless or have only one or sometimes two children. Yet, the evidence presented in Table 15.4 does not support the conventional wisdom. In fact, the division of reproduction has become more equal over educational groups, in large part because women's education has increased significantly over the past 30 years. In 1970, 31% of all newborns had mothers who were high school dropouts. Only 9% of newborn babies had highly educated mothers—those with college degrees or more. By 2000, more babies had college-educated mothers than they had mothers who dropped out of high school (25% vs. 22%).[7] This is a significant change over a short period of time. Children's mothers are older and they are more educated than in the past. From a population perspective, this is positive news for America's children if, as many studies show, children benefit in multiple ways from being raised by highly educated parents (Martin, 2003).

---

[7] Previous research also shows that highly educated women are increasingly likely to delay births, including first births, after age 30 (Martin, 2000; Rindfuss et al., 1996).

Table 15.4.
Percent of Births by Mother's Education and Year

	Education of Mother			
Year	LT12	12-15	16+	Total
1970	30.8	61.6	8.6	100
1980	23.7	62.3	14.0	100
1990	23.8	58.7	17.5	100
2000	21.7	53.6	24.7	100

Implications and Conclusion

Most Western industrial societies have experienced long-term declines in fertility, a trend that has culminated in below-replacement fertility in the majority of countries. The total fertility rate for the developed world is now only 1.6 births per woman (Bongaarts, 2002). In the past, population experts worried almost exclusively about over-population and high fertility. Today, they also worry that low or below replacement-level fertility may present serious social and economic consequences as a result of its long-term effects on age composition and economic growth (Lutz et al., 2003). Our goal has been modest—to shift the focus from quantitative changes in fertility (i.e., declines in the number of births) to qualitative changes in America's population of newborns (i.e., their social and demographic characteristics) and to their likelihood of positive developmental trajectories. Specifically, are children increasingly born of a smaller and/or more disadvantaged segment of America's female population? If so, the American fertility "problem" may be one of social reproduction rather than biological reproduction of the next generation.

Our goal, in part, was to measure the changing concentration of reproduction in the United States. As we showed here, the concentration of reproduction (using the Gini index as a measure of inequality) increased between the depression-born and baby boom-born cohorts of American women. At the same time, the childbearing observed among baby-boom women was much less concentrated than it was for turn-of-the-century women, who often remained childless or, alternatively, had large numbers of offspring (see Pullum, Tedrow, & Herting, 1989). If we extrapolate to recent cohorts, the strong negative correlation between cohort fertility and inequality in childbearing ($r = -.52$) suggests that today's very low fertility may be associated with a greater concentration of reproduction (i.e., smaller shares of women produce increasing shares of the babies). From a policy standpoint, a real concern is whether children are devalued as a public good if they are concentrated in a small segment of American women.[8]

Globally, fertility is increasingly concentrated among poorer, developing nations (Lutz, 1987). In the United States, the increasing concentration of reproduction implied by our results begs an obvious question: Are newborns increasingly concentrated among historically disadvantaged populations? If so, then the changing concentration of fertility in America implies a more disadvantaged future as today's "at risk" newborns grow into adulthood. Current trends may create built-in demographic momentum for future social and economic inequality. On this question, our results provided more good news than bad news. Newborns have become more racially diverse since 1970, but changes have been surprisingly small, which should be encouraging to those who are concerned that greater racial and ethnic diversity will undermine national unity and contribute to cultural and economic balkanization. And, while Hispanic babies represent a growing share of all newborns, it is also the case that the economic status of Hispanic families (like other minority families) has improved substantially in recent years. Over the past 30 years, the poverty rate among Hispanic children peaked at 41.5% in 1994, but declined to 28.6% by 2002 (U.S. Bureau of the Census, 2003). Our results also indicated that policy concerns about the large share of American children born to single mothers can be tempered somewhat by much higher percentages of out-of-wedlock children born to older mothers. And, unlike the past, recent research by Bumpass and Lu (2000) shows that the growing shares (about 40%) of children born to unmarried mothers also cohabit with co-residential partners, who provide economic resources, assume care-taking responsibilities, and provide mothers with emotional support. Arguably, the challenges and circumstances facing out-of-wedlock children today are much different from the past. Finally, and perhaps most significantly, newborns today are much less concentrated among poorly educated mothers. From our preliminary evidence, it is difficult to conclude that, on balance, change in the concentration of reproduction means that greater shares of children are "at risk" of developmental delays or poor socioeconomic outcomes in adulthood.

---

[8] As Morgan and Hagewen (this volume) point out, increasing shares of women intend to have two children and, significantly, are more likely than in the past to realize their fertility goals. Indeed, unwanted fertility has declined as a result of improved contraception and access to abortion and surgical sterilization, while the availability of new reproductive technologies has helped older, sub-fecund couples to meet their fertility aspirations.

In conclusion, it seems that smaller shares of American women are taking on a larger share of the burden in reproducing the next generation. Glass (1992) has suggested that there may be a widening fertility gap between housewives and employed women, which means that a growing share of American children may be reared by less educated, poorer, and more traditional families. Yet, our results suggest that there is perhaps more diversity than ever in children's social, demographic, and economic characteristics at birth, despite less diversity today in the parity distributions of children's mothers (Morgan & Hagewen, this volume). Single women, older women, and more highly educated women are contributing growing shares to the nation's newborn population. This trend occurred even as childlessness has risen among cohorts of (presumably high SES) women who have recently completed their fertility. Our results suggest that more American children today, on balance, are born to mothers with social and demographic traits that place them at less risk of long-term social and economic disadvantages.

References

Bongaarts, J. (2002). The end of the fertility transition in the developed world. *Population and Development Review, 28*, 419–444.

Bongaarts, J., & Feeney, G. (1998). On the quantum and tempo of fertility. *Population and Development Review, 24*, 271–291.

Brown, M. (1994). Using gini-style indices to evaluate the spatial patterns of health practitioners: Theoretical considerations and an application based on Alberta. *Social Science and Medicine, 38*, 1243–1256.

Bumpass, L., & Lu, H. (2000). Trends in cohabitation and implications for children's family contexts. *Population Studies, 54*, 29–41.

Eggebeen, D. J., & Lichter, D. T. (1991). Race, family structure, and changing poverty among American children. *American Sociological Review, 56*, 801–817.

Espenshade, T. J. (2001). "Replacement migration" from the perspective of equilibrium stationary populations. *Population and Environment, 22*, 383–389.

Golini, A. (1998). How low can fertility be? An empirical exploration. *Population and Development Review, 21*, 59–74.

Glass, J. (1992). Housewives and employed wives: Demographic and attitude change, 1972–1986. *Journal of Marriage and the Family, 54*, 559–569.

Lichter, D. T. (1997). Poverty and inequality among children. *Annual Review of Sociology, 23*, 121–145.

Lutz, W. (1987). *The concentration of reproduction: A global perspective* (Working Paper No. 87-051). Laxenburg, Austria: International Institute for Applied Systems Analysis.

Lutz, W., O'Neill, B. C., & Scherbov S. (2003, March 28). Demographics: Europe's population at a turning point. *Science, 299*, 1991–1992.

Martin, J. A., Hamilton, B. E., Ventura, S. J., Menacker, F., & Park, M. M. (2002). Births: Final data for 2000. *National Vital Statistics Reports, 50*(5).

Martin, S. P. (2000). Diverging fertility among U.S. women who delay childbearing past age 30. *Demography, 37,* 523–533.

Martin, S. P. (2003). *Delayed marriage and childbearing: Implications and measurement of diverging trends in family timing.* Retrieved October 15, 2003, from the Russell Sage Foundation Web site: http://www.russellsage.org/programs/proj_reviews/si/revmartin01.pdf

McLanahan, S., & Sandefur, G. (1996). *Growing up with a single parent: What hurts, what helps?* Cambridge, MA: Harvard University Press.

Morgan, S. P. (2003). Is low fertility a 21st century crisis? *Demography, 40,* 589-603.Morgan, S. P., Botev, N., Chen, R., & Huang, J. (1999). White and non-white trends in fertility timing: Comparisons using vital registration and current population surveys. *Population Research and Policy Review, 18,* 339–356.

National Center for Health Statistics. (2003). Percent distribution of women by parity, by exact age of woman according to race of child, in selected groups of cohorts from 1896-1900 to 1981-85: United States, 1940-2000. In *Vital Statistics of the United States, 1999: Volume I, Natality* (Table 1-32). Retrieved October 2, 2003, from http://www.cdc.gov/nchs/data/statab/t991x32.pdf

Pullum, T. W., Tedrow, L. M., & Herting, J. R. (1989). Measuring change and continuity in parity distributions. *Demography, 26,* 485–498.

Rindfuss, R. R., Morgan, S. P., & Swicegood, G. (1996). Education and the changing age pattern of American fertility: 1963–1989. *Demography, 33,* 277–290.

Stark, L., & Kohler, H. P. (2002). The debate over low fertility in the population press: A cross-national comparison, 1998–1999. *Population Research and Policy Review, 21,* 535–574.

U.S. Bureau of the Census. (2003). *Poverty in the United States: 2002* (Current Population Reports No. P60-222). Retrieved October 4, 2003, from http://www.census.gov/prod/2003pubs/p60-222.pdf

Vaupel, J. W., & Goodwin, D. G. (1987). The concentration of reproduction among U.S. women, 1917–80. *Population and Development Review, 13,* 723–730.

16

THE FUTURE OF LOW FERTILITY

Panel Discussion

Authors of the initial chapters of the first three sections of the book—Morgan, Barber, Axinn, and Thomson—were asked to comment on and critique the presentations by Bachrach and her colleagues, White and Lichter. Bachrach, White, and Lichter then had an opportunity to respond to their comments. This was followed by an open question-and-answer period. An edited text of the comments and discussion follows.

Morgan: A number of years ago I was invited to a conference on immigration in Italy and I began my talk with something like: "These barbarians are a problem. They come without knowing the language, they don't have relevant skills, they need lots of training, and they don't respect our customs." I was talking about our kids. Reproducing the next generation is difficult. Comparisons of immigration (and the investment required to effectively incorporate immigrants into the community) to a realistic assessment of how difficult it is to raise kids is something that should be considered when we talk about whether we'll have sufficient people in subsequent generations. Immigration and fertility are alternative mechanisms for population replacement.

Who's really concerned about low fertility? Patrick Buchanan recently wrote a book called *Death of the West* (2002). He is following on a book that many demographers know well, Ben Wattenberg's *The Birth Dearth* (1987). Now the bottom line of these books is captured in the subtitle to Buchanan's book, which is something like "how immigrant invasions and low fertility imperil our nation and our civilization." A lot of the concerns about low fertility are really about the sense that each civilization's culture is going to disappear under the weight of substantial immigration. Now this is something we may want to debate. My own position is that these concerns are about insufficient numbers of workers, warriors, and consumers. In a global economy, why is there concern about workers and consumers? In a global economy, workers and consumers need not be "home grown." At the global level, there are plenty of workers and consumers. Further, increasing the number of warriors is less important. Our military wows people with its technology, shock and awe, not its raw numbers.

Thus, I see low fertility (in terms of numbers) as a second-order problem, at least in the United States. But that's because we don't have very low fertility here. Even if our total fertility rate were to decline to 1.8, this level of fertility could easily be compensated for by moderate levels of immigration. Now the Italy story is very different. In Italy, with a 1.2 level of fertility, if you tried to solve that problem with immigration, you may not have a population size going to zero. It wouldn't. You could replace the missing babies, if you will, with immigrants. But in 100 years Italy would not be an Italy with Italians. It would be an Italy made up of immigrants. Given current immigration flows, it would consist of North Africans, Asians, and Eastern Europeans.

My own take on the U.S. problem is that the glass is half full. Women tell us that they want to have two kids, which is about what society would like for them to have. If you think about creating an environment in which women have two kids, you also have to think about having an environment that invests more in children. Policies that encourage people to have an appropriate number of kids or the number of kids they want also has to be an environment that is supportive of kids.

Axinn: I think Phil Morgan's comments are consistent with the chapter that Jennifer and I wrote for this volume. Whether or not low fertility is a problem is a matter of values, beliefs, and preferences. I also share your concern with the connection between identifying low fertility *per se* as a problem and values about immigrants and immigration. It's ironic to me that the U.S, of all countries, would consider immigration as a poor solution to a problem of low numbers of workers, warriors, and consumers given that we are a country of immigrants. I think a lot of the concern is about racial and cultural issues. I think some of it is also about poverty and not wanting to share our wealth. Not just not wanting to share our wealth within the country, but not wanting to share our wealth with poor people all over the world.

A friend of mine tells a story about flying into Nepal on a plane from Singapore with two Nepalese guys who had been in jail in Singapore for illegal labor immigration. They're on their way back to Nepal and they're talking among themselves. My friend says he overheard them say, "Gee, the jails in Singapore were so nice. You know they had television, athletic programs, three meals a day. It's really tough to have to go home now, because life in Nepal is so tough. People are incredibly poor." As a matter of fact, the British hired warriors from Nepal partly because some Nepalese were willing to come kill people for the British if they could have a taste of a British salary and maybe a few British benefits. I think there are poor people all over the world and we should share with them whether they're here in the United States or in some other country. My personal values are, why not allow them to come hang out with us? I have many friends who would like to come. In that sense, I think the more critical fertility problems for this country are not of the total quantum or pace but of the relationship between individual preferences and outcomes.

Phil mentioned unintended fertility. I think the fact that a significant number of American women are having children they don't intend to have or at the time they would prefer not to have them is a major social problem in the United States and one that we, as social scientists, should be concerned about. The fact that lots of couples in the United States would like to have a child they're unable to have is a growing problem that deserves our attention. I think those mismatches between individual preferences and fertility outcomes in terms of both unintended fertility and infertility are much more critical social scientific and policy issues for us than the total quantum of fertility *per se*.

Thomson: I appreciated Chris Bachrach's outline of the personal and the societal advantages of being a child, being a parent, and the number of children. I'm not sure about the evidence for the minor cost of childlessness in terms of social ties and especially economic well being in old age. And not just economic help, but health care. Chris wrote a very nice article several years ago that showed that women without children were no more isolated than women with children in their elderly years. But women who had had a child and no longer had living children were more isolated because they counted on their children and they hadn't constructed other mechanisms of support. It's not clear to me that the support one hopes for and the reality are the same thing, regardless of whether or not children are estranged from their parents. When parents have health or economic needs in old age, the amount of work it would take to construct a network that would provide the needed support may not be there.

One thing that has happened to the initial generation of people who had very small numbers of children or none at all is that they almost all had siblings. Siblings do a good deal of the caregiving after age 70 or 75. It's not clear to me that there aren't some real serious personal losses that can't be made up by a social security system, or maybe can't be made up even if we had a decent health care system.

One important thing Dan Lichter talked about, and Belinda Tucker mentioned earlier, is who are the parents and who are the people we worried about not having children or having children. I don't think many policy makers or the lay public are concerned if births among less well educated, young, single women disappeared. Nobody would be upset. I do think there is some interest in reproduction among the more advantaged segments of society. I agree with Lynn White that there is an interest in reproduction among some but there is also the political view that somehow we can foist the responsibility off to individuals, and hope that they'll produce the collective good that's necessary.

One of the things that happens when you don't have responsibility for children is that more people are less involved in care work. Women are less involved if they only have one child. Men are hardly parents at all, especially if they don't live with their children. If these trends continue, it means people have less of an incentive, less of a daily reminder, and less of a strong impetus to worry about the welfare of children.

It seems strange to me that with the incredible news coverage and political debate about public pension systems (that occurs more in Europe than in the United States) that politicians and the public are unwilling to invest in the children who will have to produce those goods 20 years from now. It seems obvious to me that children are public goods but if you don't have people involved with them privately, it may become more and more difficult to get the voting public to support them as a public good. I remember 25 years ago hearing a paper at the Population Association of America meeting in which the author predicted that major divisions in U.S. society would be less along age, race, and class lines (well, that was optimistic) than between parents and non-parents. Parents would increasingly be paying the cost for the larger society and non-parents would not be expected to do so. I think the authors anticipated that it wouldn't be just parents and non-parents, but female partners and male non-parents.

Bachrach: I agree with Bill Axinn and Phil Morgan that there is a great irony in the fact that the United States was built through immigration but rejects immigration as a solution to a declining population. It is especially ironic now when U.S. population diversity is mushrooming.

The gap between individual birth preferences and outcomes is worth more research. While there are questions about the extent to which technology can fix the problem, it warrants serious attention. I'm not sure how to deal with unintended pregnancy and childbearing. These are difficult concepts to define and measure with any kind of accuracy. We also have to bear in mind that unintended fertility does actually help to keep our birthrates higher and if it disappeared we would be looking more like some European countries.

Barber: I agree with Betty Thomson that the research we do on social ties between parents and children doesn't fully capture what children really mean. As a new parent I know there are very deep feelings that I couldn't obtain on any kind of survey instrument that I know about.

Thomson: I'm not so much talking about deep feelings as a new parent. I've noticed in rural areas that the children tend to provide very good care for elderly parents. Many elderly are not so isolated because they are also receiving some care from a community of peers. It is not always the same quality of care, however, that they might receive from children.

Bachrach: In my article that Betty Thomson referred to, we actually found that isolation among the elderly was related to childlessness only if the individual was in poor health or had not involved themselves in other adult roles during the prime of their adult lives. There are certain circumstances in which children are where the action is.

Audience: I think there is a global shift toward passing along the cost of reproduction to individuals. The political economy of childbearing is to lower the cost of reproduction for the state. We want to move jobs to where we don't have to pay for such things as higher education and immunizations. In addition, our immigration laws have become very selective such that we only want to bring in well-trained labor. In short, the U.S. wants to bring in people whose costs of reproduction have already been paid by someone in another country. A clear example of this is Filipino nurses in California. There's a labor shortage of nurses. Did we raise the wages of nurses? No. We just looked abroad to find adult young women who were willing to work for lower wages in the U.S. In short, globalization is going to change policies with respect to reproduction and immigration in many countries.

Morgan: In terms of the selective immigration policy, the U.S. is relatively unselective compared to Australia. In Australia you don't get there unless you're basically what they want. In Australia, as a policy, if you're from an Asian country and you can pay your tuition at an Australian university for four years, they guarantee you at the end that you can stay. That's exactly what you're talking about. For whom is this a problem? My guess is that you could pick the arguments you just made and sell this to the U.S. public as a way of making things better for us. I don't sense any broad ground swell of concern about folks in less developed countries among the U.S. population.

Audience: But people complain about the lack of support for working parents and kids.

Morgan: So you're worried about the lack of support for immigrants with children?

Audience: Anybody's kids. As long as we accept immigrants who have had the cost of their education paid for by another country, there is no incentive to create programs that are supportive.

Morgan: I think a reasonable level of immigration can easily solve the number problem if the total fertility rate is 1.8 because the number of immigrants flowing in is not so great that they can't be accommodated and assimilated. It's my own view that once the flow becomes much larger than that, it fundamentally changes the nature of the society. And for whom is that a problem?

Axinn: I want to follow up on that. I think it is also related to Chris Bachrach's comment about unintended childbearing. If we eliminated unintended childbearing our fertility would be a lot lower. That points to the distinction that Chris made between public and private costs and benefits of those children. If 50% of babies born are born in unintended pregnancies either because they're too early or weren't wanted, that cost is borne either by those particular families or society in general. Documentation of the social costs of those children is essential to convincing policy makers and voters that greater investments in children are desirable for reasons separate from the total number of people *per se*. As a voter, I like to assume that more information about the actual costs to society would result in greater investment. I don't know enough about politics to estimate whether that would actually happen. It's a very difficult fact to document. Perhaps we should invest in documenting the costs of childbearing to those who don't want to have children or don't want to have children now or who feel that the costs are higher than they're prepared to pay.

Bachrach: I think we need updated information on the cost of childbearing across the spectrum of people who plan fertility and those who don't plan. While there has been a lot of focus on the cost of teen childbearing, there's been very little focus on the cost of a professional woman giving birth at age 29 or 35.

Audience: I wanted to ask Lynn White a question. You argued that today many adults have less interest in fertility than historically. I don't have the numbers but there are a couple of trends that seem to run counter to that. According to the 2000 Census data, about 1/5 of all single parents are dads and in absolute numbers that's the largest number of single dads that we've ever had. A recent study of the changing workforce suggests that in two-parent heterosexual households dads are doing a greater share of childcare than they have done historically.

White: Suzanne Bianchi's presentation yesterday demonstrated that by a combination of reduced women's time and increased men's time, the gender gap in the amount of childcare in American households has closed dramatically, but that mothers are still doing about twice as much time in childcare as married men.

There is a relatively small fraction of single-parent families that are headed by men. The number is overestimated because the census includes fathers who are cohabiting with an unmarried woman, who were then listed on the household roster as an unrelated member of the household. So he was recorded as a single father when in fact he was a co-resident father.

Audience: Thirty percent of these custodial dads have a female partner living with them and another 10% actually live with their parents or other relatives. So, about half of those single fathers actually have support of some sort within the household.

Audience: I wanted to follow up on the immigrant issue. Clearly we're different than Europe in that regard and I see immigration as a replacement having an impact on fertility in two ways. First, the first generation has an impact because of higher levels of fertility in the first generation or two. But, what about the effect of intermarriage in the United States, particularly where there's intermarriage between Spanish and other groups? Where do you see these trends going in terms of fertility?

Morgan: Our best guide, an imperfect guide, to our future is the past and there's evidence from a broad set of immigrant groups who came to the United States at the turn of the century and had fertility rates much greater than those of the general population. People were very concerned about those differentials at the turn of the century. People thought they were going to persist. But, we now know that they've completely disappeared and they disappeared by and large by 1960. They tend to disappear by the third generation. Now will that be true for current waves of immigration from Mexico and Latin America? We don't know. The context is a bit different. It is a flow that, as Doug Massey has pointed out, is continuing. So my guess is going to be that assimilation is going to be a big factor and a lot of that has to do with intermarriage. The size of these groups in the future is entirely dependent upon the levels of intermarriage. The census recently released an estimate that said that by 2050, the U.S. is going to be, according to the projections, less than 50% White non-Hispanic.

Audience: You could also point out that there's quite a bit of evidence now that the fertility of Hispanics in the United States is higher than the fertility of many of the countries that send Hispanic immigrants to the United States.

Audience: I have a question for Christine Bachrach. Some articles I've read claim that we are actually investing more in children now than we used to in the past and some are claiming that we're investing less. Which is it?

Bachrach: It's a little bit like estimating the cost of teenage childbearing. It's one of those very slippery questions. In our chapter, we are relying on an unpublished paper put together by the Urban Institute that just focused on federal expenditures. It showed that there was a substantial increase in investment in children from 1960 on. In fact, in 1960 no social programs were directed at children in the federal budget and that is what really progressed.

Audience: So we don't know whether it has gone up or down?

Thomson: One of the reasons the federal investment may have gone up is because so many things were taken over by the federal government in that period of time and now are being shoved back to states and other entities.

White: I don't know this from my own research, but some of the material I was reading in preparing this chapter argued that one of the reasons why federal expenditures for children appear to have gone up is because of greater expenditures in higher education. Although that's good, it's not the same kind of investment that makes the most difference in terms of children's well-being and mental success.

Review the newspapers and you see that Head Start and Medicaid for children are programs that are under fire because the Medicaid funding is for children who are largely provided for by state and local governments. It is on the chopping block because they can't go into debt.

Thomson: My recollection is that of all the federal and state programs that have been evaluated with experimental and econometric research, Head Start and WIC are the only two programs—and these are directed primarily at women and children—that show substantial positive outcomes.

Audience: What is the effect of fertility on pensions?

Thomson: In the United States we're solving this with a program (Social Security) that creates a strong incentive for people not to have children. If you're going to have to provide your own pension, you better spend more time working to earn more money and not spend it on children.

Morgan: The Social Security system in the U.S. is still in surplus and I think it will be for another 15 years. This is the rare circumstance when a serious social problem is incredibly predictable and if we're unable to prepare for it, we sort of deserve what we get.

Audience: What are the implications of the rising cost of housing for fertility?

Bachrach: The silence of the panel reflects the fact that we haven't looked at this issue yet. It's very important that we do.

Thomson: It would be very interesting to take a century-long look at this issue as well as a comparative view because in the United States young couples expect to have a house or a large apartment if they want to have children. It is viewed as a necessity. The child must have its own bedroom. In Italy and Japan there are really severe housing crunches. But people learn how to live in less space. We know that there are some situations in which severe restrictions on housing have altered family patterns, but we don't know anything about the situation in the United States. I think it is because there's always been enough housing.

Axinn: Chris Bachrach brought up that what we believe is essential for children keeps growing at least as fast as our wealth, if not faster. It seems to me that standards of what has to be invested in children both in terms of housing and in terms of other forms of consumption are normatively related to how much wealth we have to spend on these things. We could adjust to the high cost of housing by deciding that having kids in an apartment or trailer is not a problem.

Audience: I want to follow up on this a little bit. I think that this issue of what we expect for our kids is an important thing. However, I don't think that our norms have changed that much. I agree that costs to achieve these norms probably have increased quite a bit, but I think that every generation says that what they want for their kids is a little bit better than what they had. This includes trying to get a house, saving for college and so forth. But the real costs associated with childbearing have gone up quite a bit as well. I'm not taking issue that our norms haven't changed, but to achieve the basic standards of what my father wanted to do before he had a family does cost a lot more. That's one of the things we haven't heard about that might limit being able to afford children.

Audience: So at issue are the rising costs of necessities and the fact that it is becoming harder and harder to have a better standard of living generation after generation?

Morgan: I don't know if I agree. I think the basket of stuff we think we have to have before we can move on has gotten a lot more stuff in it than it used to. When we don't know anything, we fall back on our own experiences. I see my kid trying to set up a household and it's not a household without cable TV. And, who can live without a cell phone? So, the basket is getting full of stuff that people think they have to have. If you look at the house size, how much square footage do people think they need? I shared a room. Every kid deserves their own room now. There were five of us—we didn't have our own rooms.

Axinn: As mentioned previously, each generation wants a little more for their children than they had as a young person. I think the same applies to father involvement in the family. People want a little bit more than the previous generation.

Linda Waite and Fran Goldscheider, in their book, *New Families, No Families* (1991), propose that if men continue to want to have wives who will take care of them, their children and everything else, those men will not get married. I think we're beginning to see that play out as the second part of the gender revolution.

Men will need to become more involved in families or there won't be as many families.

White: Just as there has been a gender increase in income equality, there has been an increase in equality with respect to the parent involvement in childcare. However, it varies along class lines. Just as there is a group of middle-class married fathers who are doing a lot more than they ever used to, there is a group of fathers who are doing far less than they used to. So there's an increase in the inequality of fathers doing a lot more or a lot less.

Audience: The U.S. Department of Agriculture does put together cost estimates of raising children and they call it a moderate standard. They don't include cell phones, a bath for every child or a bedroom for every child. So it is a modest basket of goods. If you plot that against median family income and look at the ratio of the cost of bearing and raising a child to family income, you see that they track remarkably well. The cost per child is relatively constant over the 1982 to 2000 period. What has changed, however, is the source of family income. More and more, family income reflects the earnings of a wide array of single mothers who are supporting their children. For single mothers the cost of having children has risen dramatically.

Bachrach: It doesn't surprise me that an index put together by the Department of Agriculture doesn't include a cell phone and a bathroom for every child, but it underscores the fact that fertility researchers have done a poor job of taking into account material consumption and assumptions about what we need to invest in children.

Lichter: What are the relatively affluent young adults who are not marrying and reproducing doing with their lives? How does what they're doing relate to marriage and family formation?

Thomson: In Italy and Japan a huge proportion of youth in their late 20s and early 30s stay at home until they get married. There are two parts to why they stay at home. One is they can't reproduce the parental standard of living anywhere else. The other is that their parents allow them to share that standard of living without imposing social controls that were in effect when they were adolescents. And mothers are providing services. Their rates of marriage tend to be low compared to those for other youth.

Audience: To what extent do young adolescent males get off the family track because of the juvenile justice system?

Thomson: One of the things that is really interesting to me is a study showing that working-class boys who got into trouble in fairly minor ways could not recover in terms of achievement later in life. But working- or middle-class boys who got into trouble recovered. It's the way the juvenile justice system handles young men by class that is different. For girls, it didn't differ very much by class because girls are usually drawn into the juvenile justice system for what are termed 'moral offenses' that are viewed in the same way across class. My guess is that there are variations across countries in the extent to which the juvenile justice system is not helpful to the development of young men, especially those from less well educated and minority families. In this country, the incarceration rates for Black males between the ages of 16 and 24 are horrendous and in some communities, half of the male population is either in prison or on parole.

Audience: In listening to this discussion I'm wondering if there is a way to get information based on research to a wider audience in such a way that it could have an impact on policy?

Bachrach: I think it is very important. Speaking as someone who invests many millions of dollars of the taxpayer's money on demographic research, I personally feel a great responsibility to make sure that the lessons we learn from research get out and that they're out there in a way that can inform public policy. I think the general public is aware of the fact that there is pressure on the Social Security system. One of the infrastructure programs that we funded in Child Health and Human Development goes to the Population Reference Bureau to do exactly this––to translate what we're learning in various areas and put demographic research into easily accessible sound bites and information pieces. Some of the people on this panel are involved in that effort. So yes, I think it is very important. As usual, it's often the case that the messages are complicated and not easy to communicate in the kind of sound bites that you can get across through the media.

Audience: Chris, I was wondering if you would like to say more about the mechanisms by which research knowledge can be gotten to the public.

Bachrach: I can tell you about two different ways in which I think it gets out. They don't come from formal scientific study. It is just my impression. My favorite theory of informing the public is what I call the ground-water theory. Demographic research findings get picked up in the media and they get into the ground water. They become something that everybody knows. For example, the risk of divorces is high among those who cohabit before marriage. A lot of people in the general public know that right now because it's shown up enough in the media. Because it becomes part of our general stock of knowledge, it then filters into public policy. The other mechanism is when people directly use research to craft public policy. That can be effective, too, especially if you work with policy makers in the design of your research and make sure that it's being designed in a way that is going to answer your questions. I think the ground water method, which is a more subtle type of method, is more effective.

Audience: I want to follow up by saying the ground water approach is difficult because it's hard to educate the public about things people think they already know about.

Lichter: The other problem is that policy makers think that marriage is good for people but we don't know for certain that marriage is good for people.

Bachrach: On the other hand, if we ask policy makers to wait until we nail down all the causal relations to make decisions, they won't have much use for us.

17

UNDERSTANDING LOW FERTILITY: THE IMPACT OF LIFE-COURSE COMPETITION ON FERTILITY BEHAVIOR IN DEVELOPED NATIONS

Tanja St. Pierre
Jacinda K. Dariotis
The Pennsylvania State University

The current trend of declining fertility in developed nations has sparked debate among demographers, sociologists, and policy makers with regard to its causes, consequences, and appropriate strategies to halt the process. The chapters in this volume are part of the current debate, each approaching fertility decision making from a unique perspective. Morgan and Hagewen (this volume) outline a theoretical approach to fertility decline in developed nations by introducing the concept of "life course competition" as the source of cross-national fertility differentials. The chapters that follow are variations on this theme, examining macro- and micro-level factors that are associated with fertility behavior. This concluding commentary pulls together the major themes and assumptions underlying this volume: that the production of children in developed nations is the result of women's rational choice, and that these choices are constrained by the context of reproduction.

Demographic Trends

Today, nearly 75% of developed nations are characterized by below replacement fertility (Lichter & Wooten, this volume), where the United States is an anomaly given its 2.03 total fertility rate (Morgan & Hagewen, this volume). Europe and Asia are characterized by total fertility rates close to 1.0, and the threat of population decline appears to be more acute here than in the United States. Although it is intuitive to assume that women and men simply want fewer children, research shows stable fertility intentions across nations.

On a theoretical level, Morgan and Hagewen (this volume) attributes this discrepancy to changing intentions, attitudes, and preferences over the life course, constrained by factors that compete with childbearing particular points in time. Methodologically, this implies that researchers need to measure fertility intentions, not only at the beginning of adulthood, but at different stages of the life course. Barber and Axinn (this volume) note that individuals with strong fertility preferences are more likely to act on their intentions, despite competing forces. Ultimately, most people express contentment with the number of children they have at the end of their reproductive years, although it is difficult to gauge the extent to which people realign their cognitions to match their realities (Festinger, 1957).

Family Structure Trends Related to Childbearing

The relationship between parenthood and marriage has weakened in the United States and other industrial countries over the past several decades (Thomson, this volume). This trend is often attributed to the increasing participation of women in the labor force, which results in the increasing cost of women's time, and increasing earning power. Increasing and independent earnings allow women to be more selective about their choices in general, and about marriage and childbearing in particular. Simultaneously, this trend resulted in men's weakening earnings compared to those of women (Oppenheimer, 1998) and, in turn, the declining marriageability of men. A greater proportion of men are now less suitable for marriage, increasing women's difficulty in finding suitable partners (Tucker, this volume). Women now have limited options in terms of family formation, given that marriage remains the most accepted family arrangement for childbearing. Two salient choices for women are to bear children outside of marital unions or to remain childless.

Coinciding with increasing female labor force participation, Thomson (this volume) observes an increase in non-marital childbearing that can be largely accounted for by rising cohabitation. Thus, we need to consider what makes cohabitation a desirable alternative for women. For one, cohabitation may be an alternative to marriage, depending on the quality of the relationship (Landale, this volume), which largely depends on the mother's age at birth (Jaffee, this volume). Teenage non-marital childbearing may be the result of an unplanned pregnancy and thus has different causes and consequences for individuals. Second, cohabitation may be a transitional stage en route to marriage, a period when women evaluate the qualities of their partner before committing to long-term marriage (Thomson, this volume). Lichter and Wooten (this volume) note that subsequent generations of children will be born to more educated, older, unmarried women. Despite the single-parenthood status of these women, these findings imply that the negative image of single-parenthood needs to be qualified by the mother's age and level of human capital. Childbearing within cohabiting unions may thus help to maintain the total fertility rate and prevent it from further decline.

Throughout U.S. history, over 20% of women have generally remained childless at the end of their reproductive years, increasing slightly with each subsequent decade. Because fewer families today have higher parity births, large families no longer compensate for the retreat from parenthood as they did during the first half of the twentieth century. Raley (this volume) identifies a "feedback effect" of female labor force participation in which paid employment delays childbearing to accumulate wealth and women defer the decision to have a child, a process that could continue indefinitely. Morgan and Hagewen (this volume) note that factors across the life course compete with parenthood, where the major culprit appears to be female labor force participation—the inability to combine employment and parenthood simultaneously.

An Economic Approach to Fertility

The Influence of Life-Course Competition on Fertility Behavior in Developed Nations

An underlying premise of the discussion of fertility behavior in developed nations is that childbirth is the result of individual rational choice. In the realm of fertility decision making, economic theories of fertility are at the forefront of explaining factors that influence the decision to have a(nother) child, and by default, what determines the choice to remain childless. This perspective proposes that individuals carefully evaluate the costs and benefits associated with having a(nother) child. Today, children are far from being economic assets to their parents; rather, a trend toward an elevated social reproduction requires a high financial and time investment on the part of parents. Parents' investment in children not only depends on their financial resources, but on their human capital goals as well.

Child quality refers to the direct and indirect cost of raising children. Direct costs are monetary expenditures such as clothing, food, and education, where parents may differ in the amount of money they directly invest in their children. For example, families of women who engage in the labor market contribute a large amount of their income to the purchase of childcare services (Blau & Robins, 1989). The acquisition of children may be reduced to a number that ensures a balance between resources and the goals parents have for their children. In low-income families, women required to work may limit their fertility due to childcare expenses.

Opportunity costs are indirect costs associated with raising children, costs that in industrialized nations primarily affect women. Women inevitably forgo earnings and work experience by taking time out to bear and raise their child(ren), regardless of previous employment status. Cross-national fertility differences may relate to maternity policies, where women in nations with generous maternity leaves reduce their fertility to minimize lost wages. Thus, factors related to the quality-quantity interaction depend on individuals' position in the social structure and the institutional support they receive within a given society.

An economic approach to fertility, then, directly assumes that *all births are planned*, and that individuals have the access and knowledge to effectively employ contraceptive technology and abortion services (Morgan & Hagewen, this volume; Presser, this volume). This assumption has great implications for the study of fertility because unplanned births, which are primarily related to teenage childbearing, are not assessable by rational-choice models.

Morgan and Hagewen (this volume) utilize Bongaarts' (2002) analytic framework, which presents the total fertility rate of a nation as a function of the intended family size of a woman being increased or decreased by unwanted fertility (F_u), the replacement of deceased children (F_r), gender preferences (F_g), sub- and infecundity (F_i), fertility timing (F_t), and competition (F_c). Evaluating the effect of the Bongaarts formula, Morgan and Hagewen contribute cross-national fertility difference to life-course competition (F_c), or to the fact that women reevaluate their intended family size continuously throughout the life-course in response to factors that compete with or encourage childbearing. The authors identify two key factors for fertility decline. First, nations in which women delay childbearing and that have strong norms against non-marital childbearing tend to have lower total fertility rates. Second, nations that provide an institutional setting that allows for the combination of employment and motherhood have higher total fertility rates compared to nations with low maternal and child investment.

The Utility of Children in Developed Nations

Bachrach et al. (this volume) point out that children are "goods" for both societies and individuals alike. The value of children for societies is three-fold, relating to economic growth, pension systems, and societal reproduction. Children are to a greater degree public goods and to a lesser degree private goods, and thus the responsibility of raising children in industrialized nations should be supported by national governments via institutional and monetary aids.

Compared to other industrialized countries, it is evident that public investment in children is fairly limited in the United States. For example, the U.S. ranks comparatively high on the infant mortality rate and America's children are 3.2 times more likely then children in other developed nations to live in poverty (White, this volume). Bacharach et al. (this volume) assess the increasing public rhetoric concerning children's well-being, education, and psychological development in the United States as the first step toward an increasing public investment in children. It appears that U.S. efforts are aimed to increase child quality rather than quantity, in contrast to policies in many European nations, because population decline is not an immediate concern (Morgan & Hagewen, this volume). The emphasis on child quality, however, may raise the cost of childbearing in the future by indirectly pressuring parents to invest more in their children than they originally would have intended (Bachrach et al., this volume).

Part of the underinvestment in children may be the result of a decreasing concentration of fertility among various racial and ethnic groups in the United States. Lichter and Wooten (this volume) find that births have become more racially diverse over the last three decades; the fertility of Whites has decreased little, but that of Hispanics has risen by 136%. Given the negative public attitudes toward immigrants in this country, coupled with a decline in the poverty of Hispanic children, policy makers may refrain from heavy investment to encourage fertility.

In addition, more children have been born to mothers over the age of 25, and fewer to teenagers. Similarly, more children have been born to college-educated women compared to high school dropouts (Lichter & Wooten, this volume). Theses trends are associated with positive child outcomes and, at this time, do not require urgent policy measures.

Children, while in many ways a great public value to all nations, are today, and are likely to remain, the responsibility of their parents. Research assessing the involvement of mothers and fathers in their children's lives suggests that the main responsibility for raising children lies with biological mothers, regardless of their marital status. Bachrach et al. (this volume) point out that public goods are universally accessible without any investment. It appears that as long as a nation's supply of children is adequate to maintain population size, as is currently the case in the United States, governments will see no need to actively invest in their "future."

In contrast to the United States, pro-natalist policies in Europe are designed to increase the quantity of children by decreasing the cost of children directly, through provision of financial incentives that increase with the birth of a(nother) child. Generous maternity policies, accessible to women or their husbands, are aimed at encouraging fertility. European governments invest in their citizens by providing universal health insurance, unemployment benefits, pensions, housing policies, educational standards and affordable childcare to reduce structural inequalities. It seems that Europe has responded to fertility decline by an increasing public investment in children. This cross-national variation in policy is a reminder that individuals are placed within different societal contexts and that the costs and benefits of childbearing are affected by that context as well (Morgan & Hagewen, this volume).

However, children are also resources for parents and siblings. They confer emotional support to parents, are potential old-age care-givers, and serve as a mechanism for generativity (Erikson, 1980). Bachrach et al. (this volume) acknowledge that children as private goods weakly motivate childbearing, especially given alternative mechanisms by which people can ensure old age support via private retirement funds, contribute to the world and leave their mark via professional and personal contributions, and find emotional support via stronger investment in friends, partners, and family. It is important to decipher whether declining fertility is indicative of a reduced investment of parents in children, or whether fewer high-quality children point to a heightened private investment. White (this volume) equates increasing divorces and births outside of marital unions to a lack of private investment in children by men. She refers to the fact that among adult biological parents, only 35% of White and 20% of Black men reside in the same household as their children, meaning that American fathers are less likely to parent their children compared to mothers.

The historical increase in divorce, however, may suggest that children may be fathered by non-biological fathers for parts of their lives, and by default, that fathers who remarry are more likely to father someone else's children in return. Maybe fathers do indeed invest in children, but just not in their biological offspring? Findings about stepparenting, however, are discouraging. As one would expect, stepfathers tend to lack emotional closeness and financial responsibilities for non-biological children, probably the result of late entry into the child's life as well as the absence of legal responsibility (White, this volume). More detrimental are the socioeconomic effects of this pattern: children raised in stepfamilies are comparable to those raised in single-family homes with regard to human capital acquisition and pre-marital childbearing. These poor child outcomes are further reinforced by a lack of financial support on the part of divorced fathers, placing the main responsibility of childrearing on mothers.

Residential fathers in non-marital unions also invest less in their offspring. White (this volume) reports that these men spend less time with their children and lack emotional closeness compared to biological fathers who are in marital unions. In order to assess the investment by fathers in partnered-nonmarital unions, we must consider cross-national differences in the duration and quality of cohabiting unions in order to truly understand the implications of this living arrangement for children and mothers (Landale, this volume).

Even when fathers are involved in the lives of their children, mothers still take a disproportionate responsibility for childcare. Bianchi (this volume) reports that in the U.S. women engage in twice the amount of housework and childcare compared to their husbands, and they forgo employment. While the number of single fathers is increasing in the United States, men appear to mobilize support from female relatives or partners to fulfill their parenting responsibilities. It appears as if fathers in developed nations do not equally share the responsibility of raising children with women, regardless of their union status (White, this volume).

Life-Course Competition: Explaining the Gap Between Intentions and Behavior

Individuals' experience and choices can be placed within history, a particular society, and, on the individual-level, within a particular genetic context. It follows that individuals' fertility choices are shaped by the cultural, structural, and bio-social determinants throughout the life-course. It is thus important to employ a life-course perspective when examining the discrepancy between intended family size and the fertility behavior of women. Morgan and Hagewen (2004) presents fertility behavior, relating to planned births, as events that benefit from the life course model, especially because births occur in a sequential manner. Studying the previously discussed trends in fertility in developed nations, and relating declining fertility to the rational choice of individuals related to life-course competition, forces us to examine the trend of female labor force participation and to establish how women's, and possibly men's, decisions may be influenced by role competition.

Increasing female labor force participation in developed nations means that childbearing (1) reduces net earnings of women and their families directly, and (2) diminishes the amount of leisure time women have to engage in childrearing and time they can spend on their own leisure and personal pursuits. In essence, then, making childbearing and employment compatible is a function of macro-level gender relations (Presser, this volume). We may observe cross-national differences in fertility as a result of varying pro-natalist policies (Gauthier & Hatzius, 1997), reinforcing Morgan and Hagewen's (this volume) point that "context matters." In addition, the purchase and availability of high-quality childcare and the employer's effort to support the mother's transition to work need to be considered (Bianchi, this volume). A woman's support varies by class; women who are forced to return to work to secure their family's financial position are in need of more financial and social support compared to women who seek employment for self-fulfillment. Nations vary with regard to their institutional responses, a factor deemed important to encourage childbearing (Morgan & Hagewen, this volume).

Female employment also reduces the hours of leisure time a woman (and her partner) have to devote to herself and to her children, a trend that is in discord with an ideological change toward increasing investment in children (Bianchi, this volume), as well as the right to self-actualization (Morgan & Hagewen, this volume). Bianchi (this volume) suggests that parents' investment and expectations vary by class, where individuals at the lower socioeconomic spectrum do not have the choices that middle-class women have. Economically endowed individuals, on the other hand, may choose the number of children they have, not on the basis of financial resources, but according to the time available to engage in self-enriching activities. Bianchi (this volume) presents paradoxical findings that support the trend of high parental investment: while the amount of parental time spent with children did not change over time, men and women today report not spending sufficient time with their children. Although the division of labor in the "modern" marital union has closed the female-male gap, women continue to engage in about 50% more housework and childcare compared to their spouses (Bianchi, this volume), suggesting an increasing value of parental leisure time.

There has been a shift in individual-level gender relations that has resulted from participation in the labor market, one toward greater gender equality. Not only do women have more opportunities, but also their choices are constrained by them in return. Men now seem to feel a greater necessity to "step up to the plate" and to take more responsibility within partnered unions, which has two consequences for fertility behavior. For one, the increasing time husbands and wives both spend in non-market work increases, which may reduce fertility if there is a sense of entitlement to self-actualization and leisure on the part of either partner in addition to wanting fewer, high-quality children. Second, men might choose to refrain from investing in their children if they find parenthood too costly and time-consuming.

Female paid employment and its associated consequences for women, men, and children have been related to another major trend related to childbearing: the delay of marriage. Raley (this volume) finds that female employment, that is, the result of voluntary human capital accumulation, delays marriage in favor of paid work. Thomson (this volume) does not find this trend surprising because in developed nations part of the support of parents in raising their children has been transferred to states and the market, via childcare and education. Correspondingly, the author finds evidence that the "loss" of marital births has been partially compensated by births that occur to adult cohabiting couples in the United States.

Attitudes and Bio-Social Determinants of Childbearing

Although attitudinal analyses are at the heart of traditional micro-level studies of fertility determinants, the assessment of bio-social determinants is a fairly new avenue pursued by scholars. Barber and Axinn (this volume) point to the difficulty in establishing the nature of the link between attitudes and behavior: attitudes vary across the life-course and are in part shaped by and the result of current and prior experiences on the one hand, and the societal/cultural context, on the other hand (Alwin, this volume). First, the decision to have a child depends on the roles the mother- and father-to-be currently occupy, and the degree to which individuals can and want to accommodate to this additional, optional role. To the extent that roles are incompatible, individuals may forgo parenthood or shift their fertility intentions downward, depending on their life-course stage.

Attitudes are thus indirectly linked to individuals' socialization in several ways (Barber & Axinn, this volume; Lundberg, this volume). First, early childhood experiences such as the quality and length of education have an effect on one's attitudes toward factors associated with decreasing fertility by, for example, encouraging employment careers or promoting negative attitudes toward premarital childbearing. Second, parents are known to influence children's attitudes via socialization, on the one hand, and social control techniques, on the other (Barber & Axinn, this volume). Parents will raise their children according to their beliefs and can use manipulative techniques to alter their children's behavior. However, if children are raised to respect their elders they may act in a way to please them as well. Within marital unions, partners have a say in fertility decisions as well, where marital decision making depends on the distribution of power within the union. In unequal unions, one partner's opinion may outweigh the others. In addition, Barber and Axinn (this volume) identify a variety of historical factors that influence child-bearing attitudes of individuals that are related to smaller intended family sizes, such as a large family size of origin and siblings' level of fertility. A final mechanism through which parents influence the fertility of their children is through genetic inheritance (Kohler, this volume). Barber and Axinn (this volume) state that increasing testosterone levels have been associated with a lessened desire for children. Kohler (this volume) finds that, over time, the genetic influence of fertility has become more pronounced as a result of heightened egalitarianism within developed nations. This implies that the force of socialization on attitudes may be decreasing in response to more behavioral choices. In societies where behaviors are constrained by structure, the relationship between attitudes and behavior may be weak. However, Barber and Axinn (this volume) do not examine individuals' attitudes toward competing roles, as well as fertility intentions. An individual's role preference rank and certainty about intentions are important qualifying factors when modeling and understanding disparity between attitudes and behaviors.

A further factor influencing attitudes is the number of children a woman or couple has previously conceived, or parity (Kohler, this volume; Morgan & Hagewen, this volume). Morgan and Hagewen note that the motivations for first children differ from those for second children, and that the reasons motivating a third or higher parity birth are also unique, possibly relating to the realization of gender preferences. A first birth is commonly associated with emotional gratification of parents, the second with desiring a sibling for the first child. Motivations for higher-order births in developed nations are largely unknown, given that almost 90% of all births are first- and second-order births, where only the remaining 10% are higher-order events (Morgan & Hagewen, this volume). Kohler (this volume) shows that for both parents, having a first-born male child increases the happiness for both parents, whereas additional children have no effect on the father's happiness and a negative effect on mother's happiness. These findings are in accordance with the trend toward self-realization and the unequal burden of parenthood.

Class and Fertility Attitudes

Morgan and Hagewen (this volume) argue that the total fertility rate for the United States remains above replacement level partially resulting from high minority fertility, indirectly proposing that the process underlying fertility decision making varies by race. For example, Tucker (this volume) identifies a variety of factors shaping middle-class African American women's fertility: having non-biological children in the household, increased religiosity that leads to unacceptability of non-marital childbearing, a lack of confidence in marital relationships, a cultural preference for early childbearing, coupled with medical conditions that prevent fertility, and a welfare system that especially disadvantages African American women by requiring a rapid welfare-to-work transition.

In low-income families where economic resources are insufficient to support any children, parents do not really have to choose their "plight." Having children is commonly part of everyone's life, either by choice or due to a lack of access to healthcare and contraception. Low-income families, as a result of the intergenerational transmission of poverty, expect to spend less time and money on their children, compared to higher-income parents. We tend to forget that healthcare, music lessons, education, supervision, and safe neighborhoods are upper-class ideals. Pro-natalist policy goals in the United States may have to be two-fold: (1) policies need to encourage low fertility among White Americans to increase their fertility and (2) policies should concentrate on creating equal access to healthcare and education to families and children of high-fertility minority groups.

How to Create the Next Generation? Policy and Methodological Suggestions

The previous discussion presents the dilemma of women in developed nations: while greater gender equality provides women with the choice of labor force participation and increasing personal freedoms, they continue to bear a disproportionate burden of the financial and physical responsibility of childrearing in industrialized nations. Oddly, pro-natalist policies in Western Europe have mostly failed to raise fertility, and while we have tracked those changes in behaviors related to family formation over time, empirical findings are still inconclusive with regard to what differentiates women who remain childless from those who bear one, two, or even more children. In order to relate macro-level trends to micro-level behavior, however, research must focus on the processes underlying fertility behavior. Scientific efforts to aid policy makers must move away from aggregate demographic research to multi-level, longitudinal, cross-disciplinary research designs, in order to capture the complexity of the fertility process.

Policy Recommendations

Many European nations at risk of population decline cannot afford to wait for social scientists to unravel the complexity behind the fertility process. A variety of pro-natal policies have been implemented—with a lack of success. Increasing tax breaks, low childcare costs, free and universal education, monthly monetary incentives, and generous maternity leaves and benefits have failed to convince individuals to have more than the average 1.6 children. It appears that the inability to combine motherhood and employment in these industrialized nations, a major theme throughout this chapter, needs to be addressed by policy makers in order to increase fertility in these nations.

Policy makers should reconsider the length of maternity leave. While the U.S. only provides women with a short, unpaid leave, most European mothers are able to forgo employment for up to three years. While the generosity of many European policies appears to be desirable, research supports that a woman or couple may consider forgone earnings when engaging in fertility decision making. Not only monetary losses, but the depreciation of her skills is important once a woman returns to work as well. Though many companies are required to provide the woman with her original position, or at least with a position of identical pay, the social stigma of returning after a long period of time in an age when technology changes rapidly may depress her desire to return to work. It appears as if a reduction of maternity leave and the possibility for part-time and/or flex-time employment would ease the transition to work for mothers.

Second, it would be beneficial to nations to ensure high-quality and low-cost childcare for all children whose parents are required or desire to engage in paid employment. While in the United States the availability of childcare is generally not a problem, quality, convenience, and affordability remain serious issues. It appears that middle- and upper-class parents are able to afford care in high-quality day care settings, but many lower middle-class and working-class parents cannot do so without subsidies. The European childcare system provides quality care at low cost, but lacks availability. In order to ensure that mothers are able to combine motherhood and employment, nations have to ensure that all individuals have access to high-quality and low-cost childcare. Governments ought to encourage and financially subsidize the education of early childhood educators, and implement sliding-fee scales to enable parents who would otherwise lack the resources to enroll their children in such institutions. Opening hours must be flexible to allow working parents to fulfill their work requirements—on weekdays and on weekends alike. The same logic needs to be applied to the public school system, which can be of unequal quality in the United States. In Europe many nations lack a system that allows children to attend all-day schools, which requires parents to either seek private after/ during school care or leads to women foregoing employment altogether. Only if the state supports employment and motherhood until children are self-sufficient will women find it justifiable to increase their completed fertility. Unfortunately, the current political rhetoric concentrates on the benefits of marital unions for parents and children (Lichter & Wooten, this volume), continuing to place the responsibility of parenthood on parents alone.

Alternatively, policy makers could advocate the return to gender-specialized work and family spheres. This would reduce the incompatibility of parenthood and employment by reintroducing separate spheres for men and women. Mothers would now return to exclusively raising children and men would be sole "breadwinners." Eliminating the need for paid employment might reduce the role incompatibility women currently experience, and with adequate monetary and institutional support, they may now realize their intended family size. While the retreat of women from the labor force would create numerous employment opportunities within countries at this time of high unemployment, the economic, psychological, and social benefits of employment to women will be hard to relinquish.

Increasing immigration is a fruitful alternative. Below replacement nations can utilize open immigration policies to increase their population. However, the success of these policies depends on the demographic characteristics of immigrants, such as the proportion of immigrants in the population, their age composition, their fertility level, and their sex ratio (Feichtinger & Steinmann, 1992). There are two possible ways by which immigrants contribute to a nation's population: (1) through their (numerical) presence in the population, and (2) through their offspring. Immigration policies must target young immigrant populations, preferably married couples, so that immigrants have a greater probability of contributing to population growth. While immigrants can slow population decline, the process of fertility assimilation to natives' levels over time makes immigration a short-term solution. In addition, the ethnocentric political climate of many industrialized nations prevents governments from investing in the cultural assimilation of immigrants, a process deemed essential for the public acceptance of foreigners.

Despite current pro-natalist policy implementations and reform suggestions, there appears to be no surefire solution to increase women's fertility in developed nations. Most policies have limited governmental feasibility and their effectiveness remains suspect. Past performance is the best predictor of future success; in this case, the future looks dismal. Campaigns to increase individuals' awareness of societal-level consequences of population decline, as well as highlighting how these problems will affect individuals' lives, may be the best solution to prevent further fertility decline.

Methodological Recommendations

Despite accumulating theories on below-replacement fertility behavior, empirical evidence on fertility behavior is scarce. The lack of statistical verification is the result of the complex nature of the issue. In this final section we identify methods directed toward a more sophisticated modeling of fertility processes. We recommend (a) a multi-level approach that accounts for temporal factors, (b) the utilization of mixed methods from both quantitative and qualitative paradigms, and (c) a multidisciplinary perspective to inform the scientific inquiry of fertility decision making in developed nations.

We follow Alwin's (this volume) suggestion by utilizing Bronfenbrenner and Morris's (1997) multi-level ecological model as a framework for future fertility study. First, inquiries must begin at the micro-level, by identifying *women*'s human capital expectations, their family formation intentions and their attitudes toward cohabitation and non-marital childbearing. In addition, it is important to evaluate past and childhood experiences, such as family of origin influences, i.e., one's parents' experiences with having children, parental divorce, number of siblings, and birth- and gender order. At the same time, the strengths of biological determinants need to be evaluated. Micro-level factors are important for understanding the proximal context in which individuals make their fertility decisions. For childbearing that occurs within partnered unions, it is essential to retrieve this information from the partner as well.

Second, meso-level factors include immediate relational influences of the individual, such as one's parents' ability to combine parenthood and employment, and peer's attitudes toward childbearing and childrearing. For coupled individuals, learning about the partners' child preferences and micro-level experiences aids understanding of the process, assuming that women consider their partners' opinions.

Third, exo-level factors are often discussed as contributing factors to fertility trends without being directly assessed. They include availability of family-oriented work and leave policies if a woman or her partner is employed, the availability and cost of childcare, federal family policies and marriage promotion policies, as well as individuals' perceptions of their utility. Exo-level factors have to be evaluated from the perspective of the individual, who is nested within her immediate and extended family, community, town, state, and country.

Further, macro-level factors, such as societal norms with regard to marriage and children, economic situation, and gender equality, are important for understanding the distal context in which individuals live and the degree to which culture influences their fertility behaviors. Understanding the nature of cultural norms, individuals' perceptions of cultural norms, and how much weight they give norms in influencing their preferences and decisions will help to explain the degree to which culture influences fertility behavior.

Finally, the temporal context is necessary for examining these levels across the life-course. Environmental influences change in character and significance over time. For instance, family-of-origin exerts its force during the formative years, whereas peers gain significance during adolescence and early adulthood. In order to have an accurate understanding of the proposed relationships among culture, workplace demands, personal preferences, family-of-origin influences, and biological determinants, the ideal methodological technique will require extensive data collection that surveys the same individuals into childhood through adulthood. Today, panel studies have gained acceptance among scholars who are interested in studying individual-level behavior over time. The problem with longitudinal data collection is the high rate of attrition over time, the loss of initial survey respondents. It would require an enormous amount of respondents to account for attrition in a nationally representative survey that would include multiple decades of data collection. Today, techniques such as the event-history calendar allow for the collection of retrospective information on time-varying events such as employment, childbearing, and marriage. Attitudes, however, cannot be captured by this method. Converting longitudinal data into event history files enables the researcher to take into account events that have previously taken place, e.g., the time dependency of events. Coupled with multi-level modeling techniques, research can carefully evaluate the influences of all ecological levels over time.

The Utility of Qualitative Data

Landale (this volume) highlights the utility of qualitative data to broaden our knowledge of processes. Qualitative methods (e.g., in-depth personal interviews, ethnography, focus group interviews) capture individual experiences and provide rich information precluded by close-ended quantitative interviewing and survey research. Qualitative survey methods are advantageous when examining personal issues such as the decision to have a child. Compared to impersonal quantitative survey methods, for example, personal interviews, with a skilled interviewer, can provide insights into gender equality within relationships, reduce the amount of social desirability pressure, and provide information on the intensity of fertility intentions and attitudes often not captured by survey approaches to data collection.

The Value of an Interdisciplinary Approach

Most fertility research stems from demographic approaches. Although vital information has been garnered with respect to changing behavior over time, other disciplines have made contributions that have been largely ignored by demographers. Thomson (this volume) admits that studies of aggregate fertility most likely are not appropriate if we want to discover why demographic rates have changed.

Developmentalists, family researchers, and psychologists can offer more micro-level and meso-level approaches to studying fertility, by assessing whether individuals indeed engage in cost-benefit calculations or if they simply supply a normative response to survey questions. Sociologists and demographers simply assume that individuals engage in rational decision making and that fertility behavior is thus an intentional outcome. Individual-focused disciplines would view this as a dangerous assumption leading to false conclusions. Adding a more micro-level approach to current research will provide insights into how and why individuals make decisions—especially those with regard to fertility behavior.

In sum, individuals make decisions within the context of their past, current, and anticipated future experiences. It is thus essential to examine all ecological levels, and how they relate to and influence each other, and to determine how those relationships contribute to the aggregate findings presented in the demographic literature. Currently, we have very little empirical understanding of the complexity of fertility decision making and behavior. A piecemeal approach to fertility needs to be replaced with a longitudinal, multilevel, multidisciplinary, and multi-method approach in order to begin clarifying mechanisms, processes, and problems with regard to low fertility. Using mixed methods and multidisciplinary approaches will aid in discovering the complex mechanisms and interactions underlying human fertility decisions making and behavior, and serve as a means of assessing the degree to which previous demographic and sociological findings accurately reflect these complex mechanisms.

Conclusion

The fear of population decline and its societal and individual-level consequences raises the study of human fertility to a position of importance. The perceived threat of population decline is population aging and the resulting insufficient supply of economically active individuals to support them. Today, however, we are not sure what causes fertility decline, how to solve it, or what its consequences really entail. In fact, research has just begun to unravel the process behind fertility behavior.

The diminishing personal value of children, coupled with increasing female labor force participation, can lead to decreasing fertility if the institutional responses are inadequate to ensure the combination of motherhood and employment. Increasing rights to free time required for self-actualization, coupled with the need for the necessary financial capital adequate to raise children in developed nations, may lead parents to delay or forgo childbearing in order to achieve their goals. Increasing gender equality means that women and men have opportunities that may work against accomplishing their fertility intentions over time: individuals have to weigh their options and decide how to pursue a particular goal at a particular point in time.

Pronatalist policies drafted in developed nations do not appear to compensate for the direct and opportunity costs associated with children, especially for women participating in the labor force. Why are these policies failing to increase fertility rates? What kinds of policies prevent fertility rates from continuous decline? To answer these questions, we need longitudinal, multilevel, multidisciplinary, and multi-method studies of fertility.

Acknowledgments

The authors would like to thank David Warner for helpful comments.

References

Blau, D. M., & Robins, P. K. (1989). Fertility, employment, and child-care costs. *Demography, 26,* 287–299.

Bongaarts, J. (2002). The end of the fertility transition in the developed world. *Population and Development Review, 28,* 419–444.

Bronfenbrenner, U., & Morris, P. A. (1997). The ecology of developmental processes. In W. Damon (Ed.), *Handbook of child psychology* (5th ed., pp. 993–1028). New York: Wiley.

Erikson, E. H. (1980). *Identity and the life cycle.* New York: Norton.

Feichtinger, G.,& Steinmann, G. (1992). Immigration into a population with fertility below replacement level – The case of Germany. *Population Studies, 46,* 275–284.

Festinger, L. (1957). *A theory of cognitive dissonance.* Stanford, CA: Stanford University Press.

Gauthier, A. H., & Hatzius, J. (1997). Family benefits and fertility: An economic analysis. *Population Studies, 51,* 295–306.

Morgan, S. P.,& Hagewen, K. (2004). Fertility. In L. Dudley, Jr. & M. Micklin (Eds.), *Handbook of population.* Boston, MA: Klewer Academic Publishers.

Oppenheimer, V. K. (1998). A theory of marriage timing. *American Journal of Sociology, 94,* 564–591.

AUTHOR INDEX

Note: *n* indicates footnote, *t* indicates table

SUBJECT INDEX

Note: *t* indicates table, *n* indicates footnote, *f* indicates figure.